The Late Postcolonial Condition

RECONFIGURING IDENTITIES IN THE PORTUGUESE-SPEAKING WORLD

Edited by

Paulo de Medeiros and Cláudia Pazos-Alonso

VOL. 19

PETER LANG

Oxford - Berlin - Bruxelles - Chennai - Lausanne - New York

Emanuelle Rodrigues dos Santos

The Late Postcolonial Condition

Twenty-First-Century Reconfigurations in the Literatures of Portuguese-Speaking Africa

PETER LANG

Oxford · Berlin · Bruxelles · Chennai · Lausanne · New York

Bibliographic information published by the Deutsche Nationalbibliothek.
The German National Library lists this publication in the German National Bibliography; detailed bibliographic data is available on the Internet at http://dnb.d-nb.de.

A catalogue record for this book is available from the British Library.

Library of Congress Cataloging-in-Publication Data

Names: Santos, Emanuelle Rodrigues dos, 1983- author.
Title: The late postcolonial condition : twenty-first-century
    reconfigurations in the literatures of Portuguese-speaking Africa /
    Emanuelle Rodrigues dos Santos.
Other titles: Reconfiguring identities in the Portuguese-speaking world ;
    v. no. 19. 22350144
Description: New York : Peter Lang Publishing, 2025. | Series:
    Reconfiguring identities in the Portuguese-speaking world, 22350144 ; v.
    no. 19 | Includes bibliographical references and index.
Identifiers: LCCN 2023056377 (print) | LCCN 2023056378 (ebook) |
    ISBN 9781787074507 (paperback) | ISBN 9781787076525 (ebook) |
    ISBN 9781787076532 (epub)
Subjects: LCSH: African literature (Portuguese)--21st century--History and
    criticism. | Authors, African--21st century. | Postcolonialism in
    literature. | Postcolonialism--Africa, Portuguese-speaking. | Africa,
    Portuguese-speaking. | Africa, Portuguese-speaking--In literature.
Classification: LCC PQ9900 .S265 2025 (print) | LCC PQ9900 (ebook) | DDC
    869.0996--dc23/eng/20231207
LC record available at https://lccn.loc.gov/2023056377
LC ebook record available at https://lccn.loc.gov/2023056378

Cover image: Photo by Paolo De Padova.
Cover design by Peter Lang Group AG

ISSN 2235-0144
ISBN 978-1-78707-450-7 (print)
ISBN 978-1-78707-652-5 (ePDf)
ISBN 978-1-78707-653-2 (ePub)
DOI 10.3726/b11288

© 2025 Peter Lang Group AG, Lausanne
Published by Peter Lang Ltd, Oxford, United Kingdom
info@peterlang.com – www.peterlang.com

Emanuelle Rodrigues dos Santos has asserted her right under the Copyright, Designs and
Patents Act, 1988, to be identified as Author of this Work.

Contents

Abbreviations

CEI	Casa dos Estudantes do Império
	House of The Students from the Empire
CONCP	Conferência das Organizações Nacionalistas das Colônias Portuguesas
	Conference of Nationalist Organizations of the Portuguese Colonies
FNLA	Frente Nacional de Libertação de Angola
	National Front for the Liberation of Angola
Frelimo	Frente de Libertação de Moçambique
	Mozambican Liberation Front
IMF	International Monetary Fund
MLSTP	Movimento para a Libertação de São Tomé e Príncipe
	Movement for the Liberation of São Tomé and Príncipe
MpD	Movimento para a Democracia
	Movement for Democracy
MPLA	Movimento Popular de Libertação de Angola
	Popular Movement for the Liberation of Angola
PAICV	Partido Africano para a Independência de Cabo Verde
	African Party for the Independence of Cape Verde
PAIGC	Partido Africano para a Independência da Guiné-Bissau e Cabo Verde

African Party for the Independence of Guinea-Bissau and Cape Verde

PALOP   Países Africanos de Língua Oficial Portuguesa

African Portuguese-speaking Countries

RENAMO Resistência Nacional Moçambicana

Mozambican National Resistance

UN   United Nations

UNITA   União Nacional para a Independência Total de Angola

National Union for the Total Independece of Angola

Acknowledgements

The journey leading to this book can be traced back to an optional module on Cape Verdean literature taken at the very last stage of my undergraduate in *Letras* at the Universidade de São Paulo, where Mário César Lugarinho introduced me to the African literatures in Portuguese. The research path that ensued was one marked by questioning, learning and, above all, kindness. Developed between the academic environments of the Universidade de São Paulo, Universiteit Utrecht, the University of Warwick and the University of Birmingham, this book has greatly benefitted from input from a number of transnational communities of scholars whose support was fundamental for its completion.

I must start by thanking Mário César Lugarinho, Paulo de Medeiros and Inocência Mata for all the mentoring, encouragement and support without which I wouldn't have been able to carry out the research to write this book. In Brazil, I am also indebted to Emerson da Cruz Inácio, Simone Caputo Gomes, Laura Padilha, Sílvio Renato Jorge, Rita Chaves, Tania Macedo, and Sinei Sales for the teachings and inspiration that propelled me to pursue this project. In the Netherlands, I am forever grateful for the generosity of Patricia Schor and Peter Maurits (now in Germany). From my many trips to Lisbon, I would like to thank Ana Mafalda Leite, Elena Brugioni (now in Brazil), Jessica Falconi, Livia Apa and Marta Banasiak for giving me an intellectual home in Portugal. In the UK, I am forever grateful to Mark Sabine, Rui Miranda, and Bernard McGuirk for the warm Nottingham welcome to my research in this country. At Warwick, I thank Michael Tsang and Jenny Mak for their friendship. I also express my gratitude to Hilary Owen and Robert Young whose work was instrumental to my own. Likewise, I would like to thank Eleanor Jones for holding my hand as I found my way through early career life in UK academia.

I express my gratitude to Cláudia Pazos-Alonso and Paulo de Medeiros for giving this project a home in their series at Peter Lang, and Laurel Plapp for making it a smooth process. This project benefitted from funding from the Brazilian CAPES Institute – Coordenação de Aperfeiçoamento de Pessoal de Nível Superior – and from the Portuguese Instituto Camões's Cátedra Gil Vicente, to which I am grateful.

Most of the writing of this book was completed in the UK after I joined the faculty of the Department of Modern Languages at the University of Birmingham. Here, I relied on the support of Stephen Forcer, Charlotte Ross, Sara Jones, Enea Zaramella (now in Italy) and Elliot Evans. I would like to thank Thomas Waller, Johanna Kreft and Gitanjali Patel for allowing me to learn with their doctoral projects. For their patience and relentless encouragement, I would like to thank my dearest friends in the Portuguese team, Maria Inês Castro e Silva and Gisele Orgado. To Alice Corr, my gratitude for the intellectual partnership that keeps me curious. To Aengus Ward, I am forever grateful for the push to cross the finish line.

Finally, I would like to thank Samih Fourali and Anahí Santos-Fourali, for their love and understanding without which there would be no joy and no book.

This book is dedicated to my mother, Nívia da Conceição Rodrigues dos Santos, who loved me enough to let me go.

Introduction

> [C]ritics are not merely the alchemical translators of texts into circumstantial reality or worldliness; they too are subject to and producers of circumstances, which are felt regardless of whatever objectivity the critic's methods possess. The point is that texts have ways of existing that even in their most rarified form are always enmeshed in circumstance, time, place, and society – in short they are in the world, and hence worldly. ... The same implications are undoubtedly true of critics in their capacities as readers and writers in the world.
>
> – Edward W. Said,
> *The World, the Text, and the Critic* (1983: 35)

This book engages with the literatures of Portuguese-speaking Africa from a worldly perspective, which entails a diverse range of coordinates in space and time. While its corpus takes us to Angola, Cape Verde, Guinea-Bissau, Mozambique, and São Tomé and Príncipe, its critical analysis dialogues with an international community of scholars whose organisation within literary studies takes forms ranging from Portuguese, Lusophone and Luso-Afro-Brazilian Studies in the United States, the United Kingdom, Portugal and Brazil. In terms of discipline, this work's embedding in the field of postcolonial studies conjugates intellectual perspectives of the Global North and South. Time is compressed into a palimpsestic contemporaneity that amalgamates traces of over five centuries of history, the last of which has seen developments as radically opposite as the armed Marxist revolutionary liberation movements and the adoption of neoliberal capitalism. Coupled with the methodological tools of comparative literature, an appreciation of the intersecting nature of these coordinates in time and space is essential for the proposition at the heart of this book that seeks to reinstate the crucial relevance of the concept of postcoloniality in the twenty-first century.

At a time when postcolonial studies face yet another epistemological crisis, a proposition to review one of its central features may well put off some of the trendiest readers. Since its revival at the beginning of the new century, the paradigm of world literature has been growing in Global North academia as a more up-to-date replacement of the postcolonial paradigm, now increasingly seen as *démodé*. From both sides of the political spectrum, theoreticians shape their definitions of world literature from the remains of a body of work in postcolonial theory that, they say, is no longer capable of accounting either for today's unbridled cosmopolitanism or for the current stage of late capitalism. For David Damrosch, world literature is a way to approximate a hypercanon of European works and a postcolonial countercanon of 'subaltern and "contestatory" voices of writers in languages less commonly taught and in minor literatures within great-power languages' (2006: 45). In their introduction to the issue of *The Journal of Postcolonial Writing* on 'Postcolonial Studies and World Literature', scholars James Graham, Michael Niblett and Sharae Deckard have attributed the materialist turn away from postcolonial literary studies to the field's 'failure to address the historical changes in the world-system characteristic of late capitalism' (2012: 465). Further on, evidence compels the editors to backtrack. They point out in their introduction that in addition to the fact that the essays 'exemplify and demonstrate the interpretative possibilities opened up by world-literary criticism',

> [w]hat also unites [these essays'] different approaches is a conviction that the 'post-colonial' remains vital to the critique of the capitalist world-system precisely because it names the particular configurations of social experience and traumatic historical legacies in those once-colonized peripheries which continue to exist in asymmetrical relationship to the older imperialist centres … . The historical particularity of the violence of formal imperialism and colonization clearly differentiates postcolonies from other kinds of peripheries, such as those within Europe. (Graham, Niblett and Deckard 2012:468)

Despite their professed ideological differences, a commonality emerges between the positions of Damrosch, and Graham, Niblett and Deckard. Both sides attempt to pose world literature as the next step in comparative literary studies by setting its novelty value against the scrapping of the postcolonial paradigm. What they fail to realise, however, is that this opposition is neither necessary nor true as their views of world literature do not constitute a replacement for the postcolonial approach, as they quite simply just set out to do something else. At stake for Damrosch is the desire to read the literary works of Europe and its Others comparatively, without having to bother with the aesthetic or historical consequences of the colonial difference between them. On the other hand, Graham, Niblett and Deckard may well claim that they want to read works comparatively that reveal the systemic nature of the modern capitalist world-system in a way that postcolonial studies to date has failed to do. Yet, as their piece introduces their contributors' essays, concentrated mainly on the cultures of Africa and the Caribbean, the editors are forced to recognise that the postcolonial paradigm still retains its systemic critical potential. At the end of the day – and as any materialist will know – colonialism is not only part and parcel of the history of the modern capitalist world-system, but it should also not be completely disregarded in an analysis of the development of late capitalism in peripheral societies. What becomes difficult under the postcolonial paradigm is, as the team of editors rightfully recognises, to develop an adequate set of conceptual tools to approach the formal nuances of literary registration of systemic unevenness in semi-peripheral settings located in Europe or in other places without a history of exploitation common under classic forms of colonialism. That is the kind of material whose understanding demands alternative approaches, such as the concept of world-literature coined by the Warwick Research Collective, or WReC (2015).

The decoupling of the new rise of world literature from the presumed obsolescence of the postcolonial as a critical paradigm touches on just one of the issues within the field. Even though the postcolonial should not be discarded just because several scholars from the Global North are no longer interested in the ways postcolonial aesthetics registers coloniality at a societal level, whether because they are no longer interested in these phenomena or those societies, it is true that the field's theoretical apparatus requires periodical revision. In fact, the capacity for self-critique is one of the most distinctive features of postcolonial studies as a field of enquiry. With a dialogical tradition that inherits from both its poststructuralist and materialist roots, as well as the many fruitful clashes between them, the field has grown what Ella Shohat and Robert Stam have termed a 'jiujitsu-like capacity to transform critique into renewal' (2012: 43). At every step of the way since the field's establishment, interrogations from insiders and outsiders alike have brought its body of theories forward by continuously pointing to its blind spots. Essential topics that were far from the field's theoretical constructs in the 1990s – such as settler colonialism in Palestine, indigeneity, US imperialism, the environment, gender and sexuality – today constitute solid directions of enquiry, as demonstrated by the contributors of important volumes like *What Postcolonial Theory Doesn't Say?* (2018).

Embedded in the tradition of writing 'in the necessary mode of perpetual autocritique' (Young 2012: 22) that is distinctive of postcolonial studies, this book expands the field's body of theories into one of its main epistemological, temporal and geographical blind spots: the non-anglophone contemporary postcolony. Its focus on literary works by authors speaking from Angolan, Cape Verdean, Bissau-Guinean, Mozambican and Santomean settings contributes to decentre the field's anglophone predisposition as it argues for postcolonial theory's urgent need to enlarge its analytical range in order to account for the wide array of inherited colonial practices experienced in postcolonial societies today. Moreover, the attention to the transition of the African postcolony into the twenty-first century compels a careful reconsideration of the multifaceted impact of capitalism in these societies in the *longue dureé* of modernity, something at the core of postcolonial theory whose roots lay in the anti-colonial reason. This not only allows for the much-needed historically grounded assessment of the twenty-first century postcolony but also enables a coherent assessment of cultural colonial legacies, seen in relation to its material and societal conditions of production.

Literatures of Portuguese-Speaking Africa: Notes on a comparative approach

This book dialogues with the now-established academic tradition of reading the novelistic production of the five countries of Portuguese-speaking Africa in relation to projects of national identity-building rooted in both anticolonial and post-independence efforts. The study explores if the postcolonial interpretative paradigm built to understand the literary registration of the strive for, and the consolidation of, independence is still valid for grasping how works conceived within twenthieth-century contexts register postcolonialities marked by relative stabilisation and, with it, new challenges. As such, this book not only asks whether an established reading paradigm holds, thus talking back to the field of studies of literatures in Portuguese in its many configurations, but also seeks to generate a conceptual framework to understand whether and how the postcolonial condition has changed as each country drifts further away from colonial times. To do that, this study adopted a comparative approach designed to allow the emergence of unobserved and unexplored formal and thematic literary registration patterns, which entailed the selection of a corpus of five novels, one from each of the countries of Portuguese-speaking Africa, chosen alongside the temporal axis around the first decade of the twenty-first century (1998–2012). The inclusion of authors and works followed criteria designed to mix both well-known authors and books with an established international reputation, with lesser known authors and books. In what follows, we situate this book in the comparativist tradition in the study of such literatures and, in terms of postcolonial studies, introduce the texts included in the corpus and the structure around which the book is organised.

The study of the literatures of Portuguese-speaking Africa has come to constitute an important subfield of Portuguese studies or studies of literatures in Portuguese, since the countries' independences in the 1970s. Nonetheless, the breadth of the comparative scope proposed in this book is new. While academia has produced a number of excellent thematic edited volumes that successfully bring in a multiplicity of scholars and perspectives from various parts of the Portuguese-speaking world, the field has yet to give rise to studies capable of conjugating aspects of the varied realities of the five African countries with literatures in Portuguese, as proposed in this book. Far from indulging imperial nostalgias via the essentialisation of linguistic communities, usually characterised by a particular kind of celebration of *lusofonia* popular in Portuguese academia (Brugioni 2019: 220), the present comparative approach looks for literary registrations of an African experience of colonialism capable of factoring the legacies of anticolonial revolutionary Marxist nationalism, socialist nation-building and integration into transnational capitalism that is capable of enlightening a significant blind spot in postcolonial theoretical frameworks often articulated from situated experiences expressed in English.

From a perspective grounded in the debates surrounding the establishment of the study of African literatures in Portuguese in the 1980s, Inocência Mata speaks of the refusal to name the individual national literatures in Portuguese of the five African countries as such. When they finally made it into academia, such literatures' place in reading syllabi was conditioned by a comparativism that fed imperial nostalgias, diametrically opposing their then very anticolonial contexts of emergence, hence informing these literatures' critical views of the 1990s in their commitment to carving indisputably national and singular narratives for these cultural artefacts (2013: 109–110). Our perspective, thus, matches Mata's, when she states that 'embora eu não esvazie ... a ideia de "literaturas nacionais", julgo ser produtivo captar a transnacionalidade dos estilos e a dinâmica das interlocuções entre esses sistemas, nas suas "conjunções e disjunções", tensões e distensões' [though not deflating ... the idea of 'national literatures', we believe to be productive to capture the transnationality of the styles and dynamics of the dialogues between these systems, in their 'conjunctions and disjunctions', tensions and distensions] (113).[1]

Another important aspect in which this study refers back to the criticism of the literatures of Portuguese-speaking Africa is temporality or, better yet, timeliness. Much in line with studies considering texts published in the 1960s, 1970s and 1980s, the intrinsic connection between these literatures, given their shared emergence in a context of joint anticolonial reason and armed resistance, this analysis of twentieth-century texts shows a similar trend that cannot be taken for granted. As is widely known, the texts conceived around the years in which these countries attained their respective independence displayed a notion of culture much in line with anticolonial thought and efforts towards nation-building. What is less known, and has become quite visible through our comparative analysis, is that even after the end of these countries' joint struggle and their drift in political, social and economic terms, their fiction still takes literary forms

1   Unless otherwise stated, all translations from Portuguese in this study are my own.

displaying related aesthetic choices. While it is undeniable that times have changed, this similarity indicates a literary registration of transnational phenomena, suggesting that relevant commonalities in the ways these societies are organised remain even in the aftermath of the colonial settler's departure. If one sees anticolonialism and nation-building as movements characterised by their opposition to colonial and external forms of economic exploitation and cultural subjugation, the texts analysed here show that these literatures' expressions of postcoloniality and national criticism still thematise forms of economic exploitation and cultural subjugation. What has changed is that the oppressor now seems to come from within.

Notwithstanding its value as a critical intervention in the international scholarly debate around the literatures of Portuguese-speaking Africa, the findings of this study also constitute a critique of theorisations in the field of postcolonial studies. Even when important strands of the field, such as the materialist one, acknowledge the concrete societal challenges posed by colonial legacies today, few are the systematic attempts – such as Achille Mbembe's (2001) – to refashion its concepts from a perspective that departs from the internal dynamics of the postcolonies, let alone from African and non-anglophone ones. Our study and Mbembe's differ in terms of objects and methods. He focuses on French- and English-speaking Africa through a poststructuralist-informed psychoanalytical approach, whereas we look into Portuguese-speaking Africa oriented by a postcolonial approach involving poststructural discourse analysis, anticolonial thought and world-systems theory. Yet, our shared standpoint puts our studies in a position of relative supplementarity, as we both believe that the experience from within the postcolony must be considered as an important locus of theorisation in postcolonial studies.

Texts

Aspects considered in the selection of the literary texts analysed involved form, time of publication relative to the development of their national literatures, canonic status and circulation. The aim to reassess the timeliness of current ideas of postcoloniality compelled a choice of texts whose context of production was neither too far from the context of this study, nor from each respective country's current political and economic stage. As such, the boundaries in terms of time were, on the one hand, the consolidation of each country's state sovereignty ratified by the demise of a single, main organised armed threat and, on the other hand, the consolidation of – at least nominally – democratic forms of government allied to a seemingly long-lasting adoption of a given economic system, which leaves us with three main categories to define stabilisation: absence of armed conflict with other states, formal commitment to democracy and maintenance of a liberal economic model.

Considering this specific political and economic conjuncture, we see that although in Cape Verde, São Tomé and Príncipe, Mozambique and Guinea-Bissau the military, political and economic decisions leading to the following period of stabilisation were taken at different points in the course of the 1990s, Angola still experienced civil war until 2002. For this reason, the goal was to aim for works published after the turn of the century. In a related manner, the aesthetic choice for the novel comes from the long-acknowledged intimacy between liberal ideology and the novel form, historically consubstantiated in its relations with the rise of the bourgeoisie that was immortalised by G. W. F. Hegel's formulation of the novel as the modern bourgeois epic, later furthered by Georg Lukács (1999).[2]

The coordinates for the selection of the corpus related to literary circulation were connected to each work's relative position within their national literary canon and aimed at diversifying the small pool of authors and titles already addressed in the field, especially in works published in English. Underlying this criterion was also a desire to balance the insertion of texts by authors that enjoy different levels of familiarity with the international reader. Uniting lesser-known novels by known authors and well-known novels by relatively unknown authors, we avoided works by canonic and well-studied authors such as Pepetela, Mia Couto and Germano Almeida from relatively well-known literatures of Angola, Mozambique and

---

2   The text was originally published in the Russian *Literary Encyclopedia*, Vol. IX, Moscow, 1935. This Portuguese translation was made by Letizia Zini Antunes from the text's 1976 version in Italian and from its 1974 version in French.

Cape Verde, opting instead for *Teoria Geral do Esquecimento* (2012) by the Angolan José Eduardo Agualusa, translated in 2015 as *A General Theory of Oblivion*; *Campo de Trânsito* [Transit Camp] (2007) by the Mozambican João Paulo Borges Coelho and *Marginais* [Marginals] (2010) by the Cape Verdean Evel Rocha. From São Tomé and Príncipe, we selected *Aurélia de Vento* [Aurélia of Wind] (2011) by Albertino Bragança; from Guinea-Bissau, we chose *Tiara* (1999) by Filomena Embaló.

The oldest novel considered, *Tiara* was published by the Portuguese international Camões Institute but is still less renowned than the country's widely recognised novels by Abdulai Silla: the trilogy *Eterna Paixão* (1994), *A Última Tragédia* (1995) and *Mistida* (1997). The only novel authored by a woman in our corpus, *Tiara* is Embaló's only novel, but not her only work. She has published a collection of texts and short stories – *Carta Aberta* (2005) – and a volume of poems – *Coração Cativo* (2008). Often seen under the autobiographical light, *Tiara* draws from the country's history as much as it does from its author's personal experience 'Vivi um período de grande revolta pessoal que só consegui ultrapassar através de um trabalho de introspecção que me levou à escrita e através desta à redefinição da minha identidade, desta vez numa óptica multinacional, tal como é, afinal de contas, a minha essência' ['I went through a period of great personal revolt that I was only able to overcome through a work of introspection that led me to writing and through this to redefining my identity, this time from a multinational perspective, as it is, after all, my essence'] (2009).

The novel consists of a narrative about an eponymous heroine who, just like Embaló, who was born in Angola, migrated during her youth from one African country to join the independence struggle of another, remaining there until the aftermath of independence, when, after two decades of public service, she is stripped of official duties by the independent regime. Deeply disillusioned, Tiara abandons the country's public life. This trajectory is mirrored by the reason behind Embaló's migration to France, where she was last known to have worked in an international cultural institute – dissolved in 2013. While the general lines of this novel do parallel the author's biography, its precise extent is not known as there is an entire emotional and personal aspect to the struggle of Tiara that cannot be verified in terms of the author's lived experience. In any case, my approach to

this third-person narrative novel takes it as a work of fiction whose connection is deeply enmeshed in the conflicts of the country in relation to
which it is conceived.

Campo de Trânsito is another example of the dubious and complex
connection between fiction and history, as Mozambique did, in fact, maintain prison camps that 'disciplined and punished' those who deviated from
the single-party line. *Campo*, one of the author's thirteen prose-fiction
works published from 2003 to date, is among Coelho's least studied works.
A Professor of History at the University Eduardo Mondlane in Maputo,
Coelho's PhD thesis defended at the University of Bradford (UK) thematised the colonial and post-independence resettlement of peasants in his
home country, which might have proven important in the writing of this
book. Critics hold strong views in their commentaries regarding the novel's
potential critique of the country's recent history. While some are categorical
in affirming the historical connection as the best way of reading the narrative (Moreira 2010), some seem to be much too keen on totally avoiding it
(Mendonça 2007). While the novel certainly does relate to Mozambique's
history and internal critique of its recent past, it also establishes a connection with other forms of artistic work such as Licínio Azevedo's 2012 film,
Virgem Margarida, which portrays the story of a young woman taken to
one such camp as a result of being mistaken for a prostitute. Nonetheless,
as the author has expressed himself, the novel is not only about this episode
of the country's history as it 'procura colocar algumas questões relativas ao
absurdo na nossa civilização global. Ou seja, não se trata de uma abordagem
"cautelosa" dos campos de reeducação' ['seeks to raise some questions about
the absurdity of our global civilisation. In other words, it is not a "cautious"
approach to re-education camps'] (Coelho 2010).

Largely unknown in the body of works that make up Cape Verdean literature, *Marginais* is almost metonymic. Its author, Evel Rocha, has served
as politician on the island of Sal, which is background to his literature. His
literary work first came out in 1997 and boasts seven published works to
date, including poetry and prose. *Marginais* tells the story of Sérgio do
Rosário, or Sérgio Pitbull, whose wretched existence is underlined by the
inequality on his island, and whose tourism industry preys on the poor
to fill the pockets of the local elite and foreign investors. The narrative is

coloured by an impressive naturalist aesthetics capable of portraying a very realistic picture of poverty's gruesomeness and abjection. Rocha's work is important as it has been classified as a novelty in the literature of Cape Verde. As Mário Lugarinho explains: 'Sua "novidade" consiste no [seu tratamento do] espaço, que não oferece mais sentido, como acontecia na produção mais tradicional. Se a terra, tanto na geração claridosa, quanto naquelas que lhe seguiram, oferecia sentido a um anseio de identidade nacional autônoma, em *Marginais* essa mesma terra perde o seu estatuto privilegiado – [de] espaço geográfico onde a nação se concretiza' ['Its "novelty" consists in [its treatment of] space, which no longer offers meaning, as it did in the more traditional production. If the land, both in the Claridosa generation and in those that followed, offered meaning to a yearning for an autonomous national identity, in *Marginais* that same land loses its privileged status – [as] the geographical space where the nation is realized'] (2012b: 220).[3] By moving away from the idea of nation and problematising the institutions mediating the very means of social, economic and human development, this little-known narrative is an important addition to our corpus.

Another barely known novel included in this book is the Santomean *Aurélia de Vento* by Albertino Bragança. A politician and writer, the author has published five works so far: two volumes of short stories and three novels. While his first novel, *Um Clarão sobre a Baía* (2005), has been the object of some significant critical commentary by specialists, our analysis looks into his second novel, which is a curious case precisely because the ideological, political and sociocultural aspects of society are not advertised as the main topic of the book. In *Um Clarão sobre a Baía*, the initial epigraph clearly announces the politically loaded content of the book '[à] Memória do Sr. Lereno da Mata, um patriota injustiçado e tão tragicamente desaparecido. Para todos quantos passaram, inocentes, pelo sinistro silêncio das masmorras' ['[to] the memory of Mr. Lereno da Mata, a patriot who was wronged and tragically disappeared. For all those who passed, innocent,

---

3   *Claridoso* or *claridosa* is an adjective denoting a relation with the Cape Verdean literary journal *Claridade* of the 1930s that played an important role in the rise of the country's national identity.

through the sinister silence of the dungeons'] (2011b: 10).[4] In contrast, in *Aurélia de Vento*, the epigraph is an unpublished poem by the Portuguese poet Sophia de Mello Breyner Andresen, made public for the first time posthumously in a Portuguese newspaper that examined the collection of her documents on the occasion of the fifth anniversary of her passing.[5] It is an epigraph that sets the stage for a much more personal, subjective pace, which certainly is at odds with the more openly engaged prose of the author or with the tradition of prose fiction in the country. In fact, the narrative revolves around the ethnically mixed heritage Aurélia, the beautiful, fair and strong daughter of the white widowed farmer Pedro Santos. In this story, both characters are heavily antagonised and succeed only with the support of the country's mass of peasants sensitive to their cause. While the novel sets the stage for an intimist narrative of overcoming, it delivers a much more revealing picture of the current dynamics of the class system in Santomean society. Additionally, it also adds to the number of female protagonists considered in our corpus, an aspect that connects it with the most recent of the texts contemplated in this study, José Eduardo Agualusa's *Teoria Geral do Esquecimento*.

Agualusa is, without a doubt, the most widely known and prolific writer whose work has been selected for this study. His works, which he began publishing in 1989, amount to thirty-five titles to date, including novels, collections of poems and short stories, novellas, plays and children's literature. His works have been translated into twenty-five languages and he is, arguably, the most prolific writer of Angola. Pepetela, who has been publishing since 1972 and counts twenty-six titles to date, is nonetheless

---

4   Mr da Mata, father of the Santomean academic and literary critic Inocência Mata, was arrested and killed in prison in 1978 during the single-party state regime, under the presidency of Manuel Pinto da Costa.

5   The poem, whose title 'Inocência e Possibilidades' [Inocence and Possibilities] is omitted in Bragança's quote, was written in 1943: 'As imagens eram próximas / Como coladas sobre os olhos/ O que nos dava um rosto justo e liso/ Os gestos circulavam sem choque nem ruído/ As estrelas eram maduras como frutos/ E os homens eram bons sem dar por isso' ['The images were close / Like glued over the eyes/ Which gave us a fair and smooth face/ The gestures circulated without shock or noise/ The stars were ripe like fruit/ And the men were good without realizing it'] (Bragança 2011a: 6).

arguably the Angolan writer with the most academic prestige. With so many publications to his name, Agualusa is a difficult author to follow, resulting in his earlier novels being the ones studied the most. With so much to choose from, our criteria sought to bring in a relatively understudied novel with a high degree of international prestige. Daniel Hahn's English translation of *Teoria* was shortlisted for the 2016 edition of the International Man Booker Prize and awarded the 2017 International Dublin Literary Award, making it the most accessible book for a non-Portuguese-speaking audience included in this study.

Agualusa's story revolves around twenty-eight years in the life of Ludovica Fernandes Mano, a White Portuguese spinster brought to Angola by her sister, who married a wealthy Black Angolan engineer shortly before the Carnation Revolution and the country's independence. Ludo is portrayed as a simple woman whose fear of going outdoors drives her to seal the door of her apartment after her sister and her husband mysteriously disappear. As the protagonist spends the years safely locked in the penthouse of what had been a luxurious building, the reader witnesses, with her and from above, the changes taking place in the post-independence area. Linked to the rest of the city of Luanda by the journey of her brother-in-law's forgotten diamonds, used by Ludo as bait to attract a pigeon who flies away, taking in its little stomach a small fortune onto other hands, we follow the development of a number of characters, all interlinked with the present, the past, the diamonds and each other. Conflating history and subjectivity in almost three decades into the aftermath of Angolan independence, this narrative offers a contemporary view on the postcolony that is essential to this study.

Book structure

Chapter 1 situates this work in terms of critical tradition within the international field of studies of the literatures of Portuguese-speaking Africa and disciplinary embedding in postcolonial studies. Attention is drawn to the shortcomings of established interpretative pathways for reading texts from these literatures, namely their importance for a discussion of nation-building and identity formation overly grounded in relations of *inter*-national order in detriment of *intra*-national tensions. The chapter addresses issues in postcolonial theory and proposes, through the observation of the concept of intra-colonialism, new ways to investigate contemporary formations, focusing on internal historical and social dynamics as local expressions of global systemic forces.

The next three chapters – Chapters 2 to 4 – are dedicated to the analysis of the themes that emerged from this comparative enquiry: state, violence and wealth. Each chapter is structured in a slightly different way to accommodate the literary fashioning of these themes as they emerge from the comparative method. As a result, each chapter contains an introduction that historically situates the diverse ways in which the given theme has been relevant to the texts' contexts of production – from the anticolonial struggle to the time of publication of the corpus – an analytical section focusing on convergences and divergences of the way the given theme is represented, and a conclusion where preliminary points for a transnational understanding of the given theme are brought forward.

Chapter 2, 'From Nation to State', is the most context-specific one given the essentially local aspect of the organisation of the machine of the state. For this reason, while the historical connections between these states are treated in the introduction of the chapter, the analytical section is divided into five parts, one for each novelistic representation of the state. Chapter 3, 'The Weapon of Violence' owes its structure to the array of ways in which violence is both presented and ingrained in each of the narratives. Historically contextualised, the registration of violence that emerged was in terms of state, gender and memory. It shows a change in terms of the representation of violence from physical to symbolic means of coercion that is connected to the concealment of violence inherent to democratic forms of political organisation coupled with liberal ideology. Chapter 4, 'The Matter of Wealth', looks at literary representations of wealth concentration and distribution, such as state wealth, wealth in transition from the state to private hands and private wealth. The concluding chapter, 'Towards a Late Postcoloniality', resumes our critique of postcolonial studies as it demonstrates, in light of the points raised along the analytical chapters, the necessity for a refashioning of the idea of postcolony that is addressed with the coinage of the concept of *late postcolonial condition*.

CHAPTER I

(Re)Locating Postcolonial Studies in the Postcolony

> We must begin *wherever we are* and the thought of the trace, which cannot not take the scent into account, has already taught us that it was impossible to justify a point of departure absolutely. *Wherever we are*: in a text where we believe ourselves to be.
> – Jacques Derrida, *Of Grammatology* (1997: 162).

The study of literary works that have emerged within any of the five African Portuguese countries with literatures in Portuguese is an activity marked by transnationality from the beginning. Prompted mostly by colonialism in its control of both academic and editorial activity, the intellectual diaspora of the African intelligentsia has, since very early on, set the pace for African literature outside Africa. As is already widely known, the CEI, or *Casa dos Estudantes do Império* (1944–1965) in Lisbon played an essential role in gathering African students, many of whom were committed to the cause of independence and to the end of colonialism, such as Amílcar Cabral and Agostinho Neto, among many others. The institution was also responsible for publishing the journal *Mensagem*, which, between 1949 and 1964, was an important means of diffusion of literature and ideas from the African diaspora in the metropole. Even as evidence of the transnational context in which the literatures of the Portuguese-speaking African countries emerged, the CEI was not the only instance of it. As Pires Laranjeira reports, between the 1960s and the time in which the independences were achieved, the diaspora was an important site for the literary production of the then Portuguese colonies – at the time treated by the government in Lisbon as 'Overseas Provinces' – and the places of publication would not only include the metropolis but also France, Italy, the Soviet Union and Brazil (1992: 28–29). Although the reverberations of those African publications in the developed world are yet to become subject to extensive study – reflecting the epistemic asymmetry where the only kind of intellectual exchange that matters is the Western influence in Africa, not the African influence to European thought and culture –, Laura Padilha offers an important account of the impact of Castro Soromenho's *Terra Morta* (1949) in Brazilian academia. She affirms that 'toda uma geração de universitários de letras, portanto, se formou ouvindo rumores sobre lugares africanos de nós tão distantes, mas onde se falava a nossa língua e de onde vieram homens e mulheres que sagraram as cores dos corpos de muitos de nós' ['A whole generation of university students, therefore, graduated hearing rumours about African places that were so far away from us, but where our language was spoken and where men and women came from who made the colours of the bodies of many of us sacred'] (2010b: 210). Padilha offers a witness account of the impact of the transnational circulation of African texts on the emergence of studies of African literatures in Portuguese beyond the metropolitan axis of Portugal. In Brazil, it was through the publication of Castro Soromenho's trilogy, composed of the above-mentioned *Terra Morta, Viragem* (1957) and *A Chaga* (1970), that the academic interest in such literatures started to rise.

While many critics in the field like to evoke Benedict Anderson's classic 1983 book *Immagines Communities* to speak of nation formation, not so many like to quote him when he traces the origins of national consciousness to a relationship with languages as an advent of 'print-capitalism, which made it possible for rapidly growing numbers of people to think about themselves, and to relate themselves to others, in profoundly new ways' (1991: 36). It is striking to note how often even engaged postcolonial critics tend to overlook that, in order to exist, literature depends on the book as a means and that the very conditions of production of literature as a cultural product mark the literary system as understood in its cycle from the author to the reader and from the critic to the educational system.[1] The

---

1   An issue that gained space in the field of sociology of literature and world literature thanks to the works of scholars such as Pascale Casanova, Gisèle Sapiro and Sarah Brouillette. In the field of African literatures in Portuguese, this debate has been looking at the literary impact of the political agenda of African authors. See Philip Rothwell's *Pepetela and the MPLA: The Ethical Evolution of a Revolutionary Writer* (2019) and Dorethée Boulanger's *Fiction as History: Resistance and Complicities in Angolan Postcolonial Literature* (2022).

establishment of foreign critical reception of literary works by Portuguese-speaking Africans is thus, for better or worse, in congruence with the very conditions of production of many of those literary works themselves. This does not mean, however, that the foreign critique is either above suspicion or is the *only* critique available. It is a fact that, in the same way that certain authors' literary works do not penetrate the transnational field of research of African literatures in Portuguese, so the critique by Africans is very little circulated beyond the critics' home cultures. In a 2010 text about the development and consolidation of African literature, Ana Mafalda Leite (2010), for example, traces the development of those studies in Portugal, Brazil, England and the United States, but little is said about the development of those studies within Africa, which makes it unclear whether she only meant to examine foreign studies or whether she was looking at the field as a whole. Such a distinction, followed by a brief but necessary investigation into the existent critical works conceived within Portuguese-speaking Africa, is made more clearly by Russell G. Hamilton, who acknowledged that 'foreign academics [are the ones who] have written the majority of the book-length studies of lusophone African literature' (2004: 618). It seems that while the much-needed debate about the gender and race of the African authors whose work is chosen to circulate in the transnational community of Portuguese-speakers has finally been initiated – see Mata's essay 'A Utopia Cosmopolita na Recepção das Literaturas Africanas' (2011) – the debate about the place of enunciation of such literature's criticism has yet to materialise. In a context where discussions involving the impact of socioeconomic privilege in the production and circulation of a cultural artefact as enmeshed in elitism as literature are still a problem, matters certainly get worse in the realm of criticism.[2] Whether this has to do with its close connection

2   Particularly interesting examples of this kind of heated discussion in the field could be seen during the international colloquium *Percursos, Trilhos e Margens: Recepção e Crítica das Literaturas Africanas em Língua Portuguesa,* organised by Margarida Calafate Ribeiro, Jessica Falconi and Elena Brugioni in July 2011. Although the proceedings of this colloquium are unfortunately not available, a better idea of the clash of positions can be obtained from the analysis of the conference programme, available online at <http://www.ces.uc.pt/ficheiros2/files/Programa_14_15_Ju lho.pdf>.

to the industry of education or its commitment to literatures conceived to deconstruct cultural hegemony, it is certain that queries with the potential to unveil, in the criticism of today, lingering relations of inequality dating back from the times of colonialism can be unsettling. As Mata well points out 'a questão ... comporta – disso tenho plena consciência – demasiados melindres ideológicos, muitas vezes fulanizados, nefastos num debate cultural descomprometido com julgamentos históricos' ['the question ... involves – and I am fully aware of this – too many ideological quibbles, often personalised, harmful in a cultural debate uncommitted to historical judgements'] (2011: 7).

Highlighting the foreignness that marks much of the critique of the African literatures in Portuguese is not an attempt to undermine criticism that comes from abroad. The intention here is not to depart from any essentialist perspective of truth, in which only endogenous criticism would account for the contextual reality of the literary work. Moreover, even though we value and hope for widespread endogenous criticism of African literatures precisely because of its multiple enabling possibilities, we do not believe that critical quality relies on inside or outside perspectives. When it comes to the impact of distance in sight, one must keep in mind that hypermetropia is, just like myopia, a condition that demands the use of corrective lenses.

Even if the location of the critique is not necessarily a problem, given that both endogenous and exogenous critiques offer complementary views on a given cultural artefact, pointing out the loci of enunciation of the critical discourse is important to understand both its potential and shortcomings. If one considers that critics 'too are subject to and producers of circumstances, which are felt regardless of whatever objectivity the critic's methods possess ... that texts have ways of existing that even in their most rarefied form are always enmeshed in circumstance, time, place, and society – in short they are in the world, and hence worldly' (Said 1983: 35), one should commit to read them 'with the same awareness of ambivalence that is brought to the study of non-critical literary texts' (de Man 1971: 110).

To treat the critical text as worldly demands that we consider the possibilities and constraints connected to the material contexts within and towards which the critical discourse emerges. By being worldly and thus circumstantial, the critical effort is always incomplete in the sense that it can never encompass the totality of the analysed work. It is only through this earthly, perspectival view that it is possible to look at a critical work's blind spots to unveil its insights. Once the worldly conditions of a critical text confer incompleteness upon it, its lack – or blindness, as Paul de Man wrote in *Blindness & Insight* (1971) – are the very conditions enabling the insights it brings to the fore and which constitute my point of departure.

Of blindness and insight

Critical approaches to the social implications of the cultural project of nation-building are a major blind spot of exogenous critical discourse on African works written in Portuguese. This is gradually being acknowledged, as seen through the work of Fernando Arenas who, in the closing paragraph of his book *Lusophone Africa: Beyond Independence*, states that

> [the book] aims to move the discussion beyond the heroic accounts of the liberation struggles and away from overly cautious and *acritical approaches to the political establishment* in nations such as Angola and Mozambique that have prevailed in the humanities, especially in the field of literary studies. (2011: 204; emphasis added)

Having begun in very turbulent times, the study of African works in Portuguese went hand in hand with the very political engagement whose theme constituted those literary pieces. The first systematic study of the literary history of the Portuguese-speaking African countries came initially in English, with Hamilton's *Voices from an Empire: A History of Afro-Portuguese Literature*, published in 1975, at around the same time that the independences of Angola, Mozambique, Cape Verde, Guinea-Bissau and São Tomé and Príncipe were being recognised by Portugal. Even though it was written at the tail end of the colonial period, when the five territories were still classified as Portuguese overseas provinces, not soverign states, Hamilton's option to organise his book according to the national literature study framework had a strong political connotation. With a full section on Angola, one on Mozambique, one on the Cape Verde Islands – within which we find 'The Case of Portuguese Guinea (Guinea-Bissau)' (358) – and a section on São Tomé and Príncipe, Hamilton treats almost each literary system as national and independent, as he states that 'despite their obvious interrelationships, the four parts of this study can be read independently of each other with no loss of coherence' (22).

Very much a product of its time, Hamilton's option for critical language reveals the liminal moment from which he writes. Terms such as 'Portuguese Guinea', 'Guinea-Bissau', 'African literature of Portuguese expression' and 'Afro-Portuguese' are interchangeably used in his work. The context of critical writing from an early postcolonial perspective, before the formal end of colonialism in the region, results in a vacillating choice for an anticolonial critical terminology that will sharpen and later become the new standard. In its function as gatekeeper of the canon, criticism has developed an important political role in the transnational cultural arena by promoting recently independent countries' literary systems. This is a pivotal moment in the commitment of the critique of African literatures in Portuguese to African nationalist causes.

The assertion by Arenas proposes that the political engagement that once constituted criticism's vanguardist standpoint has come to constitute one of the field's most pronounced blind spots. Recent book-length studies by Phillip Rothwell (2019) and Dorothée Boulanger (2022) have started to make a visible movement to address this aspect of textual worldliness by investigating the role played by authors' political ideology and concrete involvement in party politics in their work in the literatures of Angola, where the participation of writers in politics is especially relevant. While the focus of their study is authoritarian complicity with party politics, their remarks on critical silence on this front can be read as a tangential critique of criticism in the field. As Rothwell puts it, when speaking of one of the most canonical of the Angolan writers '[i]n their appreciation for his fiction, many literary critics remain silent about Pepetela's role in a purge of the MPLA in 1977' (2019: 3).

In its commitment to support the legitimacy of the recently independent countries, criticism has supported the nationalist movements-turned-governments, often in control of state-sponsored writer's associations and state-owned publishers, in their cultural efforts to forge their national communities' imaginations to provide a soul to their states' geopolitical bodies. Nevertheless, at the time of Arenas' book release, over three decades after the constitutional acts that legitimised the political formation of those nation-states, the situation had become much more complex. History had made it impossible to conceal the harmful societal impacts of the contradictions underlying the reinvention of the anticolonial nationalist movements from colonial opposition to the post-independence situation. Yet, despite essential political, economic and cultural changes in these works' contexts of production, mainstream critical discourse struggles to shift.

In almost half a century since political sovereignty, the victorious struggle for independence gave way to internal armed conflicts in both Angola (1975–2002) and Mozambique (1977–1992), as well as to complicated democratic processes reflected by irregular and contested presidential successions across the five countries. São Tomé and Príncipe counts two attempted *coups d'état*. Guinea-Bissau had the power given to its longest-sitting president due to a coup. João Bernadino (Nuno) Vieira held power for a total of twenty-three years, split into four mandates – although it is reported that two other unsuccessful attempted coups had taken place in 1983 and 1985 (Forrest 2002) – until a final uprising led to the 1998–1999 civil war that ended with the 2000 election. Between 2000 and 2012, Guinea-Bissau suffered yet another coup in 2003, a presidential assassination in 2009 and a coup in 2012. Cape Verde's political constitution is seen by many as one of the smoothest in Africa. Without civil wars or coups, one can only notice that the relatively long terms of the last two elected presidents for two mandates (ten years in total for each president) resulted, however, from largely uncontested elections. Apparently as smooth but not as uncontested has been Mozambique's permanence in power of the Frelimo party that, since 1975, has provided the only four presidents to govern the country. In Angola, the MPLA has been leading the country since independence, having provided the only three presidents the country has ever had, with one of them remaining in power for an astonishing thirty-eight years. In light of these facts, it is hard to believe that the literary production in Portuguese-speaking Africa would have been little engaged with these internal political developments. If this is so, how could Arenas remark on a tendency towards acritical approach to political establishments in literary studies?

In an attempt to answer this question, we can turn to Rothwell's *A Postmodern Nationalist: Truth, Orality and Gender in the Work of Mia Couto*. Published in 2004, Rothwell's study investigates Mia Couto's works published between 1987 and 2001, which are deeply grounded in aftermath of the independence in Mozambique. As the title says, Rothwell sees Couto as a nationalist. Such an idea is, alone, pretty much widespread through the field where criticism often legitimises the canonical rights of works and writers by attesting their ability to evoke a certain spirit – or a ghost – of the nation. What is new in Rothwell is his willingness to look at the postmodern features of Couto's works, seeing him (as a metonym for his works) still as a nationalist, but a postmodern one.

To see Couto in his modified nationalism, as proposed by Rothwell's title, could constitute an important step forward in the approach of an African literature in the aftermath of independence. Faced with the impossibility of portraying the grand narrative that characterises the modernist aesthetics of nation building in the twentieth century, the resort to postmodern in national(istic) contexts could be seen as indicative of an erosion of the modern certainties that once guided the national project. However, this is not the approach taken by Rothwell. Seen in its implication as the cultural logic of globalisation, the postmodern aesthetic present in Couto's productions is perceived as a contradiction to the author's presumed nationalistic aims that came into being as a by-product of transnational capitalism:

> In a world where the executives of multinational corporations and aid-agency officials often wield more influence than government ministers over supposedly sovereign states, *nationalism and an assertion of national identity is an increasingly weak refuge for those wishing to oppose the inexorable trend towards globalization.* Yet *it remains, along with religious fundamentalism, one of the principal counterbalances to unfettered neoliberal capitalism* in an age that has rejected the socialist experiment. For good or for bad, nationalism invariably operated by putting up barriers to distinguish between the national group and the foreign, making it *the perfect ideological opponent to globalization,* once class struggle is excluded from the equation … . Globalization wants to dissolve the border, which, as a range of critics have pointed out, culturally allies it with the postmodern project since postmodernism recognizes no boundary and rejects the primacy of binary demarcations. (2004: 15; emphasis added)

Rothwell analyses Couto's work from the premise of the author's 'obsession for blurring frontiers, the overriding characteristic assigned to postmodernism' (32). The book then follows in a crescendo where the critic ultimately sees the resolution of the author's contradictory traces – the conjugation of postmodern aesthetics and the modernist project of nationalism – as he completes a process of maturation that culminates at the point when Couto is seen abandoning his postmodern position and reaching a 'postcolonial maturity' (170). For Rothwell, postcolonial maturity is reached as Couto's 'evolution as a writer has reached the point where it is no longer sufficient just to ask questions. The time has come for answers to be furnished' (172), and those answers came when the author decided to centre his narrative back on the nation.

Complementary to Rothwell's perspective towards the national in detriment of the postmodern, and probably to rescue the author from eventual apolitical accusations commonly destined to those who serve themselves of that aesthetics, Rothwell affirms 'the techniques of the postmodernism, as employed by Couto, do not proscribe the creation of *a national identity*' (169; emphasis added). Consequently, Rothwell develops his analysis of Couto's postmodern style by seeing it as a deliberate strategy of destabilising Western binarisms. In his view, Couto's work disavows both Platonic and Hegelian traditions as he blurs the frontiers between oral and written 'on a repudiation of the demarcations privileged by Western traditional culture' (172), against which a Mozambican national identity should be shaped. According to this line of thought, the work of Couto is put in relation to Western thinkers such as Nietzsche, Derrida, Saussure and Lévi-Strauss, as well as to the aforementioned Plato and Hegel. Every step of Rothwell's thought reinforces its main argument that views Couto's aesthetic destruction of conceptual boundaries in relation to truth, orality and gender as an appropriation of the postmodern, and presumed apolitical, tool to meet political nationalistic ends – met when he finally reaches a 'postcolonial maturity'.

One of the gains brought by Rothwell's reflections is his postcolonial reading that recuperates Couto's works as a non-Western literary work that is capable of proposing a rethinking of Western conceptualisations of truth, orality and gender, talking back to the European centre. However, the ease with which the critic puts Couto's works in dialogue with the West certainly depicts the author more in relation to an international system than to the internal political dynamics within which the establishment of 'a' national identity would work. This move could have the unintended effect of detaching Couto from the Mozambican national scene, seeing the value of his work in terms of its ability to unsettle Western dichotomies.

Analysing a corpus that goes from Coutos' 1987 *Vozes Anoitecidas* (translated as *Nightfall Voices* in 1990), out twelve years after independence, to his 2001 *O Último Vôo do Flamingo* (translated as *The Last Flight of the Flamingo* in 2004), nine years after the end of the Mozambican destabilisation war, Rothwell's analysis of Couto's use of postmodern aesthetics sees a nationalism too much in line with the anticolonial moment and too little connected with the Mozambican postcolonial moment within which those literary works are inscribed. In the words of Rothwell, Couto's 'concern is to help develop an independent Mozambican identity' (169), which means an identity that can be seen in its separation from the foreign element and not an identity concerned with dealing with the cultural pluralities present in the country. Despite indicating his awareness of the internal social and political situations of Mozambique at the time of Couto's publications, Rothwell's work does not contemplate the possibility of Couto's reworking of the concepts of truth, orality and gender as a critique to his government's political practices, and policies in terms of language or gender. The concept of 'a' national identity is taken for granted and is never the object of analysis even when, in the face of the facts, Rothwell mentions diversity both in linguistic (42–45) and gender practices (134) as obstacles to such an endeavour by Frelimo. Mozambique's political and military convulsions are in the background, playing the role of a framework for Couto's critique expressed as the appropriation and abrogation of Western concepts. According to Rothwell's bottom line analysis, the political governance of Mozambique is not to blame for the problems of the young nation and Couto, throughout his work, 'critiques European interference in Mozambique, and extends [it] to cover the *Eurocentric* Marxist model that oppressed the nation from 1975 under Samora Machel' (171; emphasis added). What is at stake in Rothwell's interpretation of Couto's work is, almost exclusively, the inside/outside dichotomy – even when Couto's aesthetic choices are seen to point in a contrary direction – rejecting rigid dichotomies. When he chooses to blame European interference and Eurocentric Marxism for oppressing the nation instead of seeing it in relation to Frelimo's ability to run the country in the face of an international climate averse to the socialist experiment, Rothwell moves away from a closer evaluation of Mozambique's internal postcolonial political situation. This is how this work by Rothwell can be seen as an important example of the phenomenon pointed out by Arenas and where the lack of a more encompassing critique of contemporary African works can be seen as apolitical. Put against Rothwell's much more critical take later, as per his 2019 book *Pepetela and the MPLA*, it may seem that the critical panorama may have started to shift even if a more substantial work of reflection on the very place of the critic's agency and ideological agenda is yet to come.

That said, it is important to reassert the relevance, range and depth of Rothwell's reading of Couto's works. In line with de Man's study of the productivity of the analysis of critical works, my point here is 'very different from claiming that what the critic says has no immanent connection with the [literary] work, that it is an arbitrary addition or subtraction, or that the gap between his statement and his meaning can be dismissed as mere error' (de Man 1971: 109). The contradiction emerging from Rothwell's reading of postmodern aesthetics to serve a grand narrative rather than to question it seems inherent to his locus of enunciation as a critic. Although his intention appears to be the recuperation of Couto's nationalism as a trope of resistance against globalisation's invasive dissolution of borders and localisms, the analysis ends up turning Couto into a reviewer of Western thought to the extent that his work is seen, mostly, in relation to it. Following de Man, critics who, like Rothwell in this case, 'seem curiously doomed to say something quite different from what they meant to say' (105–106), result in doing so because of a 'peculiar blindness: their language could grope toward a certain degree of insight only because their method remained oblivious to the perception of this insight' (106). As such, Rothwell's oversight is the imbrication of his methodology and his locus of enunciation, resulting in a mismatch between his aim to place Couto at the forefront of the fight against globalisation and his use of Couto's work to destabilise concepts of truth, orality and gender forged and upheld in the West. In keeping with de Man's proposition that it is through its analysis that a critical text can reveal its utmost productivity, what Rothwell's reading allows us to see is the significant lack of an analysis of Couto's works in relation to the internal political situation of Mozambique.

The phenomenon verified in Rothwell's analysis should not be seen as exclusive to critics speaking from the anglophone cores of the capitalist world-system. Brazil is another place from which much criticism of African literatures in Portuguese has been done. Situated across the Atlantic from West Africa, Brazil was for 322 years part of the same colonial enterprise that connected its history with those of Angola, Mozambique, Guinea-Bissau, Cape Verde and São Tomé and Príncipe. In more than 500 years of history since the arrival of the Portuguese in what is today the surroundings of the Brazilian city of Porto Seguro, in the northeast of the country, Brazil has been an independent state for less than half of that time. As the chosen jewel of the colonial metropolis, Brazil was the colony that most benefitted from metropolitan investments. This explains why roughly 5 million Black Africans were sent there as enslaved labour to feed various economic activities undertaken by the Portuguese in the Brazilian colony, such as sugarcane plantations, cocoa plantations, or the exploitation, extraction, and appropriation of gold, silver and diamonds, among other resources.[3] If anyone were to claim that Rothwell's critical bias would be determined by the historical and cultural distance from Mozambique whence he writes, one might be surprised that a Brazilian critique could go the same way.

One of the most renowned and respected Brazilian critics, researchers and professors in the field of African literatures in Portuguese, the work of Laura Cavalcante Padilha constitutes an important example of Brazilian critical trends in the area. In her 2010 article titled 'O Ensino e a Crítica das Literaturas Africanas no Brasil: um Caso de Neocolonialidade e Enfrentamento', Padilha reflects on forty years of history of the Brazilian practices of research and teaching of the considered five African literary

---

3   The website SlaveVoyages.org, developed by researchers of the Hutchins Center for African and African American Research at the University of Harvard in partnership with universities in Brazil, the United Kingdom and New Zealand, informs that of 5,848,266 people embarked as slaves in Africa with a destination of Brazil, 5,099,816 were disembarked alive on the shores of the country.

works in Brazil. Starting by providing us with important historical facts connected with the establishment of the bachelor in language and literature in the country, Padilha recalls the inhospitable environment surrounding African literatures in Brazil and its gradual overcoming, with the blooming and expanding of the field from the 1990s onwards, whose drive is defined by the critic:

> pela tentativa de, por um viés transdisciplinar, tornarem-se mais visíveis alguns recessos da cultura nacional -, nós, estudiosos, *acreditamos estar contribuindo para a reversão da opacidade por tanto tempo existente. Só assim cremos ser possível mudar o contorno da imagem de nossa distorcida face projetada no espelho da história, espelho em que, por muito tempo se elidiu a pluralidade do sujeito nacional,* pelo fato mesmo de que a contribuição simbólica dos primeiros habitantes da terra e dos que para cá vieram como escravos foi sempre considerada, sumariamente, de menor ou quase nenhuma importância. (2010a: 6; emphasis added)

> [by attempting, through a transdisciplinary approach, to make some of the recesses of national culture more visible – we, scholars, believe to be contributing to reversing the opacity that has existed for so long. Only in this way do we believe it is possible to change the contour of the image of our distorted face projected in the mirror of history, a mirror in which, for a long time, the plurality of the national subject was elided, due to the very fact that the symbolic contribution of the first inhabitants of the land and those who came here as slaves was always summarily considered to be of lesser or almost no importance.]

Imbued with such a drive, Padilha reports that the Brazilian critic works as a translator whose aim is 'trazer, à cena contemporânea, as tradições que sempre foram apagadas e/ou se apresentavam como incompreensivelmente exóticas ou diferentes, no olhar dos agentes do vetor considerado alto, da cultura brasileira' ['to bring to the contemporary scene traditions that have always been erased and/or presented as incomprehensibly exotic or different, in the eyes of the agents of the vector considered high, of Brazilian culture'] (7). Looking for a reconnection with Africa, the critic wishes 'tornar mais visíveis "o significante" e a "metáfora" que a África representa, na busca de construir … "novas fronteiras de solidariedade"' ['to make more visible "the signifier" and the "metaphor" that Africa represents, in the quest to build … "new frontiers of solidarity"'] (2010a: 9) in a movement that reflects the search 'através da construção literária e cultural que as produções artístico-verbais africanas acabam por nos oferecer, das "rotas" que, ao fim e ao cabo, subsistiam, como afirma o teórico jamaicano [Stuart Hall] "no interior de complexas configurações" de nossa própria cultura' ['through the literary and cultural construction that African artistic-verbal productions end up offering us, of the "routes" that, in the end, subsisted, as the Jamaican theorist [Stuart Hall] says, "within the complex configurations" of our own culture'] (2010a 9–10).

Through the coordinates given by Padilha, we can see that, in their search for Africa, the Brazilian critique proposes to decentre and dis-occidentalize the notions of literary canon in the country. Having the research on Africa as an attempt to confront Brazil's strongly neocolonial cultural heritage – as expressed by the critic already in the title of her article – Padilha's concern with this field not only points to the Global South but also to the subaltern Global South, with an aim to change the geographies and displace hegemonic notions of cultural and artistic value. Additionally, the political drive of such a critique addresses the very pungent socio-economic problem of racism in Brazil. Even though the country sells an image of racial democracy, a 2008 study reveals that for 63.7 per cent of the population, colour or race are still factors of influence in their everyday lives (2011: 37). Moreover, if we take the 2010 census as a point of reference, which, for the first time in history, reports the number of people identifying as non-White as larger than those identifying as White, the high indexes of extreme poverty to which the Black population in Brazil is subjected constitute evidence of the subaltern connotation of African heritage in Brazilian culture.[4]

Notwithstanding this, the political inclination aiming for a change in Brazilian society shows that a critique in line with Padilha's view turns out to be centred on its own identitarian needs. Padilha's metaphor in which the search for Africa serves the Brazilian aim of changing its own

---

4   In Brazil, race is usually denoted in terms of skin colour. Of the total recorded re-
     spondents on the question of race or colour, 52.3 per cent identified as non-White
     while 47.7 per cent identified as White. Under 'non-White', we have 43.1 per cent
     of respondents identifying as 'pardo' (mix of Brown and Black ethnicities), 7.6 per
     cent said Black, 1.1 per cent identified as 'yellow' (East Asian heritage) and 0.5 per
     cent identified as Indigenous Brazilian.

distorted image projected in the mirror of history, a distortion that refers to the obliteration of the Black people's relevance in Brazil's racial and cultural identity, we are reminded of Jacques Lacan in his 'The Mirror Stage as Formative of the Function of the I' essay. According to the French psychoanalyst, the mirror stage is the first stage of identification for the subject, resulting from the process in which the subject identifies itself with the image of their whole body reflected in the mirror. Lacan also remarks that the mirror stage is just an initial step in a larger process of identification of the subject, occurring very early in the child's development (between the ages of eighteen months and six years), and that it is an intrinsically individual process in which the other is merely the child's own image – what Lacan calls *imago*. This means that, at the mirror stage, 'the I is precipitated in a primordial form, before it is objectified in the dialectic of identification with the other' (1989: 2). With that in mind, looking for Africa to reinforce its own identitarian needs would not put the Brazilian approach much further apart from Rothwell's to the extent in which it also talks back to the social urgencies of the place of enunciation of the critic rather than to the literary contexts of emergency. If the approach that Padilha reports is indeed connected with the Lacanian mirror stage of the Brazilian psyche, as she points out throughout her text and as Lacan himself reminds us, this is a stage of identification that does not consider a relation with the other, meaning that it does not contemplate Africa in its alterity.

Rothwell's analysis of Couto's works ends up not addressing the possible critical relations those works could establish with Mozambique's internal political affairs in order not to defeat his purpose of maintaining nationalism as a 'refuge' – even though 'weak' – to fight globalisation. Similarly, Padilha's choice, resonating with the 'mirror stage' in her commitment to the creation of a positive image of Black heritage in Brazil, betrays her own declared desire to look for Africa because it does not relate to it in its alterity. Such an approach, which aims at accessing an 'other who is in us', invades the alterity of the African other by giving it relevance only insofar as it works as a component of Brazilian identity. Although different from the colonial process of othering in nature, this view still shares its procedure. While the classic type of colonial othering sought to mark a hierarchical separation between coloniser 'Other' and colonised 'other', Padilha's view takes the African cultural element 'other' to legitimise Blackness in a Brazilian cultural identity conceived as 'Other', revealing her slippage into the very logic she appears to contest.[5]

The conceptualisation of the other's alterity has been central to twentieth-century philosophy. Brought up by Derrida in *Writing and Difference*, Levinas' relations with Husserl and Heidegger's ideas about the other are criticised and supplemented in what came to be worked on his own ideas of the other (*l'autre*) throughout his later works. Derrida's conceptualisation can be seen as moving away from Levinas' thought of a divinely absolute Other (*Autrui*), which, in its unreachability, 'increases the neutrality of the other' (2001: 130), making it unsuitable for the play – according to the Derridan concept of play (*jeu*)– through which other people and other things would signify. He minds Levinas' concern with alterity, though, whose expression he also sees in the Husserlian concept of alter ego. Even though establishing a relation of symmetry between the 'I' and the 'other', Husserl's proposal preserves alterity once it implies 'an ego which I know *to be in relation to me as to an other*' (15; emphasis added). To think of the other as alter ego, in its unreachable sameness brought about by the impossibility of any consubstantiation with the other, becomes key to the play through which the other can, asymmetrically – to the extent that the Derridean relation between opposites is always hierarchical – signify.

This conceptualisation of alterity implies that the purpose of the study of Africa described by Padilha denies the symmetry between the 'I' and the 'other' to the extent it regards the 'other' only as within the 'I'. This leads to the situation that, once they are not similar in their alterity and do not relate to each other as other, both the Brazilian and the African element can never define each other, neither in terms of the synthetically Hegelian *aufhebung* nor the oppositional Derridian *différance*. And again, evoking de Man, it is noticeable that what Padilha described bears a blindness towards its own methodology, which defeats the purpose of

5   A thought-provoking discussion on the (in)utility of the concept of other in the light of both practices of colonial otherness and philosophical attempts to bear the other in mind in its alterity can be found in Robert J. C. Young's essay 'Postcolonial Remains' (2012).

her study to the extent that it does not really imply the knowledge of Africa as other – by only focusing on its sameness, not its difference. By not doing so, it refutes the possibility for the Brazilian identity to define itself either in terms of synthesis with or in opposition to Africa, ending up, as de Man has termed it, doing something quite different from what she seems to have intended. In its insight, Padillha's approach recuperates the importance of alterity, as very well remarked by Rita Chaves in her own reflection on the study of African literatures in Portuguese produced in Brazil titled 'A Pesquisa em Torno das Literaturas Africanas: Pontos para um Balanço':

> Acabo, nesse momento, de tocar num outro aspecto que me parece essencial: a nossa condição de estrangeiro, ou melhor, a importância de não perdermos de vista, ao lidarmos com esses textos, que estamos diante de uma literatura que não é nossa. E, nesse ponto, contrariando algumas correntes, ouso arriscar que a língua portuguesa pode ser um complicador. Porque ela nos dá a ilusão de que estamos perante uma situação muito familiar. Muitas convergências existem, muitos laços nos unem, e creio que, como todos que têm a África como tema, eu desejo vê-los apertados; no entanto, acho que a viabilidade desse desejo depende também da consciência serena das nossas diferenças. (2010: 9; emphasis added)

> [I have now touched on another aspect that seems essential to me: our condition as foreigners, or rather, the importance of not losing sight, when dealing with these texts, of the fact that we are dealing with a literature that is not our own. And on this point, contrary to some trends, I dare to venture that the Portuguese language can be a complicating factor. Because it gives us the illusion that we are dealing with a very familiar situation. There are many convergences, many ties that bind us, and I believe that, like everyone who has Africa as a theme, I want to see them tightened; however, I think that the viability of this desire also depends on the serene awareness of our differences.]

Both Rothwell and Padilha's receptions of African literary texts support Arenas' assessment of the field, as both critics fall short of analysing such literatures' responses to their local socio-political contexts of emergence. Given that both critics are extremely capable academics whose contributions to the field are incontestable, such oversight could be explained by their positionality. Going back to Said's proposition for a criticism that is worldly (1983: 35), committed to the society in which it is inserted and to which it speaks, we can understand how both critics engage very productively with their own places of enunciation. As Rothwell criticises the current hegemonic model in which the West explains the rest, by using Couto's work as a supplementary discourse to Western thought, he engages actively with the political discourse of his own Anglo-American space, both by challenging the unidirectional flows of thought from an active north to a passive south and by offering routes of resistance to globalisation, the moving force in the realm of the capital that perpetuated the unidirectionality of those flows. Padilha, in her turn, works with similar political engagement with Brazil's socio-economic problems to the point she openly addresses, in an active way, the country's racial problems reflected by the oblivion affecting the Black person as a valued historical agent and, at the same time, proposes an epistemological decentring of a culture locked in a vicious tradition of moving towards the West. Returning to de Man's proposition of critical blindness as the necessary condition for critical insight, it is important to look at what these critical works miss if we are to come to terms with our own worldly engagement with foreign critical discourse in the field of African literatures in Portuguese. A critic's blindness, according to de Man,

> can take on the form of a recurrently aberrant pattern of interpretation with regard to a particular writer. The pattern extends from highly specialized commentators to the vague *idées reçues* by means of which this writer is identified and classified in general histories of literature. It can even include other writers who have been influenced by him. (1971: 111)

In this sense, rather than reproducing perspectives, this study challenges them from a supplementary position. de Man's proposition can aid in understanding Arena's detection of a pattern of avoidance in terms of critical engagement with the political situation of the postcolonial states in question, suggesting that there may be a need for greater critical engagement with the political situation of the postcolonial states. Since the analysis of these works, specifically in relation to their internal situation, constitutes the core of this study, this book *comes from* and is situated *in relation* to this same criticism, giving it insight and strength from which to depart.

Towards the postcolony: From between states to within states

Most of the foreign criticism of African literatures in Portuguese is made with the help of postcolonial theory. Embedded in a field that came to be known as postcolonial studies, almost every book, article or essay on postcolonialism comes supplied with a 'clarifying' genealogy of the field.[6] Although most of the definitions come with an interesting disclaimer stating that the field cannot be circumscribed within the genealogies given, most of them locate the roots of postcolonial thought in the post-World War II wave of independences of British colonies and locate its condensation as a field recognised under the 'postcolonial' rubric from the 1970s. There are even those who would declare its beginning with the publication of Said's *Orientalism* in 1978, setting its institutionalisation in the Anglo-American academia in the 1980s, and there are some who would speak of these beginnings as the moment 'when Third World intellectuals have arrived in First World academe' (Dirlik 1994: 329).[7] Interestingly, even though the line of thought in the field is often said to be heavily marked by poststructuralism, postcolonial studies seem unable to deny its Marxist heritage, expressed by its everlasting need for historicity, beginning with its own.

With time, however, it has become clear that genealogies dialogue, in fact, with the place of enunciation of the critic that will always play a role in guiding their interpretative work. It is for this reason that accepting Derrida's advice and beginning wherever we are is seen here as the most

---

6   Stuart Hall, in his essay 'When was the postcolonial? Thinking at the limit' (2003) summarises well the discussion around the term 'postcolonial' as it was posed by scholars such as Ella Shohat, Anne McClintock and Arif Dirlik in the early 1990s. In the 2000s, refashions of the discussions can be found in 'What postcolonialism doesn't say' (2011) by Neil Lazarus, 'Postcolonial remains' (2012) by Young, Benita Parry's 'What is left in postcolonial studies?' (2012), Ella Shohat e Robert Stam's 'Whence and whither postcolonial theory' (2012) and Timothy Brennan's *Borrowed Light* (2014).

7   Such as Ana Mafalda Leite's *Literaturas Africanas e Formações Pós-coloniais* (2003) and Aschroft et al.'s *The Empire Writes Back* (1989).

appropriate way to take off, as, given the vastness of both territories and phenomena it concerns, any genealogy of postcolonial studies will always be incomplete. As Shohat and Stam recently stated:

> we should see it [Postcolonial Studies] as a potentially polycentric and open-ended discourse to be defined from multiple sites and perspectives. Our key argument about the multidirectionalities of ideas is that the Postcolonial project and similar projects emerge out of many, many contexts. There are so many antecedents along-side the usual postcolonial triad of Edward Said, Homi Bhabha, and Gayatri Spivak. Important as they are, we have to remember figures like Frantz Fanon, Aimé Césaire [and Almícar Cabral]. (2012: 18)[8]

When it comes to critics occupied with Portuguese-speaking Africa, their relations with postcolonial theory are influenced by the hierarchical position of the critic's place of enunciation in the global market of epistem-ologies. While the critique coming from English-speaking spaces shows little resistance to the theoretical corpus available, as Shohat and Stam point out, the 'Latins' represented here by Portugal and Brazil tend to receive an 'Anglo-Saxon' postcolonial theory with distrust (13). When it comes to the Portuguese critique, besides being very well informed of what is published in the English-speaking world, it tends to highlight its need to drift away from Anglo-American academic theories based on British postcolonial experiences, expressing the need for local theories able to deal with the spe-cificity of Portuguese colonialism, a project that has been long embraced by Boaventura de Sousa Santos and has taken the shape of *Epistemologias do Sul* [Epistemologies of the South].[9] When it comes to Brazilian critics, the point made by the Portuguese is usually taken into consideration and reinforced by a sense of belonging to Latin America, which adds to their idea of the theoretical body, and de Sousa Santos is joined by local flavours

---

8   In this interview, Shohat and Stam discuss at length other places of enunciation of critical reflections on the postcolonial as well as the enduring tendency to trace its beginning to what has been called the 'Anglo-Saxon' academe.

9   Initially elaborated on Boaventura de Sousa Santos' *Toward a New Common Sense: Law, Science and Politics in the Paradigmatic Transition*, the concept of 'epistemologias do sul' (Southern epistemologies) was the theme of an eponymous book organized by Maria Paula Meneses and de Sousa Santos.

such as Antonio Candido, Roberto Schwarz, Silviano Santiago and Walter Mignolo, along with the widespread anglophone canonical counterparts Said, Bhabha and Spivak. Precisely because it is performed from a post-colonial perspective, foreign literary criticism of African literatures in Portuguese tends not to turn a blind eye to the epistemological hierarchy of the north towards the south, for it re-enacts the same dominant logic of the colonial practices that this form of criticism is committed to contesting. In an 2008 interview, Mbembe makes an interesting distinction between 'thinking about the postcolony' and 'postcolonial thought':

> In many respects my book [*On the Postcolony*] adopts a different approach from that of most postcolonial thinking, if only over the privileged position accorded by the latter to questions of identity and difference, and over the central role that the theme of resistance plays in it. *There is a difference, to my mind, between thinking about the 'postcolony' and 'postcolonial' thought.* The question running through my book is this: 'What is "today", and what are we, today?' What are the lines of fragility, the lines of precariousness, the fissures in contemporary African life? And, possibly, how could what is, be no more, how could it give birth to something else? And so, if you like, it's a way of reflecting on the fractures, on what remains of the promise of life when the enemy is no longer the colonist in a strict sense, but the 'brother'? So the book is a critique of the African discourse on community and brotherhood. (2008: 11; emphasis added)

It is clear that for Mbembe, there is a disjuncture between the postcolony as a space and postcolonial thought as an epistemological practice. According to his perspective, while the latter demands a concern with contemporary African political realities, the former is a

> product of the encounter between Europe and the worlds it once made into its dis-tant possessions … . It calls upon Europe to live what it declares to be its origins, its future and its promise, and to live all that responsibly … postcolonial thought calls upon Europe to open and continually relaunch that future in a singular fashion, re-sponsible for itself, for the Other, and before the Other. (11)

Although Mbembe's statement sets the stage for a number of important questions – including whether it would be fair to reduce postcolonial thought to a European sense of responsibility for the other that continues colonial practices – for the moment, and according to the pertinence of our object, one could ask whether Mbembe is right in his distinction and therefore whether postcolonial thought would be enough to understand the social materiality of the postcolony.

Between *inter-* and *intra-*national dimensions

Although the term colony is not a recent concept, nor is the existence of ex-colonies, if we take into account the US declaration of independence from Great Britain in 1776, for example, postcolony as a critical term is a product of the late twentieth century. In contrast to the wave of independence that started in the Americas in the eighteenth and nineteenth centuries, emancipation following World War II came intertwined with anticolonial nationalism, often revolutionary in nature. Besides the fact that nationalism is a widely studied phenomenon, the majority of what is done comprises the nationalism responsible for the European processes of national unification. This leaves aside a more detailed study of the socio-ideological movements that brought independence to the Americas, shaking the basis of the British, French, Spanish and Portuguese colonial empires – an epistemological move that is questionable and hardly innocent.[10] Differently from the nationalism of the Americas, although similarly subaltern if compared to the attention given to European ones, much can be found about the study of the nationalist wave that led the postwar world into the end of colonialism. Even though it tends to be seen as a European derivative movement – given that it had European colonialism as a common enemy – anticolonial nationalism happened in diverse ways, both as a response to the specific contexts in which they emerged and as a means to face the specific challenges colonialism put to them. Robert Young, for example, makes a clear distinction between what he calls 'colonial nationalism', as it happened in India, and 'Marxist internationalism with armed national liberation movements', as happened

10   Interesting reflections about the academic neglect of nationalism in the Americas are found in Doyle and Pamplona's *Nationalism in the New World* (2006).

in Angola and Mozambique. Nonetheless, despite its differences, it is also important to state that, just as colonialism puts those movements together, '[h]istorically, postcolonial theory is the product of all these [forms of anticolonial nationalism]' (Young 2001: 166).

Before the political entity of the postcolony, anticolonial thought was a counterideology in relation to colonialism. As the works of Fanon and Cabral show, way before Said, Spivak or Bhabha, the basis of what is currently known as 'postcolonial theory' was forged within anticolonial struggles as the intellectual weapon of counterattack to colonialism. And if, on the one hand, anticolonial consciousness has helped to forge the postcolony, its very connection with the armed movements within which it emerged can be regarded as one of the main reasons for its apparent inadequacy to handle the current postcolony. Given that it rests upon the nationalist principle that rejects the domination of one nation, or even a group of different nations, by an alien dominating one, which is reflected in the fight against the advance of global capitalism through the practice of colonialism inherited from anticolonial thought, postcolonial theory was born much more prepared to deal with the international agenda of its time. In this sense, as a body of theory, postcolonial studies have evolved to be better equipped to handle relations *between* states rather than *within* states, endorsing Mbembe's perspective. Such seems to be the heritage of a current of thought conceived by the clash between *inter*-national capitalism and *inter*-national Marxism: the *intra*-national dimension of these struggles is often regarded as redundant.

The inability of postcolonial criticism to go *intra*-national has been slowly addressed since the turn of this century as the contradictions of anticolonial nationalism condense into political and economically disappointing postcolonial realities. As Arif Dirlik puts it:

> [i]n many ways, contemporary postcolonial criticism is most important as a reflection on the history of postcolonial discourse (a self-criticism of the discourse, in other words), bringing to the same surface contradictions that were rendered invisible earlier by barely examined and fundamentally teleological assumptions concerning capitalism, socialism and the nation, but above all revolutionary national liberation movements against colonialism – the failure of which has done much to provoke an awareness of these contradictions. (2002: 432)

Those contradictions, termed by Dirlik also as '[t]he tragedy of anticolonial revolutionary nationalism' (437), are of special interest here as they encompass the contradictions of the very kind of nationalism that set forth independence and constituted the governments in each of the five Portuguese-speaking African countries. Still, according to Dirlik, the most contradictory aspect of anticolonial revolutionary nationalism was nation-building. Since the anticolonial aim to liberate the colonial spaces and to constitute sovereign nations was the very result of colonial inter-vention – as the boundaries of the new states were based on those of the colonies whose drawing was made taking into account European interests and not the cohesion of cultural groups within them, as is widely known – 'what were the consequences of their imaginings for the populations that colonialism had gathered under its administrative aegis, which they now sought to make into a nation? Is it possible that they would end up as colonialist themselves where these populations were concerned?' (437).

The points made by Dirlik support the critical perspective of Mbembe. While one may not entirely agree with Mbembe's assertion that post-colonial thought is only concerned with a European agency towards its other, as much of the seminal thought in what came to be later recognised as postcolonial studies has been actively done by non-Europeans with their situated perspectives, one must accept that postcolonial thought is a product of interaction with European intervention, whose inheritance has proved itself, in the long run of history, irremediable.[11] On the other hand, as postcolonial studies march on and follow in constant reorienta-tion and self-criticism, one may be led to disagree with Mbembe's inferred proposition of the inadequacy of postcolonial thought to understand the contemporary dynamic of the postcolony. Once postcoloni*al* is an adver-bial mode born from the interaction with colonialism as an ideological basis for the fight against it, so is postcolon*y*, the ideology's ultimate goal, and a term that Mbembe does not refuse to employ even when his aim is

11   Mbembe's usage of the words other and Other in the works cited in this study is
       in line with the definition of Lacan, which implies a relationship of inequality and
       subordination.

to talk about what could be termed 'African States that are former colonies of European States'.

The mismatch between postcolonial thought and postcolony discussed by Mbembe is a good example of the limiting effect that the obsession with the genealogy of postcolonial studies can have on the still untapped critical potential of the field. The excessive focus on the fact that postcolonial thought was widespread via US academia at a time of US hegemonic global position obfuscates its non-linear, multidirectional loci of emergence, as pointed out by Shohat and Stam. This further invisibilises the contributions by scholars in the field thinking from elsewhere, discouraging others from engaging with and modifying the field, then turning criticism into a self-fulfilling prophecy that falls short of the field's potential. A move that is especially counterproductive at a time when what the postcolonial condition means is everchanging.

As Young argues, postcolonial theory can still be useful to address inequality in situations striking the world in the twenty-first century. Taking up the challenge of the *intra*, Young's article 'Postcolonial Remains' (2012) shows how the postcolonial eye remains operative in making the invisible visible. It argues that, as a postcolonial body of theory born from the heart of anticolonial movements, conjugated with its diversity-oriented perspective and emerging from the very non-European cultures it engaged with, postcolonial reason is extremely transferrable. For this reason, its political- and cultural-oriented awareness has been useful in addressing the case of Indigenous struggles against sovereign states, as Stam and Shohat elaborate in their response to Young's essay titled 'Whence and Whiter Postcolonial Theory'.[12] Challenging postcolonialism's own Marxist rules of secularism and modernity, the case of Indigenous struggles also demands a critique of colonial practices perpetrated by postcolonial states, insofar as they subalternize cultures and dispossess properties in the name of sovereignty and economic advantage in global capitalism. Thus, accepting Said's advice, it becomes visible that what those critics propose carries an 'awareness of

---

12   For more on this topic, see Shohat and Stam's *Race in Translation: Cultural Wars around the Postcolonial Atlantic* (2012).

the resistances to theory, [and] reactions to it elicited by those concrete experiences or interpretations with which it is in conflict' (1983: 242).

In the case of the postcolonial critic of African literatures in Portuguese, as the earlier discussion on its criticism shows, a lasting preference for the *inter* seems to happen in detriment of the *intra*. This preference, however, shows itself much more indebted to a commitment to the Marxist revolutionary aspects of the anticolonial struggle that shaped the first awareness of postcolonial thought rather than to later unfolding events connected, as shown by Dirlik, Stam, Shohat and Young, with the tendency of the field, to 'continu[e] in the necessary mode of perpetual autocritique' (Young 2012: 22). In this sense, the avoidance of a politically critical position on the current critique of the literatures of Portuguese-speaking Africa comes precisely from its postcolonial engagement with the contradictory processes of nation-building that were at the heart of the revolutionary anticolonial nationalism that freed those states from colonial rule.

To evoke the Marxist orientation of the anticolonial struggle is to remember that '[i]f postcolonial theory is the cultural product of decolonization, it is also the historical product of Marxism in the anti-colonial arena' (Young 2001: 168). With the vantage point of historical distance, we can see that on behalf of nation-building, revolutionary anticolonialism used the same logic of appropriation of weapons of violence used by the colonial enterprise, being 'condemned almost from the beginning to replicate the practices of the colonialists in their very efforts at nation-building', a process that had to be 'sufficient[ly] unified to struggle against colonialism and withstand its pressures, which meant in practice puritanical intolerance of any sign of disunity or less centrist and integrationist views of the nation' (Dirlik 2004: 437). The realm of culture, which was one of the most important elements in the building of the national consciousness during the nationalist movements of the Portuguese-speaking countries, became a field of dispute and a site that provides a privileged view of how the systematic promotion of cultural homogenisation was a necessary part of the fight against imperialism. According to Cabral:

> For culture to play the important role which falls to it in the framework of development of the liberation movement, the movement must be able to conserve the positive cultural values of every well-defined social group, of every category, and

to achieve the *confluence* of these values into the stream of struggle, giving them a new dimension - the *national dimension*. Faced with such a necessity, the liberation struggle is, above all, a struggle as much for the conservation and survival of the cultural values of the people as for the harmonizing and development of these values within a national framework.

...

As we know, the armed liberation struggle demands the mobilization and organization of a significant majority of the population, the political and moral unity of the various social categories, the efficient use of modern weapons and other means of warfare, the gradual elimination of the remnants of tribal mentality, and the rejection of social and religious rules and taboos contrary to development of the struggle (gerontocracy, nepotism, social inferiority of women, rites and practices which are incompatible with the rational and national character of the struggle, etc.). The struggle brings about many other profound changes in the life of the populations. The armed liberation struggle implies, therefore, a veritable forced march along the road to cultural progress. (Cabral Cabral 1979: 147;152; emphasis in the original)

Despite the revolutionary anticolonial nationalist movements in Portuguese-speaking Africa's valuation of local culture, the need to use culture as a tool for national cohesion led to a careful selection of traditional cultural practices, thereby privileging only those that served the purpose of the fight against colonialism. Combined with the Marxist values and morals of modernity, this selection, which can be seen as violent by entailing a degree of cultural erasure, was the basis of a cultural dialectic whose aim was a synthesis of national identity. As Dirlik puts it 'Fanon, like many others [such as Cabral], ignored that those masses, in particular the peasantry, might be the most averse of all to the homogenizing urges of nationalism' (2002: 437).

If earlier we discussed the impact of a critic's worldiness on the reception of a literary work, to the extent that it influences the ways in which the critic unveils the work's significant aspects to the society in which he is inserted, here we can see another dimension of the critic's worldiness, very common to the postcolonial critic, which rests on the role of the critic's political engagement with the place of enunciation in which the literary work is inserted. In their commitment to support the establishment of these countries by legitimising the weight and relevance of their cultures in the international arena, the foreign postcolonial critic will support those

African national identities from their relatively privileged position as cultural gatekeepers in academia. From this perspective, it becomes clear why a critic would be unwilling to read a literary work in its most critical *intra*-national potentialities or to look too closely at the peasants' cultural suppression on behalf of the forging of a national identity. In this context, literary displays of discontent that could serve as arguments to undermine the national achievements in the international arena can be easily swept under the carpet 'for the greater good'.

The examples by Rothwell and Padilha show their engagement as postcolonial critics not only in the treatment they give to the literatures they analyse, reading it most productively in relation to their place of enunciation but also by engaging politically with the literature's places of emergence to the extent that both support those countries projects of national culture. Rothwell draws his analysis of the works of Couto disregarding any major critique of the Mozambican postcolonial state or of the idea of national identity and ends up suggesting that there is, in fact, an image of national identity developed throughout the writer's work. For this critic, the writer's 'postcolonial maturity' was reached with a novel whose plot focused on the interventionist policies of international organs such as the United Nations and showed that the fight against imperialism had not ended with the end of colonialism. Different from what is read in Mbembe, the bottom line for Rothwell seems to be that the postcolony is still striving to build up its identity as an opposition to what comes from outside. Hence, the focus on the *inter*-, in the face of which an untroubled condensation of the *intra*-national would be possible. Padilha, in her turn, also subscribes to a homogenising view of the African continent, giving preference to highlighting its points of connection with Brazil rather than dwelling on the plurality of its cultures and different literary systems. Again, on the realm of the *inter*, as well as with the aim of identity-building through opposition with a foreign element – focusing, this time, on Brazil – Padilha suggests the existence of an African unification and tradition that is necessary to the dialectical process of identity-building in an Afro-Brazilian culture. The idea of a group of 'African countries' that is coherent enough to be valued as a singular element of Brazil's national culture draws on views derived from myths about European national unification of the nation that fetishise cultural homogeneity.[13] Here, Padilha's search for synthesis is in line with a left that is not only of revolutionary anticolonial aim but also one that is entrenched in the Brazilian humanities' academe. As Antonio Candido's case of 'sequestro do barroco' ['kidnapping the baroque'] demonstrates, Brazilian mainstream literary critique is well used to the ideologically oriented construction of a literary system capable of displaying enough cohesion to portray the country's national identity face the hegemonic literary traditions of Western Europe.[14]

Critiquing the politics of nation-building generated within revolutionary anticolonial movements and employed by postcolonial political regimes does not lessen the relevance of those movements or the greatness of their achievements, without which neither the world we know today nor the very possibility of this reflection would exist. In common with Stam, Shohat and Young, who propose the opening of postcolonial theory

13   An interesting reflection on Brazili's dialectic/anthropophagic process of cultural identity building can be found in Bernard McGuirk's 'Laughing Again he's Awake: de Campos *à l'oreille de l'autre celte*' and in McGuirk and Else Vieira's *Haroldo de Campos in Conversation* (2009).

14   'O sequestro do barroco' is a curtailment of the book *O sequestro do barroco na formação da literatura brasileira: o caso Gregório de Matos* (partially published in English as 'The Disappearance of the Baroque in Brazilian Literature: The Case of Gregório de Matos' in 2007) by the Brazilian poet and critic Haroldo de Campos and refers to an unresolved polemic in Brazilian literary studies. In his 1989 text, Campos sets out to critique Antonio Candido, arguably the most import literary theorist of the country to date, for not having included the baroque works by Gregório de Matos (1636–1696) on his *magnum opus Formação da Literatura Brasileira* (1959). Candido's argument was that Matos' works' were not included in his idea of the country's literary system because, in the seventeenth century, Brazilian literature still did not have a system in place, with producers and consumers of literature capable of assuring Matos' influence in the system's posterity. Campos, in his turn, denounces Candido's exclusion of Matos as a signal that Candido's idea of the formation of a literary system was only a prescriptive theoretical construct willing to exclude or include anything that would prove its logic. The polemic, which remains unresolved and has now been rendered pointless to the very debate on the makeover of the Brazilian literary system, serves as a good example of the discussion around literature and national identity in Brazil that is important for the understanding of the positioning of many of its critics.

towards Indigenous claims, we too believe that it is the critic's job to resist
theory, stretch it, put it to the test of different possible dimensions, and
then tear it, open it, criticise and adapt it to the very social materiality –
to the very worldliness – of the context of the emergence of literature. As
such, to look at the contradictions of nation-building in African literatures
in Portuguese and to take up the challenge of going *intra* does not disrupt
nation-building but furthers it.

Intra-colonialism: Praxis of postcolonial times

> [U]ma teoria não é um simples aparelho conceptual e muito menos um corpo
> doutrinal ou um conjunto de princípios metodológicos, cabe-lhe, sim, ocupar o
> espaço crítico da desestabilização da *doxa* estabelecida e do questionamento das
> aparentes evidências do senso comum. E cabe-lhe, do mesmo passo, construir uma
> metalinguagem que permita articular uma permanente perspectivação interrogativa
> do seu campo de incidência. Essa metalinguagem, evidentemente, não surge a partir
> do nada, constrói-se a partir da ressignificação de conceitos geralmente pré-existentes
> cuja operatividade no novo contexto teórico e no novo campo discursivo está na
> medida exacta da sua capacidade de alargar e definir o espaço da interrogação.

> [A theory is not a simple conceptual apparatus, much less a body of doctrine or a set
> of methodological principles. Rather, it has to occupy the critical space of destabilising
> the established doxa and questioning the apparent evidence of common sense. At
> the same time, it has to build a metalanguage that allows it to articulate a permanent
> interrogative perspective on its field of influence. This metalanguage, of course, does
> not come out of nowhere, but is built from the re-signification of generally pre-
> existing concepts whose operability in the new theoretical context and discursive field
> is to the exact extent of their ability to broaden and define the space of questioning.]

> – António Sousa Ribeiro, 'Vítimas do Próprio Sucesso?
> Lugares Comuns do Pós-Colonial' (2012: 39)

To go *intra* and analyse how identity building is portrayed in the twenty-
first century African literary works written in Portuguese also demands
a critical look at the postcolony. The concept of postcolony, as proposed

here, follows the definition of Mbembe, to whom the African 'postcolony' means age and a *durée*:

> By age, is meant not a simple category of time but a number of relationships and a configuration of events… . As an age, the postcolony encloses multiples *durées* made up of discontinuities, reversals, inertias, and swings that overlay one another, interpenetrate one another, and develop one another: an *entanglement*. (2001: 14)

In his defiant challenge to linear historicity, Mbembe proposes the abandonment of a Eurocentric idea of linear time in which the present necessarily derives from the past and engenders the future. He argues for an idea of postcolony more suitable to African social formations, thus representing a 'time of existence and experience, a time entanglement' once that

> [African social formations] harbor the possibility of a variety of trajectories neither convergent nor divergent, but interlocked, paradoxical. More philosophically, it may be supposed that the present as *experience of a time* is precisely that moment when different forms of absence become mixed together: absence of those presences that are no longer so and that one remembers (the past), and the absence of those other that are yet to come and are anticipated (the future). (16; emphasis in the original)

To see the postcolony as an age of entangled temporality constitutes a proposition that addresses much of the criticism directed towards the 'postcolonial' as a term. Without ignoring its relation to 'colony', both in its historical, cultural and material aspects, Mbembe recuperates the 'postcolony' from a fallacious conceptualisation of overcoming the colonial that prevents more fruitful discussions about the potential of the postcolonial as an analytical framework today. While for those concerned with the relevance of colonialism for capitalist world-system relations, the *post-* in postcolonial would imply an apolitical movement beyond colonialism (Shohat 1992: 101), for many interested in the development of the sovereign African states that emerged from colonialism, independence brought the beginning of a political new era in which the birth of the 'New Man, fully conscious of his national, continental and international rights and duties' (Cabral 1979: 170) would take place. In the face of this scenario, although Mbembe's formulation does not entirely dispense with the novelty inherent in the term, by emphasising the lingering of colonial practices as constitutive of postcolonial times, he readjusts the 'weapon of theory' for going *intra*. Something that certainly would not go down well for anyone interested in inaugurating new beginnings within the postcolony, as to think of continuations might be an inconvenience given that 'keeping alive memories of colonialism ... [is] likely to create cultural and psychological obstacles to assimilation into the [new] system, while forgetting makes for easier assimilation – and acceptance' (Dirlik 2004: 439–440).

Looking at it from an *intra*-national perspective, the suggestion of the postcolony as an entangled temporality denies the rupture with colonial practices so desired by anticolonial nationalisms. Writing from the vantage point of historical distance, Mbembe's reflections on the postcolony consider around fifty years of post-independence historical development and the nation-building process in Africa to address the achievements and problems of the nationalistic projects. Different from those whose political commitment sees such a critique in its potential undermining of post-independence accomplishments, the conceptual perspective of Mbembe into the temporality of the postcolony considers the agency of the subaltern. It calls into question the responsibility of African elites for appropriating several colonial practices to subjugate the same people they were once committed to liberating.

Derrida's proposition that 'we can pronounce not a single destructive proposition which has not already had to slip in the form, the logic and the implicit postulations of precisely what it seeks to contest' (2001: 354), can help to understand the principle of entangled temporality in the postcolony. Trapped within a play of difference with 'colony', the 'postcolony' can only exist in opposition to that which it contests, thus being defined by the very logic it seeks to displace. Before the poststructuralist scent of this view puts off any committed materialist reader, it would be useful to remember that the praxis of such a play of sameness and difference was already inscribed in the history of the postcolony way before Derrida became mainstream. It was part of the anticolonial thought that put colonialism down and installed the *commandment* of the independent postcolony. As Fanon has put it '[d]ecolonization is the meeting of two forces, opposed to each other by nature, which in fact owe their originality to that sort of substantification which results from and is nourished by the situation in the colonies' (2001: 36).

To think of the entanglement between colonial and postcolonial is key to understanding the pitfalls to which the anticolonial nationalisms of the Portuguese-speaking African countries succumbed. Its critique, as the following chapters demonstrate, constitutes an important feature in the literary works of Portuguese-speaking Africa, conceived almost five decades after their independence. Now, however, departing from Mbembe's wider conceptualisation of postcolony as a time of entanglement to think about the 'postcolonial African subject, his/her history and his/her present in the world' (2001:17), we move towards a related concept tailored to address the Portuguese-speaking African subjectivity: the idea of *intra*-colonialism.

Intra-colonialism is a concept coined by Bernard McGuirk to analyse postcolonial Angolan processes of identity-building in relation to its colonial past based on the reading of Agualusa's novel *O Vendedor de Passados* (published in English as *The Book of Chameleons*).[15] Analysing the novel's fictionalisation of the selective reweaving of memory, McGuirk deepens a critique of postcolonial forgetting by proposing that the process is not only used to promote the obliteration of colonial continuities in the aftermath of independence. He asserts that the practice becomes fundamental as an attempt to dress the more recent wounds carved by decades of civil war in which the enemy was the very 'brother' that anticolonial nationalism sought to liberate.

In his analysis of Agualusa's fictional rendition of the interplay of memory and forgetting behind the programmatic efforts to build up some sort of national identity for a postcolony thirsty for new beginnings, McGuirk identifies the state appropriation of the authoritative colonial ideological mode of discourse to rewrite its misdeeds as a form of intra-colonialism:[16]

---

15   Besides McGuirk's use of the term 'intra-colonialism' in regard to his 2009 article titled 'Intra-Colonialism or l'Animotion Mosaïque of the Black Atlantic: Re(p) tiling Angola in J. E. Agualusa's *O Vendedor de Passados/The Book of Chameleons*', the term can be found in the critic's work as early as 1997, as found in the book *Latin American Literature: Symptoms, Risks and Strategies of Poststructuralist Criticism*.

16   For an extensive analysis of the representation of memory throughout Agualusa's oeuvre, see Ana Margarida Fonseca's 'A Invenção do Futuro: (Re) Escritas do

'Memory is a landscape watched from the window of a moving train'... Intra-colonialism would rattle along, discursive lapses on track, halting not at some recu-perable or necessary past ... but forever in a present which has moved on, re-tracing, re-mapping, that History in which rewriting is a norm. (2009: 300)

When Mbembe states that 'African regimes have not invented what they know of government from scratch ... part of [their] knowledge or rationality is *colonial rationality*' (2001: 24–25; emphasis in the original), we have to remember that, although historically colonialism is often de-scribed as direct domination through political power promoted by alien agents to the dominated people (Cabral 1979: 128), the main instrument of domination holding the colony together was violence (Cabral 1979: 134). If we think of intra-colonialism as a set of colonial practices perpetrating postcolonial structures, a product of entangled temporalities, what we see is the elimination of the alien political dominance after independence that accounts for the *intra*-prefixation of a lasting colonialism in the form of a praxis of violence. According to Albert Memmi:

> In addition to economic exploitation and cultural alienation, colonization is the history of a succession of unbearable constraints.....Yet, even with liberation, the vio-lence continued, the faces were just about the same, the executioners the same. There are not many ways to torture, to deprive someone of his freedom or his life. Some commentators will say that this was necessary to consolidate the country's growing power against potential enemies, sometimes even against militants in the independ-ence movement, men and women who had until then been completely devoted but who failed to understand that the revolution was over and was absurd – dangerous, in fact – to assume that every promise would be kept. (2006: 49)

The violence to which Memmi refers is a well known but little dis-cussed historical issue throughout most of the Portuguese-speaking African countries. Although the violence that swept the postcolonial societies of Angola, Mozambique and Guinea-Bissau, for example, is seen by some as a direct legacy of the population's militarisation required to fight the anticolonial war (Coelho 2003: 177), it is important not to forget the role of violence in these countries' politics. Violence is one of the most widely

---

Passado nos Contos de José Eduardo Agualusa' [The Invention of the Future: (Re) Writing the Past in José Eduardo Agualusa's Short Stories].

employed repressive tools for dictatorship, which has been argued to be
the de facto political system in place disguised as single-party 'guided democracy' models (Sklar 1986: 20–21) of those three countries for almost
twenty years – the first multiparty elections in Angola were held in 1992,
and Guinea-Bissau and Mozambique in 1994. According to Patrick Chabal,

> [i]n those three countries, as in the whole of postcolonial Africa, the construction
> of the nation-state involved three distinct, but crucial, steps. The first was to mo-
> bilise support for the nation-building party. The second was to *neutralize internal
> (political, ethic, religious or regional) opposition*. The third was to establish a political
> system able to balance the demands for representation with the need for consoli-
> dating 'national' unity. (2002: 54; emphasis added)

In light of these historical facts, the resurgence of the Angolan purge of
1977 at the heart of *O Vendedor de Passados* as the unforgettable memory
of politically and ideologically motivated violence is the major element
connecting the dots of the story.[17] It exposes the type of inconvenient
fact that any intra-colonial search for a postcolonial *tabula rasa* tends to
erase and that most pieces of critical literature will try to recuperate. The
understanding of the postcolonial as a synthesis of a dialectical process –
à la Hegel – between the colonial and the anticolonial erases the continuation and reconfiguration of cultures and institutions by implying a
neutralisation of hierarchies and oppositions within itself. Consequently,
the conciliatory view of the postcolony in terms of time and space as an
aufhebung, the Hegelian sublation, of the colonial/anticolonial clash is
scarcely productive. While this perspective can be useful to prove the case
against international capitalism, especially in unveiling its behaviour as
an *inter*-national phenomenon, it can still be quite ineffective as a way
to address the *intra*-national issues of the postcolony itself. In this sense,

---

17 The purge of 1977 is a reference to a bloody period in the history of Angola.
    Following what is referred to as a coup by different fractions of the MPLA on the
    night of 27 May 1977, quickly suffocated with the help of the Cuban troops in the
    country, came a time of terror and political persecution involving illegal arrests, tor-
    ture and the execution of whoever could be considered a threat to those in power.
    A comprehensive analysis of this chapter of Angolan history is found in *Purga em
    Angola* (2007) by Dalila Cabrita Mateus and Alvaro Mateus.

the intra-colonial is useful because it interrupts the sublation of the colonial as *aufgehaben*.[18] It rescues the operative oppositions from within the
postcolony and constitutes a fruitful critical perspective for approaching
the complex projections of the postcolonial condition in contemporary
African literature.

While politically motivated violence is one of the intra-colonial practices of nation-building in the postcolonial time-spaces of Portuguese-
speaking Africa, the 'dictatorship of material poverty' (Sklar 1986: 29) is
another. Even when the states of Cape Verde and São Tomé and Príncipe
are seen as less politically violent than their continental counterparts, it
is deep poverty and inequality that victimise their populations. In both
countries, the main issue seems to have been the concentration of wealth
in the hands of those in power during the single-party political period.
While in Cape Verde the privatisation processes that followed the country's
economic opening are opaque and suspicious (Silva Andrade 2002: 290),
in São Tomé and Príncipe it is possible to note that '[n]ationalization allowed the ruling elite to monopolize access to land, jobs and other resources
through the state in order to maintain political control and attract followers'
(Seibert 2002: 300). Yet, as those problems are not exclusive trademarks
of these two particular countries and given that material poverty dictates
the rules for the majority of the population in Angola, Guinea-Bissau
and Mozambique, it is possible to identify a set of shared intra-colonial
practices throughout the postcoloniality of the five Portuguese-speaking
African countries concerning their consolidation of state, their use of violence and their distribution of wealth.

Therefore, in an effort to depart from and respond to a critical concern much more proccupied by those literatures' external relevance than
by their portraits of internal dissonance, this study shares Memmi's query
that if '[t]he writer is a storyteller, but often, also an accuser … [on such
contexts, perpetrated by contradictions, w]hat does the literature of the
ex-colonized tell us?' He states that:

18   While the terms 'anticolonial' and 'postcolonial' are not hyphenated to demon-
      strate the entanglement between colonial logic/praxis and its prefixal inflexion,
      'intra-colonial' and its derivatives are hyphenated to maintain the spelling used by
      McGuirk.

what is referred to as an independent thinker, exercising a critical intellect directed towards his peers still doesn't exist in the new society … all writing is suspected and controlled. The only writing that is tolerated is conformist, the praise of politicians and religious leaders, bland folkloric tales, reminders of a supposedly glorious past that will help the people forget the mediocrity of the present. (2006: 36)

Besides the inevitable existence of acritical literature in any society, the case of what has been written recently in Portuguese-speaking Africa is far from that. Partially favoured by a foreign editorial industry that publishes and sells works of African authors outside Africa – namely Portugal and Brazil – thereby releasing authors from the authoritative control of their works by internal political interests, the works that have been published in the last two decades show vigorous fictional denunciations of the post-independence/colonial state of affairs of their countries. However, as the critical potential of literature might never be released if it does not find a critical reader, one should maybe give up looking for critical books and concentrate on trying to develop critical readings.

It is through the key of *intra*-colonial dimensions that the following analysis tries to critically write back to the *inter*-national field of critique of the African literatures in Portuguese. Aiming to contribute to the field's unfolding and critical productivity, what follows in this study seeks alternative ways to look at the postcolony, which, as an entangled time-space concept, is always in motion, regardless of its direction.

From Nation to State

We have seen in the preceding pages that nationalism, that magnificent song that made the people rise against their oppressors, stops short, falters and dies away on the day that independence is proclaimed. Nationalism is not a political doctrine, nor a programme. If you really wish your country to avoid regression, or at best halts and uncertainties, a rapid step must be taken from national consciousness to political and social consciousness.
> – Frantz Fanon, *The Wretched of the Earth* (2001: 163)

O grande desafio da literatura moçambicana, assim como o da literatura das restantes ex-colónias portuguesas, é porventura como transitar do velho paradigma nacionalista para um novo paradigma democrático.

[The great challenge facing Mozambican literature, as well as the literature of the other former Portuguese colonies, is perhaps how to move from the old nationalist paradigm to a new democratic one.]
> – João Paulo Borges Coelho, 'Writing in a Changing World' (2013: 21)

The intrinsic connection between literature and history subjacent to the rise of literature in Portuguese-speaking Africa has made the nation one of the most studied themes in the field. The approach, often informed by the worldliness of critics residing abroad and sympathetic to the causes of the liberation movements, has generated a respectable body of literary criticism that ends up resonating, albeit inadvertently, with one of the most criticised aspects of Fredric Jameson's famous text 'Third-World Literature in the Era of Multinational Capitalism' (1986). In their tendency to focus on the significance of nationalism, especially revolutionary nationalism, as a force capable of changing the world order through the dislodgement of colonialism, this literary criticism tends to sideline nationalism's own internal dimensions and contradictions, along with the impact of nationalist projects on the lives of people living in the postcolonial condition. As such, while an alignment regarding the relevance and assessment of the nation and nationalism can be seen in the literary critique of works from Portuguese-speaking Africa and Jameson's view that '[a]ll third-world texts are necessarily ... *national allegories*'(1986: 69; emphasis in the original) can be identified, this is more indebted to historically situated critical blindspots than to homogenising whims.

To bring up the positionality of literary criticism and theory is essential to one's committed to a critical dialectic capable of exploring further nuances in the literatures of Portuguese-speaking Africa, be it in terms of representation of themes or registration in terms of form. This type of contextualisation allows an understanding of the intrinsic relation between reach and limitation that is inherent to established pathways of reading the nation in these contexts. It helps to see how these approaches seek to pursue an understanding of these countries' literary registration of postcolonial experience in systemic proportions. It is due to their historical development that the literatures of the countries in question lend themselves quite well to Jameson's categorisation, which is perhaps one of the reasons why the essay was reprinted without changes in Jameson's 2019 book *Allegory and Ideology*. Yet, while Aijaz Ahmad's (1987) critique of Jameson's essay's potential for further othering what is known today as postcolonial literature in 'Jameson Rhetoric of Otherness and the "National Allegory"', may not reverberate the same way if applied to the critique of African literatures in Portuguese, given that most works in the field take these productions not only as national allegories but also as allegories of nation formation, Ahmad's argument is an important and relatively early warning of a potential pitfall in the field, at a time when the positionality of the critic was only rarely discussed.

As the review of this debate by Lazarus in *The Postcolonial Unconscious* shows – despite the author's open advocacy for Jameson and declared impatience with Ahmad – the polemic between the two theorists gave way to a 'curious process through which his [Ahmad's] intended Marxist critique of Jameson's "Third-Worldism" came to be taken up as ' "Third-Wordist" critique of Jameson's Marxism and of Marxism as such' (2011: 100). Capturing the generational debate of materialist versus poststructuralist-inclined critical approaches at the heart – or the unconscious – of postcolonial studies, Lazarus' account speaks of an academic debate that does not seem to keep many of the postcolonial-informed critics occupied with the literatures in question here awake at night, leading me to the provocative question: *whose* postcolonial unconscious? Speaking to the structural unevenness underlying Aristotelian views of structures of knowledge-making that prime theory and critique as episteme and case study as techne, the Jameson–Ahmad debate furthers the idea of critical worldliness as it sheds light on its positionality.

In his essay, Ahmad positions himself as an India-born Pakistani author of poetry and prose in Urdu who, upon his encounter with Jameson's statement about the nature of all third-world texts, 'realized that what was being theorised was, among many other things, myself ... the farther I read the more I realized, ... that the man whom I had for so long, so affectionate, ... taken as a comrade was, in his own opinion, my civilizational Other. It was not a good feeling' (1987: 3–4). In his critique of Jameson's third-worldism, Ahmad calls attention to the diverse nature of experience in postcolonial contexts driven by internal socio-historic dynamics that tend to become invisible in the sweeping nature of systemic statements of which it is nonetheless part. Alerting for the danger of romanticising the revolutionary machine of nationalism, Jameson's exultation of what third-world nationalism constituted a situated effort to preach the wonders of social mobilisation amidst the individualist culture of a postmodern United States, Ahmad notes:

> Whether or not a nationalism will produce a progressive cultural practice depends, to put it in Gramscian terms, upon the political character of the power bloc which takes hold of it and utilizes it, as a material force, in the process of constituting its own hegemony. There is neither theoretical ground nor empirical evidence to support the notion that bourgeois nationalisms of the so-called third world will have any difficulty with postmodernism; they *want* it. (1987: 8)

Ahmad's plea for the dissociation of nationalism as a revolutionary force and the political project of the parties that took over power in any former colony is significant. It not only echoes Fanon's seminal 'Pitfalls of national consciousness' (1961), but also relates to Cabral's advice in 'The Weapon of Theory' (1966), where he affirms that the national liberation struggle is incomplete if political independence is not followed by a social revolution that starts with the bourgeoisie's suicide as a class. Despite its pertinence – or perhaps because of it – Ahmad's appeal remains largely ignored, evoked mostly in its relevance as a critique of Jameson. Even if one might not sign up to Ahmad's frontal attack on the 'Three Worlds Theory', one can surely gain from his considerations regarding what is left behind when the transnational aspect of economic systems of production is seen as the only determining factor by critics who promote an 'over-valorization of nationalist ideology' (1987: 8).

> If this 'third-world' is *constituted* by the singular 'experience of colonialism and imperialism,' and if the only possible response is a nationalist one, then what else is there that is more urgent to narrate than this 'experience'; in fact, there is *nothing else* to narrate. For if societies here are defined not by relations of production but by relations of intra-national domination; if they are forever suspended outside the sphere of conflict between capitalism (first world) and socialism (second world); if the motivating force for history here is neither class formation and class struggle nor the multiplicities of intersecting conflicts based upon class, gender, nation, race, region and so on, but by the unitary 'experience' of national oppression … then what else can one narrate but that national oppression? (1697: 8–9, italics from the original)

It is understandable that the points raised by Ahmad could, in times of Cold War, seem unsatisfactory from the viewpoint of an engaged Marxist critique located in the developed world, to whom anticolonial nationalism, as well as their post-independence socialist experiences, served as argument and inspiration for change. If we are willing to understand contemporary national imaginations as portrayed in the literatures of Portuguese-speaking Africa, however, the multiplicity of intersecting conflicts within postcolonial societies gains greater relevance.

The quote by Fanon opening this chapter reminds us that the understanding of nationalism as a revolutionary force and not as a governmental platform is nothing new. Yet, Fanon's conceptualisation of a quick transition from national to political consciousness has worked more as an aspiration than as an attainable goal. In multiethnic and multinational postcolonial societies, the process can only continue on a larger scale in the aftermath of colonial resistance, after independence. It is for that reason that the two processes that Fanon imagined following one another had, in the case of the contexts of the works analyse, to overlap. At the same time, the nationalism of anticolonial orientation did not die away on the day that independence was proclaimed. Instead, it was turned into an ideological weapon of the single-party state that followed independence in each of the five African countries that attained independence from Portugal.[1] The recently created states also had to strive to reorganise themselves along with raising a social and political consciousness with a Marxist-Leninist orientation.[2]

The consolidation of postcolonial states under a mix of anticolonial nationalism and Marxism-Leninism is a distinctive commonality among Portuguese-speaking African countries. Such a mix, which 'those in the west call 'third world nationalism'[,] has never been successfully analyzed by theorists of nationalism because it never operated according to a general model, or even ideology' (Young 2001: 172). Its implications for post-independence nation-building, although inescapable, remain largely undebated, especially in the analysis concerned with their artistic representation. In an insightful

---

1   Agostinho Neto, in his speech during the sixth conference of the Afro-Asian Writers in Luanda on 1 July 1979, proclaimed that: 'O problema que se põe agora em Angola, como em todas as outras regiões do mundo, é o da transformação do carácter da sociedade. É entre o Socialismo que avança e o capitalismo moribundo. Assim acontece entre o colonialismo e a Independência, entre o racismo e a igualdade, entre o poder burocrático e o poder popular. Não há Independência verdadeira sem o Socialismo. Mas estamos ainda na era das unidades nacionais, e por isso mesmo o nacionalismo. Cada unidade nacional vive a sua história, explicando-a de modo a preservar direitos soberanos e a integridade territorial. De modo também a desenvolver a cultura e a valorizar os temas que servem a sua atividade'. ['The problem now facing Angola, as in all other regions of the world, is that of transforming the character of society. It is between an advancing socialism and a dying capitalism. So it is between colonialism and independence, between racism and equality, between bureaucratic power and popular power. There can be no true independence without socialism. But we are still in the era of national units, and therefore nationalism. Each national unit lives its history, explaining it in such a way as to preserve sovereign rights and territorial integrity. It also develops culture and valorises the themes that serve its activity'.]. (Neto 1980: 72)

2   It is largely accepted that state-building and nation-building are processes that overlap. The focus on these processes as separate phenomena allows the observation of the state's influence on the raising of national consciousness that is necessary to transform the sovereign postcolonial state into a nation-state. A detailed conceptual analysis of these two terms can be found in Linz (1993: 355–369).

essay titled 'Pontos comuns e heterogeneidade das culturas políticas nos PALOPs' (2015) Michel Cahen argues for a nuanced understanding of the ways in which Marxism-Leninism was lived in the five countries of this transnational region. While his view that it was due to the local bourgeoisies' desire for single-party states that they embraced a Marxism-Leninism that was, in fact, a Stalinised version of Marxism may be controversial, his call to differentiate what this doctrine meant in terms of political imagination from what it meant in terms of social imagination is relevant (2015: 33–34). To make sense of literary representations of the nation in a context of apparent contradiction between a self-professed socialist political project for the nation-state that endures beyond the abandonment of a commitment to the socialist mode of production and the embracing of capitalism in the 1990s, one needs more refined ways to understand how the socialist project was lived in these multiple contexts, as well as in its discursive and actual aspects. Yet, Cahen's view of the revolutionary state in Portuguese-speaking Africa as Stalinist in its promotion of cultural homogeneity via political disenfranchisement of views unaligned with the ones defended by the core of the party, along with the demonisation of difference seen as 'traição, arrogância, intriga, tribalismo, etc' ['betrayal, arrogance, intrigue, tribalism, etc'], is contested by a more in-depth analysis of the type of state developed in the post-revolutionary Soviet Union (2015: 31).

The Soviet-type state was the name used by Gianfranco Poggi (1990) to designate non-fascist single-party states of communist orientation, such as the one erected by the Soviet Union after the Bolshevik Revolution of 1917. What is interesting in Poggi's analysis is the extent to which he links the statist Soviet use of coercive tools to maintain its party (in) power with the very revolutionary drive to exterminate capitalism by eliminating the market and private property. For Poggi, it was only through the control of a public sphere 'within which the composition of the political leadership and ... the content of policy would be at issue in a legitimate and orderly contest for public support among competing parties' that the state could keep itself in power, thus ensuring the continuation of revolutionary achievements. This method of manipulating the public sphere, still according to Poggi, was inherited from the Tsarist's time, which 'had never previously allowed a public sphere and a constitutional order to come into being' (1990: 147). Consequently, as soon as they were in power, the revolutionary feared the very conspiratorial political and cultural conditions through which it came into being. 'In this sense, we might say, Bolshevik rule was forced upon a novel and (from a Western standpoint) abhorrent path to the exercise of state power because of *where it came from*' (1990: 148; emphasis in the original). Here, Poggi categorically diverts from Cahen's position as he comments on Lenin's mistake in expressing that the danger of the abuse of the party-state power that became a reality after his death was due to a failing of Stalin's character 'rather than to the dictatorial nature of the powers in question, and to the fact that society as a whole was defenceless against them' (1990: 151).

In the same way, an assessment of the means employed by the post-colonial governments of Portuguese-speaking Africa to legitimate their power and to build their countries after independence during their single-party years ought to take into consideration the series of continuations that characterise the postcolonial – with the colonial intervention as a departure point – or post-revolutionary – as a time of entanglement and becoming. Since 'tricontinental Marxism has emphasized what one might call untranslatability of revolutionary practices, the need for attention to local forms, and the translation of the universal into the idiom of the local' (Young 2001: 169), the series of forces at play in those countries' postcolonial present cannot be delinked from their colonial past.[3] In a process that seems to be similar to what Poggi saw in the Soviet Union, the single-party state regimes from the mid-1970s until the political opening in the early 1990s that were in place in all five countries of Portuguese-speaking Africa were instituted and ruled by state parties that stemmed directly from their respective local anticolonial movements run by the local elites. These, according to Cahen, were weakened by the failings of a colonial capitalism that was itself peripheral, thus not capable of offering

---

3   As Amílcar Cabral clearly stated on the occasion of the first Conference of Solidarity with the People of Asia, Africa and Latin America, 'national liberation and social revolution are not exportable commodities. They are (and increasingly so every day) a local, national product – more or less influenced by (favourable and unfavourable) external factors, but essentially determined and conditioned by the historical reality of each people' (Cabral 1979: 122).

conditions for strong African elites to rise. As a result, these possible elites established a dependence of the colonial state that shaped their political imagination of the single-party state as well as a social imagination of their new countries. They relied on a view of national cohesion that was urban, undisturbed by the territorial borders drawn by colonisers, dependent of a linguistic homogeneity privileging the colonial language, and embracing a modernising ideology rooted in the civilisational principals of colonial capitalist ideology that opposed elements clearly identified as traditionally African (2015: 33).

Irrespective of whether they drew from a Stalinist or classic Bolshevik approach to the single-party state in the development of their respective national projects, if their view of nation-building was committed to the socialist revolution or with serving the interests of selected ethic groups whose hegemony hardened under colonialism, the fact that these revolutionary elites maintained their political power after the abandonment of their socialist experiment is a testament to the complexity of transculturation of Marxism that characterised tricontinental Marxism in its untranslatability of revolutionary practices. Added to a decoupling of socialism as political imagination, along with the role of the nation in it, from socialism as social imagination, concerned with the organisation of the intra-state modes of production, we argue for a framework that allows to understand the literary registration of local renditions of the socialist experiment in terms of aesthetic diversity rather than solely in terms of contradiction. This shift enables us to draw from these situated realities to challenge situated universalisms in the realm of theory and criticism that insist on a separation between episteme and techne in which episteme, or the very definition of what socialism is for Marxism, is located in an Euro-American view of the world, while other regions' lived techne are seen in relation to their adherence or deviation to the epistemic standard.

Written around the first decade of the current century, the novels examined in this study portray sovereign states' experiences of postcoloniality that reflect the multiplicity of contexts, ideologies and practices that are simultaneously post-revolutionary, postsocialist, democratic and neoliberal. In scenarios such as these, where the postcolonial present entangled with the legacies of such a number of 'post-s', literary representations of the countries in question can engage with a variety of historical, social and cultural projects of nation-building deployed continuously over the course of their first four decades since their achievement of independence. In what follows, the representations of nation and state in each novel will be analysed with attention to how these institutions are conceptualised and the role they play in the selected fictional rendition of each society. At the end of this chapter, a comparative analysis of these portrayals assesses the status of the nation as a paradigm from which to read the contemporary literatures of Portuguese-speaking Africa.

Literary projections of state

The state in the time of becoming

Having achieved its independence much more as a result of the Portuguese Carnation Revolution than for any victory on the battlefield, São Tomé and Príncipe's non-violent transition from colony to sovereign state did not account for a free and peaceful independent society. The single-party Soviet-style state installed by the country's first government in July 1975 brought along its typical iron-handed approach seasoned with civil vigilance and conspiracy paranoia. As Gerhard Seibert puts it '[i]t was an intra-elite struggle for power and resources, conducted by intrigues and conspiracies, and accompanied by actual or alleged coup attempts, which in return served to increase the authoritarian and repressive character of the regime' (2002: 297). Despite the relatively small amount of attention given to the literary imprint of the archipelago's political regime between 1975 and 1990, as researchers interested in African literatures in Portuguese tend to focus on the works of Angola and Mozambique, the weight of the state in literary imagination is no less expressive in Santomean fiction.

In fact, the very history and make-up of the Santomean literary system pushes the boundaries of comparativism, given that its unique characteristics in terms of size, shape and history challenge set pathways of interpretation devised to understand literary representation in countries enjoying more hegemonic positions in the Portuguese-speaking world. As Santomean literary critic Mata asserted when a Brazilian interviewer asked if São Tomé and Príncipe had managed to establish a literary system like that of Angola, Mozambique and Cape Verde: '[o] fato de um escritor não ser publicado em Portugal não quer dizer que ele não exista. ... Gosto daquela afirmação do vosso Antonio Candido acerca da literatura brasileira: "Comparada às grandes, a nossa literatura é pobre e fraca. Mas é ela, não outra, que nos exprime". É isso.' ['[T]he fact that a writer isn't published in Portugal doesn't mean that he doesn't exist. ... I like your Antonio Candido's statement about Brazilian literature: "Compared to the great ones, our literature is poor and weak. But it is that, not others, which expresses us". That's it.] (Leite 2009). Moreover, while prose stands for the literary form that most notoriety gives to a national literatures in the field, the Santomean experience has often found its expression in poetry rather than in prose. As Mata describes in detail in her *Polifonias Insulares: Cultura e Literatura de São Tomé e Príncipe*, poetry was already a prolific genre in pre-independence days and kept its pace after a short period of literary silence after independence. Prose, on the other hand, with the exception of the work of Sum Marky, whose first publication took place in 1956, developed mostly after independence. In this context, the works of Albertino Bragança can be distinguished by what Mata terms as a writing that 'centra-se no ideológico, no político e no sociocultural do pós-independência: o universo é agora o das relações internas de poder entre os vários atores sociais, no diálogo entre a tradição e os imperativos da sua actualização, marcas afinal da escrita pós-colonial' ['it focuses on the ideological, political and socio-cultural of post-independence: the universe is now that of the internal power relations between the various social actors, in the dialogue between tradition and the imperatives of updating it, the hallmarks of post-colonial writing.'] (2010: 88).

This is the kind of postcolonial writing that we encounter in Bragança's *Aurélia de Vento*. Labelled as a novel by its publisher but called by critics a novella (Laranjeira 2011) or paranovel (Xavier 2012), which stands as a postmodern hybrid between the two forms, this narrative centres around a woman. Aurélia is a correct, honest, beautiful and fearless woman who lives life her own way. As president of the Civil Association for Mutual

Help, she is portrayed as someone committed to helping those in need. She is known to seek justice and conciliation even when her own reputation is at stake, and the vindication of her heroism comes when she survives an assassination attempt ordered by her own stepmother, Clotilde. Nevertheless, the story within the story seems to betray the author's declared aim to simply 'trazer as nossas raízes, encontrar também muitos dos nossos medos, as nossas superstições. Não obstante estar de acordo com elas as trouxe ao público, para que pudéssemos reflectir sobre as mesmas e chegarmos a consenso' ['Bringing back our roots, I also found many of our fears, our superstitions. Despite disagreeing with them, I brought them to the public so that we could reflect on them and reach a consensus'] (Veiga 2011). Taking up six of the seventeen chapters of the narrative, the story of Aurélia's father, the Portuguese-born White farmer Pedro Santos, from whom the state – with a capital 'S' as the word *Estado* is capitalised throughout the book – wants to misappropriate what in the novel is referred to as a legitimately owned plot of land.

Regardless of Aurélia's alleged place as protagonist in the narrative, her heroic posture, fairness and serene strength, her presence is substantially eroded by the flagrant voicelessness of the character. All we get to know about Aurélia comes from the voices of men, such as the male omniscient narrator and other male characters, some of whom do not even know her personally in the story but feel compelled to risk their lives for her. This establishes a strong contrast with the way in which the quest for justice of Pedro Santos against the state is narrated, where we get plenty of direct speech seasoned with the distinctiveness of his variety of Portuguese, flashbacks and accounts for his back story. The intensity in the tone of Santos' struggle in the narrative only matches Aurelia's assassination attempt, which is supposedly the climax of the heroine's story, clearly putting his quest at the centre of the story, narratologically speaking. Santos is the one character actively seeking to achieve a concrete goal – justice to the ownership rights to his farm – and through whose struggle the wider fabric of society is represented. After a quick introduction of Aurélia in the first chapter, where we hear about her rather than from her, the book turns to Santos' voice in a conversation with his partner Clotilde, the one that opens the narrative's second chapter:

– Infelizmente, parece que você tem razão. Pela conversa que eu tive com o diretor, fiquei a pensar que há gente que julga que tem mais direito sobre aquelas terras do que eu que sou o seu dono. ... Mas, eu digo você, eu vou até o fim nesse negócio. Para já o terreno de Potó Zamblala nunca foi do Estado...

– É verdade, mas se Governo quer comprar, como é que você faz?

– Comprar? Qual Comprar? Eles querem obrigar-me a vender contra a minha vontade e a um preço mais do que barato, para mais tarde facilitar as terras aos amigos deles. Isso é o que eles querem. Mas eu é que não vou calar a boca nesse assunto. Você vai ver!... (Bragança 2011: 23–24)

['Unfortunately, it seems you're right. From the conversation I had with the director, I realised that there are people who think they have more rights to that land than I do. ... But, I tell you, I'm going all the way with this issue. The plot in Potó Zamblala land has never belonged to the state...'

'True, but if the government wants to buy, how do you do it?'

'Buy? Is that buiyng? They want to force me to sell against my will and at a more than cheap price, so that they can later give the land to their friends. That's what they want. But I'm not going to shut up about it. You'll see!...']

In its very first mention, the state is designated for its corruption. Embodied in the narrative by Minister Domingos Ventura, the state is actually the only place where corruption is to be found, as all other villanies in the narrative are not motivated by material gain. The defamation of Aurélia by her husband's cousin is an act of jealousy. Clotilde's commissioning of the attempt against Aurélia's life is a crime of passion, and there is no material compensation for the actual hired assassin mentioned in the course of the story. It seems as if, in contrast to the immoral pursuit of material advantage sought by those in government, the whole population of the country is portrayed as living in some sort of social harmony where the rich and poor help each other in the absence of class struggle. Conflict is confined to the realm of social conviviality, more specifically in the clash between non-modern and modern emboldened by the opposition between Clotilde and Aurélia that structures what is supposed to be the core story of the novel. The only person or entity in pursuit of financial advantage is the state, under the guise of Minister Ventura. In doing so, this specific novel seems to suggest that the nation, imagined as a harmonious community bound by language and culture, is already there; it is the state that has to be reinvented.

It is almost as if the feeling of brotherhood that underlines the national sentiment arises as a result of mass opposition not to the invader or coloniser but to the state. The dislocation of the traditional image of the public enemy is reflected in the popular galvanisation against the state in Santos' court case, as well as in the popular mobilisation on behalf of Aurélia in the wake of her assassination attempt, regardless of the social abyss separating her from the ordinary people who admire and support her. Towards the end of the narrative, Aurélia's attacker is even captured and brought to justice by the free initiative of three simple men of the people who, although not knowing the victim personally, feel compelled to risk their lives to bring justice to Aurélia.

The description of popular support that Aurélia and her father receive, despite not being part of the impoverished Black majority themselves, is another paradigmatic point in the narrative. After Santos' victory in court, his backyard was flooded by people who were following the case and celebrating his victory against the State as their own. Aurélia '[r]econhecia que o pai, pessoa de poucas falas, não era um homem verdadeiramente popular; por isso, considerava a enchente no quintal mais como à espontânea reação de quem não se habituara ainda à ideia de que um ministro pudesse, em qualquer caso, sair derrotado perante um qualquer cidadão...' ['[r]ecognised that her father, a man of few words, was not a truly popular man; therefore, she considered the crowd in the backyard more like the spontaneous reaction of people who had not yet got used to the idea that a minister could, in any case, be defeated by any citizen...'] (86–87). Would it be a 'iniludível sinal dos tempos ou um facto isolado, casual, a que se não deva atribuir especial significado?' ['an inescapable sign of the times or an isolated, casual fact, to which no particular significance should be attached?'] (86).

New times or not, the solidarity and collaboration between social classes in *Aurélia* resonate with the not-so-new, yet powerful, idea of Cabral for an alliance between the bourgeoisie and peasantry, in which it was the duty of the first to use its privileged position to come to terms with its historical responsibility and pave the way against colonialism towards a more equal future in post-independence society (2008: 198). The meaningful difference in the context of this novel is that Santos and Aurélia – along with the lawyer Altino Castro – are not fighting colonialism but a sovereign independent state formed by the very political class that opposed the colonial system. On the other hand, the conciliatory scene of the narrative's final chapter where state, religion and law – given the presence of two ministers, one of whom is Ventura, the Bishop and the Director of the Judiciary Police – come together to pay their respects to Aurélia as she recovers from the attempt on her life – does not signal a disillusioned critique of the state. In an ending where the postcolonial state, defeated on lawful grounds by a citizen who is a White man born as a colonial settler, still agrees to pay respects to the victor's daughter, we have a fictional projection pointing towards a constructive and positive future. A future where people can organise and elicit enough power to sway the heavy hand of the state parallels the writing of a *devenir* of active postcolonial political and social consciousness in which it can be possible to dream of a State that can truly serve the people.

The experience of time as entanglement in *Aurélia de Vento* articulates the postcolonial present in the terms put forward by Mbembe and discussed in Chapter 1 as 'precisely that moment when different forms of absence become mixed together: the absence of those presences that are no longer so and that one remembers (the past), and the absence of those others that are yet to come and are anticipated (the future)' (2001: 16). As a result, the narrative portrays the critical aspect of postcolonial time in which both the absent colonial past, making itself present in the deployment of (anti)colonial reason, and the promise of a future with equality, based on the performance of justice, cling together. In that way, the juxtaposition of colonial, anticolonial and intra-colonial mentalities and practices in the postcolonial present constitutes a structuring feature embodied by the central characters of the story and the pace of the narrative itself.

Santos's character and struggle illustrate the different strands intertwined in the Santomean postcoloniality woven in *Aurélia de Vento*. The same way the colour of his skin signifies the colonial difference of the past, his defiance of the post-independence intra-colonial intransigence of the state signals the lingering of a colonial logic of race whose surpassing is already anticipated:

> – Pedro, outra coisa é que você esquece que você é estrangeiro, num país em que a independência nem tem ainda muito tempo, raiva contra branco ainda não passou tudo. É preciso você compreender isso. Nem sempre coisa anda com pressa que a gente quer...

> – Estrangeiro, eu? Não nasci aqui, mas a filha que fiz, todo o amor que demonstrei ter para com este povo? Só fiquei em S. Tomé porque é aqui onde eu quero viver, onde me sinto bem. É por eu defender os meus direitos que têm que esquecer todo o passado? (Bragança 2011: 24)

> [Pedro, the other thing is that you forget that you're a foreigner, in a country where independence isn't even long ago, and anger against Whites hasn't all gone away yet. You have to realise that. Things don't always go as quickly as you'd like...

> A foreigner, me? I wasn't born here, but the daughter I've raised, all the love I've shown this people? I only stayed in São Tomé because this is where I want to live, where I feel good. Is it because I defend my rights that you have to forget the past?]

The state's choice to forget Santos' personal history in the promotion of a homogenising and Manichean version of a collective history sheds light on the processes of erasure inherent to the establishment of grand narratives. This is further illustrated throughout the novel in the arguments used by state officials to persuade others to collaborate in the attempt to expropriate Pedro's land. In the following extract, Minister Ventura seeks to convince his lawyer of the legitimacy of his claim against Santos:

> mas, diga-me lá doutor, afinal de contas, desde quando é que o Estado tem de se submeter à vontade [refere-se na verdade ao direito] de um cidadão, ainda por cima estrangeiro?
>
> ...
>
> Acha mesmo que eu baixo os braços assim à primeira, podendo invocar o interesse público e expropriar o terreno ao maldito agricultor? Será que não existe mesmo nenhuma hipótese de forçar o tipo a vender ou, tratando-se de um estrangeiro, ameaçar expulsá-lo senão se dispuser a fazê-lo? (Bragança 2011: 46–47)

> [But tell me, doctor, at the end of the day, since when the State has to submit to the will [in actuality he refers to the right] of a citizen, a foreign citizen on top of that?
>
> ...
>
> Do you really believe that I give up so quickly when I can evoke public interest to take the land from the damned farmer? Isn't there really any way to force the guy to sell it or, since he is a foreigner, threaten to expel him if unwilling to do so?]

The minister's manipulation of Santos' belonging as an argument to strip him of his legal rights, clearly marked by the narrator's intervention

between brackets, reflects the intra-colonial appropriation of the colonial discourse of exclusion based on race. Despite referring to Santos as
a foreigner – a term that would not, in itself, necessarily imply a connection with the former colonising power – his Portuguese birthplace, white
skin and landowner status are enough to surround the proposal of his
expulsion with the spectres of an (anti)colonial resentment all too present in Ventura's words. As stated by Fanon in a segment of 'Concerning
Violence' where he describes the challenging circumstances framing the
pursuit for independence 'we see that the primary Manichaeism which
governed colonial society is preserved intact during the period of decolonization; that is to say that the settler never ceases to be the enemy, the
opponent, the foe that must be overthrown' (Fanon 2001: 39).

Within a post-independence context, the resort to anticolonial reason
in *Aurélia* is made into a mode of critique. Shown to be contradictory and
embedded in the very colonial reason it sought to dismantle, the nationalist roots of the state apparatus constructed in the narrative are conceived
in their spectrality. Personified by the late mother of Ventura's faithful
secretary, Aydi, San Labeca is described as 'uma nacionalista exacerbada
tentando impor aos outros os padrões da sua visão das coisas' [an exacer-
bated nationalist trying to impose the standards of her vision of things on
others] (Bragança 2011: 42), Labeca's intransigence is regarded as a problematic legacy: 'Desde jovem San Labeca guardava no peito o sonho de um
país livre e por isso se juntou à Cívica logo no início da fase final da luta.
Fê-lo de forma quase religiosa, fanática mesmo, tal como acontecia com a
grande maioria. Ela era dos que consideravam que a verdade só havia uma,
a do Movimento e mais nenhuma' ['Ever since he was young, San Labeca
had harboured the dream of a free country in her heart and that's why she
joined the Civic right at the start of the final phase of the struggle. She
did so almost religiously, fanatically even, as was the case with the vast majority. She was one of those who considered that there was only one truth,
that of the Movement and no other'] (Bragança 2011: 36).[4] As a result, the

4   *Cívica* was the name of the group created in 1974 in São Tomé and Príncipe to mo-
     bilise the local populations for the independence cause. The members of this group
     were supporters of the MLSTP – or *Movimento* – whose members, at the time,
     lived abroad for many years and were virtually unknown to the local population.

righteous lawyer Castro moves away from both Minister Ventura and Aydi, as he refuses to represent the state against Santos and decides to separate from Aydi, the wife who could not escape the extremist influence of her nationalist late mother. On the allegorical level, the law, then, distances itself from the corrupt state and nationalist discourse to move towards its commitment to the rule of law, which, in the Hegelian terms that sustain modern European law, is a condition for the state to live up to its potential as a conduit for freedom (Smith 1983: 5).

Albertino Bragança's fictional construction of the intra-colonial power of the state in a postcolonial present of time as entanglement spells out a grammar of becoming that is pregnant with hope for the future. The portrayal of the state as an intra-colonial agent, insofar as it appropriates from the colonial logic of race, is passed on by its anticolonial resignification – 'le movement armés anticoloniaux considéraient que l'ennemi était toujours, par principe, d'une autre race' ['the armed anti-colonial movement considered that the enemy was always, as a matter of principle, of another race'] (Mbembe 2010: 230). This resignification, used to manipulate the sense and the right to belong required to define the limits of the nation-state, points to the problem while, at the same time, signalling its solution. It is through a deconstructive construction of the postcolony, showing its inner character as a site of entangled time, that the intra-colonial state is historicised. Such historicisation, despite challenging linearity, reveals the underlying processes of resignification that are in place in the postcolonial state, indicating that 'le passage de l'État racial à l'État démocratique est en train de s'accomplir' ['the transition from the racial state to the democratic state is taking place'.] (Mbembe 2010: 237).

It is in this context that the rise of law as a resource for the achievement of justice, which for Hegel is an important moment for the achievement of freedom as it is when an individual's particular and social dimensions are acknowledged by the institution of the state (Poiraud 2019), completes the entangled portrait of the narrative as the anticipation of a future *pour s'accomplir*. A future in which the force of law is there to face the muscular corpulence of the nationalist-oriented state – whose proportions are a mix of San Labeca's 'temíveis metro e noventa . . . e reconhecida irascibilidade de character' ['fearsome metre and ninety ... and recognised irascibility of character'] (Bragança 2011: 42) and Ventura's reach, through his 'dedos compridos, mais se assemelhando a garras e, sobretudo aquele olhar penetrante e desconfiado que dir-se-ia procurar devassar o interlocutor à sua frente' ['long fingers, more like claws and, above all, that penetrating and suspicious look that would seem to seek to devour the interlocutor in front of him'] (Bragança 2010: 44). A law which, according to Castro, believes that '[s]e são os cidadãos que fazem os Estados, seus interesses devem estar em primeiro lugar' ['[i]f it is citizens who make states, their interests must come first'] (Bragança 2011: 81), and who are thus the only resource capable of keeping 'bourgeois leaders … [from] imprison[ing] national consciousness in sterile formalism', making the nation into the actual 'moving consciousness of the whole of the people; … the coherent, enlighten[ing] action of men and women' (Fanon 2001: 165).

The investment in the rule of law as an overarching force of internal cohesion, justice and an index of hope for the future marks, in *Aurélia de Vento*, the progression from national consciousness to political and social consciousness in that postcolonial society. In an Derridan sense, an *avenir* whose *devenir*, inscribed in a time of juxtaposition, can only be possible through the resignification of the use of force. In this sense, the emergence of law in the advocacy of the people indicates the assignment of a new meaning to the use of violence by the state. Employed by colonialism, appropriated by anticolonialism and monopolised by the intra-colonialism of the state, violence's future incarnation, in *Aurélia*, is to serve justice by enforcing the law and only then, finally, serving the people and achieving the desired freedom.

State as discursive actualisation

Departing from the Santomean *Aurélia de Vento* on a tour through the remaining four novels included in this study, one notes the permanence of the depiction of the state as an important force organising their fictional national universes. When compared, each of these novels sheds light on different but interrelated aspects of the modern state, as described by European philosophy. Yet, in speaking from their specific loci of enunciation, each novel offers a singular and yet related interpretation of the state in its existence within the postcolonial entangled time of becoming.

The Mozambican *Campo de Trânsito* (2006) is the most allegoric novel in our group of five. The story neither takes place in Mozambique, nor are any connections with the country made explicitly throughout the narrative, which has led a number of critics to highlight its universality (Mendonça 2007; Can 2009) in place of its potential local historicity (Moreira 2010) in digging up the controversial memory of the post-independence re-education camps. Universal or not – as discussions concerning the novel's disputed rescue of national memory will be deepened in Chapter 3 – and leaving aside discussions about what one can even mean by universality in the twenty-first century, it would be valuable to concentrate on the enormous role ascribed to the state as the organising power of the plot.

The story of the journey of protagonist J. Mungau starts with his abduction from his city apartment and incarceration in a prisoners' camp, the Transit Camp, which is where the action is centred until he leaves, at the end of the story, under the custody of the same coercive authority that detained him in the first place. Through the strategic use of showing instead of telling, the omniscient narrator makes a hostage of the reader, as we know nothing except what is presented to the character. We get to know Mungau is under arrest via a piece of direct speech 'Estás detido!' ['You're under arrest!'] (Borges Coelho 2007: 10); likewise, we are kept guessing as to who takes him and where he is taken to by a narrator limited to describing the action and its setting '[t]ranspõem os altos portões de ferro, dão uma curva larga no pátio do Comando e estacionam junto ao edifício principal' ['[t]ranspose the high iron gates, make a wide turn into the Command courtyard and park next to the main building'] (Coelho 2007: 15). In the subsequent paragraphs, the description of Mungau's captors implies that he was taken by agents of the state to a place that is always hinted at, but never named, as a prison.

Following Mungau's experiences in our role as readers, we experience that 'to read is to struggle to name, to subject the sentences of the text to a semantic transformation. This transformation is erratic; it consists in hesitating among several names' (Barthes 1974: 92). Mungau's hesitation in naming 'police' or 'prison' is passed onto the reader. A process permeated by an undecidability whose political significance is underlined by the performative meaning of the character's silence and the reader's potential discomfort in the face of this responsibility to decide. Up to page thirty-six, we are obliged to decide for ourselves the name of the institution that is holding the protagonist. After all, we are all too aware of who has the monopoly on violence in such settings. In a Hegelian fashion, the state is only named for the uncivilised, whom inhabiting deep into the interior are kept from reason and from the 'universal' as hostages of nature and tradition, to whom it cannot signify:[5]

> 'Missão de Estado!', vocifera [o agente], pretendendo com isso intimidar os marinheiros.
>
> Mas ninguém conhece alí o Estado, palpável apenas quando grupos como esse chegam e partem, nada de concreto que se veja e possa incutir respeito. Prossegue por isso a negociação enquanto os detidos, imóveis e expectantes, se deixam sobrevoar pelas libélulas e devorar pelos mosquitos. Por pouco chegam a vias extremas, o Bexigoso fora de si sublinhando os argumentos com o cano das espingardas. (Borges Coelho, 2007: 36)
>
> ["State mission!" [the agent] shouts, trying to intimidate the sailors.
>
> But nobody knows the State there, it's only tangible when groups like this arrive and leave, nothing concrete that can be seen and instil respect. So the negotiations continue while the detainees, motionless and expectant, allow themselves to be flown over by dragonflies and devoured by mosquitoes. It's not long before they go to extremes, Bexigoso out of his mind, emphasising his arguments with the barrel of his rifle.]

The architecture of the state in *Campo de Trânsito* relates to Hegel's philosophical blueprint, where it is the mechanism 'in society that binds people

---

5   'Indeed, this perplexity and difficulty of theirs [who have unsophisticated hearts] is proof rather that they want as the substance of the right and the ethical not what is universally recognized and valid, but something else. If they had been serious with what is universally accepted instead of busying themselves with the vanity and particularity of opinions and things, they would have clung to what is substantively right, namely to the commands of the ethical order and the state, and would have regulated their lives in accordance with these.' (Hegel 1978: 3–4)

together by completely transcending individual self-interest' (Magee 2010: 229), entering the revolutionary repertoire of ideas via interpretations of Marxism that will later solidify into state ideology, in a variety of ways, in diverse parts of Portuguese-speaking Africa. Considering the situated reality in post-independence Mozambique, one could see Coelho's fictional projection of the state as an allegory of the potential distortions of the 'external positive' and 'necessary authority of the state' (Hegel 1978: 161) *vis-à-vis* the loss that has to take place via the dialectical movement concerning the becoming of the individual into part of the collectivity of the state. An assimilative process fully supported by Marx in his fight against constitutional monarchy in *Critique of Hegel's Philosophy of History* (1844), embraced by Marxism, theorised by Engels in *The Origin of the Family, Private Property and the State* (1884), and incorporated in Marxism-Leninism as the notion of the individual. This notion is then occluded by the urgency of the struggle against private property on a way to more equal societies before being adopted by the anticolonial revolutionary movements in Portuguese-speaking Africa and materialised as the project for the 'Homem Novo' ['New Man'] embraced in Mozambique. In this respect, the passage of the novel quoted above shows three different moments of men in relation to the full realisation of civil society into the Ethical Idea, according to Hegel: men who are away from reason, connected to the realm of untamed nature and tradition, and therefore unable to recognise the state; men who are in their transitional moment – metaphorically and materially as they are actually in transit at that point in the narrative – towards reason as they recognise the state but are still inactive. They do not transform nature, and allow themselves to be devoured by it. Also, the men of state themselves are on duty to bring reason to the other two groups by leading them into the exercise of labour as a mode of mediation (Hegel 1977: 117). This is done in the interest of the whole, or the state, by 'sensitising' the ferry operators regarding the urgencies of state missions and by transporting individuals to their educational experience of labour at the camps.

The camps of the novel work as institutions for the labour-mediated dialectical transformation in which the state, in its role as 'the actuality of the ethical Idea' (Hegel 1978: 155), is actualised by the objectification

of individual subjectivities through stripping inmates of their names, (hi)
stories, past and future. They are then called by the nouns denoting their
function in the construction of the camp as a collectivity (prisoner, director, teacher, teacher's wife, tea seller, etc). In so being, one of the initial
moments of Mungau's transformation – he was named as such by the omniscient narrator but never by any of his interlocutors, who address him as
'prisoner' – is the important loss of his name upon arrival at the camp. As
he is rebaptised 15.6, which stands for the location of his small, hut-like private accommodation, Mungau is therefore named after a place. According
to Hegel, place as a concept is itself a token for becoming, as it is identified
by the concrete point of the transition of space into time (1970: 236–237).
While Mungau, now sublated into 15.6, refers to the materiality of his subjective moment (and place) of becoming, the Director of the three-camp
complex (including the Transit, the Old and the New camps) is named
according to his location in the objective realm of the idea. His designa-
tion, if we follow Hegel, cannot be material like Mungau's, for the state is
the actuality of the ethical Idea, thus absolute and suspended in space and
time. This prevents the Director from having a place, defined precisely
in terms of space and time as the 'unity of here and now'. The objectified
Director, thus, can be read as the personification of the state in its role of
ethical synthesis between subject and object – 'O Director é o Estado,
se é que este último pode se resumir numa única pessoa' ['The Director
is the state, if the latter can be summarised in a single person'] (Coelho
2007: 134). Furthermore, as the dialectic principle stands, the synthesis
represented by the Director carries on characteristics of the elements it
heben auf, or sublates. Besides being absolute – or maybe because of being
absolute – the Director masters both space, represented by the camps, and
time, as he also embodies the present.

In their role as the promoter of change, development and the enlight-
enment of arbitrarily caught prisoners who are made into an enlightened
society, the camps work as an interesting system. The Transit Camp is the
place for learning, specifically at the hands of the Teacher. It is a place of
indoctrination, which evokes Louis Althusser's definition of ideological
state apparatus (1971: 143), through schooling and farming – or reason and
labour. Through being tested for their exercise of thought or their ability to

triumph over nature, prisoners could be sent either to the Old or the New Camp. The Old Camp, designed to host those more attached to reason, received prisoners in need of 'expiação do crime de memória' [expiation of the crime of memory] (Coelho 2007: 96). To the New Camp went the prisoners that would have been successfully collected in the Transit Camp so that their strength would be worn out, preventing them from developing a future. Past and future become mere abstractions of a timeless state grounded in the self-perpetuating eternal time of the present:

> O Director é um homem verdadeiramente enigmático. E também muito agarrado ao presente. Agarrado a ponto de convocar o passado e o futuro como instrumentos para a realização das obras do presente. Domina-os com segurança, como se dominasse dóceis animais domésticos. Para ele o tempo não passa de uma abstração, boa para manter os outros presos a ela e nada mais. O que verdadeiramente importa é o presente. O presente e o cumprimento do dever. (Borges Coelho 2007: 140–141)

> [The Director is a truly enigmatic man. He's also very attached to the present. So attached that he calls on the past and the future as instruments for realising the works of the present. He masters them with confidence, as if he were mastering docile domestic animals. For him, time is nothing more than an abstraction, good for keeping others tied to it and nothing more. What really matters is the present. The present and the fulfilment of duty.]

While Hegel's state is the actualisation of the ethical Idea, and therefore of freedom, the version of state in *Campo de Trânsito* reveals itself to be a fictional projection that actualises the freedom-through-reason objectified in the state's potential deviations by depicting the process of realisation of this idea from the point of view of an individual character, a constitutive trace of the novel itself. Such a perspective might point a critical finger at what is lost, and very often forgotten, in the dialectical process in which the state emerges as freedom after the surpassing of the subjective moment towards an objectified ethical construct of freedom and truth. The fact that Coelho's state is conceived as a prison complex already questions absolutism by clearly relativising the notion of freedom by its constitutive opposite, captivity. In fact, the impossibility of true collective sublation, or transformation of the individual, that will later result in the downfall of the system of camps due to the unethical ways in which the camps work as institutions constitutes a fictional distortion of Hegel's philosophical conceptualisations, since his philosophy cannot be said to be represented in a projection where the state denies the constitutive importance of individual freedom and subjective being. The state of *Campo* is, therefore, irrational in Hegelian terms; hence, it cannot constitute the actualisation of the ethical Idea. The novel points out the misuse of Hegelianism by totalitarian states, for which '[s]ociety becomes an armed camp in the service of those great interests that have survived the economic competitive struggle' (Marcuse 1955: 410).

It is, thus, for its own present self-serving urgency that *Campo de Trânsito*'s totalitarian state manipulates the past and the future for profit, as we come to know that both camps are forced-labour camps. The Old Camp is a producer of truffle mushrooms, and the New Camp is a site for the extraction of naphtha. Equally, it is for the state's own self-serving needs that it manipulates the concepts of belonging and justice. Prisoners are presented with the idea of collectivity as a given, a collectivity where belonging is only possible through the complete abandonment of one's individuality, and meanwhile, they are prepared for their role as controllable mass labour. The cancellation of individuality redefines the concept of justice to justify captivity:

> A justiça, caro 15.6, é uma categoria universal a que só por meio da colectividade se chega. A singularidade não passa de uma fase transitória, antiquada, incapaz de estabelecer relação significativa com a justiça. A singularidade vem do tempo em que não havia justiça, o tempo da barbárie! Por conseguinte, 15.6, transforme-se primeiro, colectivize-se, e depois venha colocar-nos a questão da justiça! Teremos nessa altura todo o gosto em debatê-la! (Borges Coelho, 2007: 81)

> [Justice, dear 15.6, is a universal category that can only be reached through the collective. Singularity is nothing more than a transitory, outdated phase, incapable of establishing a meaningful relationship with justice. Singularity comes from a time when there was no justice, the time of barbarism! So, 15.6, transform yourself first, collectivise yourself, and then come and ask us about justice! Then we'll be happy to debate it!]

Such a caricature of Hegel's conceptualisation of justice completes *Campo de Trânsito*'s depiction of the system of rules upon which the state rests. While the Hegelian proposal sustains that '[i]n the administration of

justice, however, civil society returns to its concept, to the unity of the implicit universal with the subjective particular' (1978: 145), the complete
cancellation of the subjective particular as proposed by the Director of
the camps in the narrative spells out an error that leads to a totalitarian
state of exception instead of the actualisation of the ethical Idea. The
ease with which Coelho conceives of a world structured upon the strategic slippage from the sublation into the subtraction of the subjective
particular and of the state as an Idea, whose very definition relies on the
notion of freedom –conceived in Hegelian terms – reveals dialectics'
constitutive feature of actualisation as, above all, discourse. An idea that,
when brought back to our transnational picture of imaginations of and
from postcolonial states, charges the distorted appropriation of Hegel in
Coelho's novel with a critique that signals the largely unnoticed changes
of meaning, route and orientation materially verifiable in the conception
of the state in postcoloniality.

State as power

If *Campo de Trânsito* speaks of structures and institutions in the space-
time of entanglement of the postcolonial present, *Tiara* (1999), by the
Angola-born Guinean Filomena Embaló takes a more personal approach in her account of the juxtaposition of times and practices in post-
independence Africa. Similarly to its Mozambican counterpart, *Tiara*
is also a novel suspended in time and space. An important difference,
however, arises from the resources adopted to operate what seems to be a
calculated distance from reality. *Tiara* is set among fictional countries in
an exclusively internal linear temporality whose progress is determined
relationally in its self-contained fictional structure. Time in this novel
is never marked by any mention of a specific year, but always in a re-
lational manner that marks the number of years between the fictional
events. Through that, we witness twenty-four years of Tiara's life trajectory, starting when she was eighteen years old with her escape from her
country on the brink of a civil war. In exile, she graduates, falls in love
and marries an international student. Upon moving to her husband's

country, she joins the liberation struggle. From that moment on, the novel's time is marked both by references to events in the protagonist's life journey and to her new country's progress from struggle to independence. This feature, which substantially differs from the focus on a timeless present in *Campo de Trânsito*, also differs – although to a lesser extent – from *Aurélia de Vento*'s internal temporality. The Santomean narrative focuses on the five-year present trajectory in the life of the protagonist rather than on her country's progress in historical time. Instead, Tiara's twenty-four-year trajectory runs parallel with her husband's country, Muriti, developing from its struggle for independence to its postcolonial consolidation.

Due to its structure, *Tiara* offers a much more historical account of the juxtaposed practices of the postcolonial state, articulating a critical approach to the pervasiveness of colonial racial logic in the anticolonial movement, its lingering in the post-independent state apparatus, as well as the betrayal of the national ideals that such practices entangle. Tiara's mixed ethnic heritage, as the daughter of a White man and a Black woman, was the reason why her family had to flee to exile. It remains an obstacle to her acceptance in her husband's country from the moment she arrives to join them in their struggle for independence:

> – Kenum, porque é que as pessoas quando me vêem têm uma reacção... estranha?
> – Por duas razões: A primeira é que não contavam ver-me casado tão de repente a segunda é, certamente, a tua cor. Aqui, no campo, não estão muito acostumados a ver mestiços. Aliás, há muito pouca mestiçagem no Muriti. Em geral, ou se é preto ou se é branco... os mestiços são quase considerados acidentes de percurso... – disse, espicaçando a mulher. (Embaló 1999: 139–140)

['Kenum, why is it that when people see me they have an... odd reaction?'

'For two reasons: The first is that they didn't expect to see me married so suddenly, and the second is certainly your skin colour. Here, in the countryside, they're not used to seeing mestizos. In fact, there's very little racial mixing in Muriti. In general, you're either Black or White... mestizos are almost considered accidents on the way... – he said, prodding his wife.]

The argument of Kenun – Tiara's husband – is confirmed in the following paragraphs, as the next scene shows his conversation with the general secretary of the liberation movement:

– Tenho notado uma certa... animosidade da tua parte, desde que regressei de Terra Branca. O que se passa?

...

– Queres realmente saber o que tenho contra ti? Gostaria de saber se no Muriti não havia mulheres suficientes para que tu fosses buscar uma lá fora!
– Ah! Então era isso?! Bem que eu devia ter desconfiado! A tua xenofobia não é segredo pra ninguém! Voltou-lhe as costas e encaminhou-se para a porta. Não iria perder tempo a discutir quinhas. ... Apenas disse antes de sair:
– Um homem como tu não mereces o lugar que ocupas! – Saiu, ciente de que tinha arranjado um inimigo na guerra, mas também para a paz. (1999:141–142)

['I've noticed a certain... animosity on your part since I returned from White Land. What's going on?'

...

'Do you really want to know what I have against you? I'd like to know if there weren't enough women in Muriti for you to pick one up abroad!'

'Ah! So that was it?! I should have known! Your xenophobia is no secret to anyone! He turned his back on him and headed for the door. He wasn't going to waste time arguing ... He just said before leaving:

'A man like you doesn't deserve the position you hold! – He left, realising that he had made an enemy in the war, but also for peace.]

And as we see throughout the novel, the animosity towards Tiara expressed by the adjunct general secretary, Kito, does not diminish. This animosity perpetrates the state apparatus of the postcolonial Murity as the members of the liberation movement form the political party that rules the fictional country for its first five years through a single-party state period. As a result of that, despite Tiara's clear professional capabilities, she is denied job positions and intimidated within the state-owned company she finally manages to find work in. With the state in the hands of the party – '[o partido] tem a maioria absoluta e dita as ordens que entender!' (1999: 206) ['[the party] has an absolute majority and dictates whatever orders it wants!'] – justice is not a possibility. Besides being a lawyer herself, Tiara knows she cannot fight such a powerful enemy – 'Kenum tinha razão, seria uma guerra perdida de antemão.' (1999: 206) ['Kenum was right, it would be a war lost beforehand.'] – and as the story proceeds to its end, the tone openly changes from hope to disillusion-ment. As the narrator puts it:

> Os anos foram passando iguais uns aos outros. O país tinha feito muitos progressos, mas, como o decorrer do tempo, os ânimos foram-se acalmando. Já lá ia longe o tempo do trabalho militante, voluntário, dos primeiros anos de independência. Talvez por um certo desencanto de não se ter obtido o que se esperava com a independência. Sonhos muito altos tinham-se tornado inatingíveis. Talvez por serem utópicos ou talvez por não estarem a altura de consegui-los. O MLM [Movimento de Libertação do Muriti] acusava uma decadência. A corrupção tinha-se tornado prática corrente no seio dos seus dirigentes e os ideais revolucionários tinham dado lugar à luta pelos interesses pessoais. O aparelho do Estado também reflectia essa crise. Os partidos da oposição tinham dificuldade em afirmarem-se como forças catalisadoras para uma mudança, cada vez mais inelutável, por falta de uma estratégia adequada. (1999: 207–208)

> [The years passed one after the other. The country had made much progress but, as time went on, tempers began to cool down. The days of the militant, voluntary work of the first years of independence were long gone. Perhaps this was due to a certain disenchantment at not having achieved what had been hoped for with independence. High dreams had become unattainable. Perhaps because they were utopian dreams or because they weren't within reach. The MLM [Muriti Liberation Movement] was in decline. Corruption had become a common practice among its leaders and revolutionary ideals had given way to the fight for personal interests. The state apparatus also reflected this crisis. The opposition parties found it difficult to assert themselves as catalysing forces for change, which was increasingly inevitable, for lack of an adequate strategy.]

Tiara's closing, marked by the protagonist's divorce as she finds out her husband had been lured by his mother into holding a secret second wife in the village where he grew up, marks a rupture with the present of the country she fought for and a retreat from public service: 'Tenciono ir viver para a aldeia onde estive durante a Luta, quando cá cheguei.' (1999: 259) ['I plan to go and live in the village where I was during the struggle when I first came here.'] An ending harbouring another beginning for Tiara, whose life would be no longer connected with the history of the country, leaving space for the pursuit of personal happiness suggested by the resurgence, in the last pages of the novel, of a lover from adolescence. A future with no resolution, no justice, no promise, in which the opportunity of a restart lies in the act of disengagement from the state, in which happiness can only be found in the individual, private sphere. A postcolonial novel pointing to the abandonment of the grand narrative?

State as performance

While it may be premature to speak of the complete abandonment of the grand narrative in the novelistic production of Portuguese-speaking Africa in the first decade of this century, it is worth remarking on the radical power and critical productivity of postmodern aesthetics for discussions posed by certain pieces of postcolonial literature when it comes to the postcolony's internal affairs. While the erection of grand narratives was certainly an important cultural feature of anticolonial nationalist struggles, contributing to the rise of national consciousness amongst literate elites at home, in the metropole and abroad as it underlied the social union necessary to defeat the colonial enemy, it has also served to legitimise the State's right to rule in the aftermath of independence. The grand narrative's importance to the legitimation of the State is openly addressed by Lyotard in *The Postmodern Condition* when he says that '[t]he state spends large amounts of money to enable science to pass itself off as an epic: the State's own credibility is based on that epic, which it uses to obtain the public consent its decision makers need.' (1991: 28). While these novels are not strictly postmodern narratives, they do carry certain postmodern features. In their own way, each of them relativises the legitimacy of the state, 'de-doxifying' (Hutcheon 2002: 7) its almightiness and posing the possibility of its contestation. Their postmodern features, thus, point to the need for alternative imaginations of yet 'unpresentable' (Lyotard 1991: 82), more participative modes of democracy.

It is due to its deconstructive agency and reconstructive possibilities that the fragmentation of the grand narrative is useful to *Teoria Geral do Esquecimento* (2012). Deployed as a structuring feature of the novel, fragmentation marks the plot, the characters, the narrative perspective and the institutions represented. The story of the protagonist, the Portuguese Ludovica Fernandes Mano – or simply Ludo – a woman who literally immured herself for twenty-eight years, sealing the door of her flat in Luanda from 1975 to 2003, entangles with the bits and pieces of the other characters' stories, themselves shattered, scrambled and reordered according to the revolutions inherent to the country's historical circumstances.

In Agualusa's fictional construct, the state is not conceived as an entire and complete self-standing institution. In a broken world whose fragments are organised by war, be it the struggle for independence or the civil war that followed, both the state and colonialism are where statists and colonialists are. The novel thus foregrounds the people usually hidden behind the institutions, but who are the embodiments of the regimes their actions institute. It is a strategy that bears a radical possibility, given its emphasis on individual agency and preference to focus on institutions' performative dimension. Once it restores focus to the action, it foregrounds the personal dimension of those embodying the state, whose campaign of terror, historically and fictionally inscribed by the events of 27 May 1977, in Angola, is portrayed as a series of individual decisions between compliance and defiance; the liminal moments in which violence and peace, as well as revenge and forgiveness, are always present as attainable possibilities.

It can be said that all major characters in the novel undergo deep changes throughout the course of the narrative. Those changes, arguably, could have occurred as a direct result of the process of transformation undergone by the country itself in the course of almost thirty years covered by the story.

> Após a morte do primeiro presidente, o regime ensaiou uma tímida abertura. Os presos políticos, não ligados à oposição armada, foram libertados. Alguns receberam convites para ocupar posições no aparelho do Estado.
>
> ...
>
> [R]olaram anos. Caíram muros. Veio a paz, realizaram-se eleições, a guerra regressou. O sistema socialista foi desmantelado, *pelas mesmas pessoas que o haviam erguido*, e o capitalismo ressurgiu das cinzas, mais feroz do que nunca. (Agualusa 2012: 90–91, my emphasis)
>
> [After the death of the first president, the regime experimented with a hesitant opening up. Those political prisoners not linked to the armed opposition were released. Some received invitations to occupy positions in the apparatus of the State.
>
> ...

In the meantime, the years went by. The socialist system was dismantled by the very *same people who had set it up*, and capitalism rose from the ashes, as fierce as ever.] (Agualusa 2015: 90; 91, my emphasis)

The narrative emphasis on agency, however, seems to suggest otherwise, as shown by the disruption of the descriptive sequence on the opening of the country's regime, operated by the intrusive addition of adverbial information of *by whom*. The breakup, in the second paragraph, of the performative fact-making (ab)use of verbs in the passive voice, a common practice in the literary representation of institutional actions, insinuates the significance of individual transformation for country change, not the opposite. This argument is further illustrated through the analysis of the transformation experienced by *camarada* [comrade] Monte in the story.

Magno Moreira Monte embodies the iron hand of the revolutionary movement and, subsequently, of the state throughout the novel. He is the one whose story, similar to what happens to Ludo, is connected to all the other characters. On the brink of independence, Monte orders the execution of Jeremias Carrasco, a deserted captain-turned mercenary of the Portuguese army. After independence, Monte tortures and kills in the name of the regime, having arrested and tortured two other characters. Later, after the opening of the regime, Monte attempted to kill the Jewish journalist Daniel Benchimol, although his accidental failure led him to murder a French writer instead. As the enforcement of the postcolonial regime is delegated to his hands, it is interesting to observe how Monte progresses from the remorseless killing of Carrasco – '[l]embra-me um tipo que conheci há muitos anos. Morreu. Uma pena, porque teria muito gosto em matá-lo outra vez.' (2012: 142) [He reminds me of a guy I met many years ago. He died. A shame, as I'd have really liked to kill him again] (2015: 146) – to a more conscious and questioning approach to state violence, until finally he quits 'public' service. As readers, we first witness his discomfort with the memories of the witchhunting he perpetrated for the regime: 'Monte não gostava de interrogatórios. Ainda hoje se esquiva a falar sobre o assunto. Evita, inclusive, recordar os anos setenta, quando, para preservar a revolução socialista, se permitiram, utilizando um eufemismo grato aos agentes da polícia política, certos excessos.' (2012: 65) [Monte didn't like interrogations. For years he avoided discussing the subject. He'd even avoided recalling the seventies, when in order to preserve the socialist revolution, certain excesses – to use an euphemism for which we're indebted to the agents of the political police – were permitted.] (2015: 63) Finally, we get to the point where we see a complete separation between the demands of his job and his will:

> Lá de cima – de algum gabinete faustoso e climatizado – viera a ordem para silenciar um jornalista, Daniel Benchimol, especializado em casos de desaparecimentos.
>
> ...
>
> Ao receber a ordem para o silenciar, o detetive [Monte] não conteve a revolta:
>
> Este país está virado do avesso. Pagam os justos pelos pecadores.
>
> A observação, dita em voz alta, firme, diante de dois generais, não caiu bem. Um deles empertigou-se:
>
> O mundo evoluiu. O partido soube avançar com o mundo, modernizar-se e, por isso, ainda aqui estamos. O camarada devia refletir sobre o processo histórico. Estudar um pouco. Há quantos anos trabalha connosco? Desde sempre, penso. Acho demasiado tarde para se voltar contra nós.
>
> O segundo general encolheu os ombros:
>
> O camarada Monte gosta de provocar. Foi sempre assim, um agente provocador. Questão de estilo.
>
> Monte conformou-se. *Cumprir* ordens. *Fazer cumprir* ordens. *Nisso se resumia, afinal, uma vida inteira.* (2012: 151–152, my emphasis)
>
> [From upstairs – some lavish, air-conditioned office – the order had come to silence a journalist, Daniel Benchimol, who was a specialist in disappearances.
>
> ...
>
> When he received the order to silence him, the detective couldn't contain his disgust: 'This country's turned inside out. The just pay for the sinners.'
>
> This observation, made out loud in a confident voice in front of two generals, did not go down well. One of them straightened up:
>
> 'The world has changed. The party knew how to progress along with the world, to modernise, and that's why we're still here. You ought to give some thought, comrade, to the historical process. Study a bit. How many years have you been working with us? Forever, right? I think it's too late for you to turn against us.'

The second general shrugged:

'Comrade Monte likes being provocative. He's always been like that, an agent pro-vocateur. Just his style.'

Monte got into line. *Obeying orders. Giving orders. That was all a life added up to, after all.*] (2015: 153–154)

The gradual process of Monte's awareness is reached through the per-formative repetition of orders that keeps him in the role of captive-captor within a system he no longer believes in. As theorised by Homi Bhabha in 'Dissemination: time, narrative and the margins of the modern nation', the nation as discourse is only possible in the aporetic self-generative en-deavour of double-time, in which people are both active subjects and passive objects. The nation's undeniable historical youth, as a political construct invented in modernity, entails a constant need for legitim-isation through the resignifying rescue of myths and events capable of endowing it with a historical origin in any unmemorable past. From such an inherent contradiction of the national discourse, says Bhabha, comes the tension between its peoples' own performative and pedagogical functions, the first consisting of the individual as an active performer of a narrative tradition designed to fulfil the second, in which the people are to play the role of pedagogic object. The space 'in-between' opened up by the intervention of the performative thus harbours the possibility of staging the same cultural difference that the homogenising national narrative is designed to replace. Changing the focus of Bhabha's theory from 'the nation's *self-generation*' (1990: 212) to the state as the enforcer of the national discourse within which the nation comes to exist, explains how Monte's performance of obedient repetition rendered its own end.[6] Monte's alienation, ironically set afoot by a regime committed to Marx's philosophy, is then revolutionary as it makes room for the recuperation

6   Although Bhabha's focus on the nation as a discursive agent distances itself from 'political languages' in order to 'displace the historicism that has dominated discus-sions of the nation as a cultural force' (1990: 201) is of secondary importance, his occlusion of the role of the state as enforcer of national discourse blurs the power games at stake that are part and parcel of the process he theorises.

of the undecidable moment. For Derrida, the undecidable moment is a trial without which '[t]here can be no moral or political responsibility' (1988: 116). Here, in a context where people are portrayed as de facto drivers of institutions like the state, the recuperation of the undecidability suggests the embracing of one's ethical-political responsibility. This moment, always pregnant with the opportunity for change, can also gesture towards a horizon of justice through the possibility of accountability.

Change through transformation is this novel's incarnation of a becoming that touches every character as it is built through every new decision. In that way, Carrasco is redeemed through the second chance offered by the benefactor figure of the ex-nun-now-nurse Madalena. She is a woman who, named after one of the most widely known symbols of Christian conversion from sin to virtue, chooses not to cast the first stone and helps the man – who had his speech impaired by the bullet that should have killed him – to take refuge in the south of the country amidst the Mucubal people. It is there that Jeremias, like the author of the biblical 'Book of Lamentations' who witnesses the destruction of a city – Luanda – becomes (St.) Jerónimo. He is the great translator whose masterpiece is his own silent rewriting from greedy Portuguese – 'Combato pela civilização ocidental, contra o imperialismo soviético. Combato pela sobrevivência de Portugal' (Agualusa 2012: 33) [I'm fighting for Western civilisation, against Soviet imperialism. I'm fighting for Portugal's survival] (Agualusa 2015: 25) – into a socially conscious Mucubal. '[R]enascera não outra pessoa mas outras pessoas, um povo. Antes, ele era ele no meio dos outros. No melhor dos casos, ele, abraçado a outros. No deserto sentira-se pela primeira vez parte de um todo. … [U]m mucubal não existe sem os outros.' (2012: 221) [In his isolation among the Mucubals, Jeremias had been reborn not as another person, but as many – as another people. Before then he had been surrounded by others. At the very best, he was an individual with his arms around others. In the desert, he felt for the first time as though he were a part of it all. … A Mucubal, too, can exist only with others.] (2015: 229–230)

Ludo, likewise, undergoes a deep transformation as her fear and distance from Angola – '*Sinto medo do que está para além das janelas, do ar que entra às golfadas, e dos ruídos que traz. … Sou estrangeira a tudo, como*

uma ave caída na correnteza de um rio' (2012: 37, emphasis in the original)
[*I am afraid of what's outside the window, of the air that arrives in bursts, and
the noise it brings with it. ... I am foreign to everything, like a bird that has
fallen into the current of a river*] (2015: 31, emphasis of the original) – turns
into her dwelling place, constituting her *heimlich* home – 'Filha, esta é a
minha terra. Já não me resta outra.' (2012: 208) [This is my country, child.
I no longer have any other.] (2015: 214). The unbelievable course of her
change resembles the accidental way in which her actions affect the other
characters and the narrative as a whole. As her very name – the Latin word
for 'a game' – suggests, Ludo is the sad joker in the pack. She is a pivotal
character embodying the Portuguese flag-coloured board game, evoking the
element of chance, breaking with the authority of predictable sequentiality
and 'exceed[ing] the calculable program that would destroy all responsibility by transforming it into a programmable effect of determinate causes.'
(Derrida 1988: 116). She is the unpredictable incarnation of providence
and damnation, inadvertently interfering with the city from her Olympian
cloister on the rooftop of the *Prédio dos Invejados* [Building of the Envied],
where she locked herself in. Ludo is, at the same time, a Portuguese mad-
woman who feeds diamonds to pigeons and an avatar to the Angolan god-
dess Kianda – a deity to which a neighbour attributed the disappearance
of a chicken that Ludo stole – which is referred to in the novel as a 'uma
entidade, uma energia capaz do bem e do mal' (Agualusa 2012: 48) [is a
being, an energy capable of good and evil.] (Agualusa 2015: 43)

Through the conjunction of the elements of chance and power of will
as structural elements, the narrative foregrounds the act of deciding on its
myriad of open-ended possibilities that harbour the potential for war and
destruction as well as for justice and reconciliation. By concentrating on
the moment of decision, therefore rescuing the power of the undecidable
moment, the narrative deconstructs the comforting idea of the facelessness
of institutions to the extent that it scales down their almightiness to the
level of the everyday individual and the singular act of responsible choice.
In such a universe, a better future in postcolonial time is encapsulated in
a present individual action that, coming to terms with the past, can lead
to a cathartic moment of justice. Once again, will meets chance, and at
the climax of the narrative, Monte survives the attack perpetrated by one

of his past victims, who carries out his vengeful attempt with a knife that was, in fact, a toy blade.

> Monte, vendo-se cercado por Jeremias, António, Pequeno Soba, Daniel Benchimol e Nasser Evangelista, começou a recuar em direção às escadas:
>
> Calma, calma, o que passou, passou. Somos todos angolanos.
>
> Nasser Evangelista não o ouviu. Escutava os próprios gritos, um quarto de século antes, numa cela estreita, a cheirar a merda e a mijo ... . Avançou dois passos e empurrou a lâmina de encontro ao peito de Monte. Surpreendeu-se por não encontrar resistência. Repetiu o gesto uma e outra vez. O detetive cambaleou, muito pálido, e levou as mãos à camisa. Não viu sangue. As roupas estavam intactas. Jeremias agarrou Nasser pelos ombros e puxou-o para si. Daniel arrancou-lhe a navalha da mão:
>
> É falsa. Graças a Deus, é uma faca de circo.
>
> Assim era. A navalha possuía um cabo oco, com uma mola , para o qual a lâmina deslizava, escondendo-se, sempre que pressionada.
>
> Daniel golpeou-se a si mesmo, no peito e no pescoço, para mostrar aos outros a falsidade da arma. A seguir saltou para cima de Jeremias. Esfaqueou Nasser. Ria alto, em gargalhadas amplas, histéricas, que os restantes acompanhavam. Também Ludo se ria, agarrada a Sabalu, as lágrimas correndo-lhe dos olhos. (2012: 186–187)
>
> [Finding himself surrounded by Jeremias, António, Little Chief, Daniel Benchimol and Nasser Evangelista, Monte began to back towards the staircase:
>
> 'Take it easy, take it easy – what happened, happened. We're all of us Angolans.'
>
> Nasser Evangelista didn't hear him. He heard only his own cries, a quarter of a century earlier, in a narrow cell that stank of shit and piss ... . He took two steps forward and pressed the blade to Monte's chest. He was surprised to meet no resistance. He repeated the gesture again and again. The detective staggered, very pale, and brought his hands up to his shirt. He saw no blood. His clothes were intact. Jeremias took Nasser by the shoulders and pulled him towards himself. Daniel grabbed the knife from his hand.
>
> 'It's fake, thank God. It's a circus knife.'
>
> So it was. The knife had a hollow handle, with a spring, into which the blade slid, disappearing when something pushed against it.
>
> Daniel stabbed himself in the chest and the neck to demonstrate to the others the fakeness of the weapon. Then he leaped onto Jeremias. He stabbed Nasser. He laughed a loud, big, hysterical laughter, and the others joined in. Ludo laughed too, holding on to Sabalu, tears running from her eyes.] (2015: 193)

The passage illustrates a failed lust for blood ending in a simultaneous burst of laughter and tears. It constitutes the symbolic act of justice required to proceed with the series of reconciliations with which the narrative concludes. The attainment of justice and reconciliation through the impact of personal change on social transformation in *Teoria Geral do Esquecimento* recuperates the revolutionary potential of a postcolonial agency, responsibility and accountability. The ways in which the fictional communities of the novel manage to heal from the trauma of pain, abuse and dispossession once the institutional facelessness of the state is deconstructed gesture towards a myriad of future possibilities of fairer, more accountable and more participative forms of democratic state.

State as ideological apparatus

Marginais (2010) by Cape Verdean author Evel Rocha seems to test the limits of *Teoria Geral do Esquecimento's* empowering possibilities of societal change. Frequently regarded as 'the success story of democratization in Africa' (Silva Andrade 2002: 271), Cape Verde is also the most liberal of the five Portuguese-speaking ones.[7] Despite never turning its back completely on the capitalist world during the country's socialist experience between 1975 and 1991 under the PAIGC/PAICV government, it was the decade following the multiparty turn of 1991 that saw the rise of economic liberalism. As stated by Luís Batalha '[a]s MpD took power

---

7   Cape Verde's relatively early resort to liberalism is deeply connected with the country's difficult economic conditions related to the lack of natural resources and climatic conditions subject to long periods of drought, which, allied to the colonial underdevelopment of which it was a victim, posed great challenges to its postcolonial government's ability to feed its population. The country then was largely dependent on financial aid, accepting both socialist and capitalist contributions in addition to the contributions sent by Cape Verdean émigrés, who were compelled to leave for better economic prospects and who were mostly located in the capitalist-oriented United States and Western Europe. Later, argues Patrick Chabal, the Cape Verdean emigrants abroad would also play a crucial role in voting the left-wing PAICV out of office and electing the openly liberal economic proposal of the MpD. (Chabal 2002: 93)

there was a shift toward privatization and market economy; the central role of the state in the economy was progressively replaced with new private initiative.' (2004: 29). This is the economic environment framing the social background of misery, abuse and dispossession in which the narrative of Sérgio do Rosário Araújo, or Sérgio Pitboy, is set.

Sérgio was born and raised on the island of Sal in Cape Verde. This epistolary novel consists of a fictional journal containing his first-person account of a miserable and marginalised life, from childhood until the eve of his death. Furthering the naturalist-realist aesthetics of the text, it is through a fictional editor that the journal becomes a book. At the end of his life, stricken by poverty and ill-health, Sérgio passes his accounts on to a former schoolmate, then a successful engineer, whom he casually meets on the street. The editor of Sergio's story openly intervenes in the narrative in two clearly marked moments: at the beginning, before the opening of the story, when he introduces Sérgio and describes their encounter; and at the very end, reporting the protagonist's suicide and the revelation that takes place at his burial – the fact that his neighbour's twelve-year-old daughter, whose sad debut into the world of misery and sexual exploitation constitutes Sérgio's last account of life in his neighbourhood, is, in fact, his daughter. Despite edited, as the fictional editor admits to intervening in the text 'tomei a iniciativa de substituir algumas passagens ... [a]lguns trechos foram suprimidos por serem demasiados realistas e por descreverem factos que poderiam pôr em causa a dignidade de muitas pessoas da ilha' (Rocha 2010: 13) [I took the initiative to replace some brief parts ... some passages were suppressed for being too realistic and for bringing up facts that could contest the dignity of many people on the island] – the narrative is loaded with vividly narrated scenes of physical, sexual and psychological violence, seasoned with generous doses of filth, abuse and scatology. The novel's open social critique is also part of the plot, as the reader comes to know from what Sérgio says to his posthumous editor upon their meeting: 'Aqui, procurei descrever os dois mundos onde vivi comprimido: o mundo da pobreza e dos abastados, como alguns chamam, mas para mim são os mundos dos exploradores e explorados.' (13) ['Here I've tried to describe the two worlds in which I've been compressed: the world of poverty and the world of the well-off, as some people call them, but for me they are the worlds of the exploiters and the exploited.']

Those sharing with Sérgio the world of *Marginais* are confronted with a state whose role in the class struggle is that of a gatekeeper, making sure the poor remain poor, uneducated and starving. It is a means through which the dominant classes are provided with a multitude of heavily deprived people to exploit. Through the combination of systemic and subjective approaches towards the society of the Aspargos neighbourhood, Sérgio provides a searing critique of the political and economic order. At the same time, he takes us on a very realistic journey through the subjectivity of his fellow 'marginals', vividly narrated in a fierce battle between individual will and socioeconomic determination heavily influenced by the power of the state.

Sérgio grew up on a street that was 'de terra solta e ferros velhos, crateras onde se amontoavam lixos varridos pelo vento e poças de água de esfregadura misturada com urina que as mulheres despejavam na calada da noite' (Rocha 2010: 19) [unpaved, filled with scraps and craters where rubbish swept by the wind piled up and puddles of foul water mixed with urine that women poured out in the dead of night]. His family structure was broken by a patriarchal culture that allowed his father to be unreliable, giving his loving but overwhelmed mother the sole responsibility for the family, earning a living as a washerwoman. Having little to eat at home, Sérgio starts stealing eggs, which was his first crime. Later on, Sérgio recollects the relevance of his formative years to the life of social transgressions he leads, especially when it comes to crime and illegal substance abuse. According to him, in childhood '[t]eimosamente, soubemos sobreviver à desigualdade que havia entre nós e filhos de pais abastados, contudo, na nossa adolescência e juventude não soubemos superar essa mesma desigualdade' (2010: 20) [stubbornly, we managed to survive the inequality between us and the kids of wealthy parents. However, during our adolescence and youth we could not get over the very same inequality].

The novel not only thematises the gap between the rich and poor along with the stigmatisation of poverty in marginalised communities, but it also emphasises the role played by the state in maintaining the status quo. Sérgio's first lesson on how democracy worked in his society came in primary school, when he was voted to represent his class during an event but was denied the position by his Portuguese language teacher, who 'declarou que os votos atribuídos ao Sérgio do Rosário não contavam.

Não faz sentido eleger um indisciplinado, um bandido para representar a turma' (2010: 56) ['declared that the votes attributed to Sérgio do Rosário did not count. It doesn't make sense to elect an undisciplined, thug to represent the class']. Sérgio then quickly learnt that 'a escola é o centro de formação do carácter de um homem, mas é, acima de tudo, o lugar onde aprendemos o ódio, a desigualdade e passamos a compreender que pobreza é uma doença incurável' (2010: 55) ['school is the centre where a man's character is formed, but above all it is the place where we learn hatred, inequality and come to understand that poverty is an incurable disease'] (2010: 55). The school election aimed at teaching the young students to vote, given the country's first steps into multiparty democracy. As such, it taught students the limits representational democracy, ready to be trumped by the will of those already in power as evidenced by the language teacher's overruling of the election result and direct appointment of the blond and blue-eyed daughter of an Europea merchant. In its symbolism, this passage's critique of public institutions such as the state and education is one that will be reiterated throughout the narrative. The fact that the teacher in question is the Portuguese language teacher, given the former colonial language's official status in a multilingual country where it enjoys prestige under diglossia, points to the colonial legacies of post-independence Cape Verde. The teacher's power to overrule the result of the class election, too, signals the way in which the type of inequality based on Eurocentrism and racism prevents institutions from changing direction, even if that is the express wish of the people. The relevance of this episode to Sérgio's future descent into a life of violence and crime that will result in his premature death in the narrative further stresses the power of the themes and imagery for the social critique posed by the book.

The importance of the school's role in the reproduction of the systems of production is therefore discussed at length by Louis Althusser in 'Ideology and Ideological State Apparatus (Notes Towards and Investigation)'. Drawing on the understanding of the state apparatus as a repressive apparatus composed of the police, the courts, prisons, and the government itself, Althusser argues that this apparatus' has a twofold structure: the repressive state apparatus and the ideological state apparatus. While both structures work in tandem, their difference would reside in their primary way of functioning. The repressive state apparatus, located in the public domain, encompasses the organs tasked with the use of physical violence, such as the police and the army, while the ideological state apparatus, located both in the public and the private domain, includes a multiplicity of organs in the ideological domain, such as the church, the family, cultural ventures, the legal system, politics and, most importantly, the school, which, according to Althusser:

> takes children from every class at infant-school age, and then for years, the years in which the child is most 'vulnerable', squeezed between the family State apparatus and the educational State apparatus, it drums into them, whether it uses new or old methods, a certain amount of 'know-how' wrapped in the ruling ideology (French, arithmetic, natural history, the sciences, literature) or simply the ruling ideology in its pure state (ethics, civic instruction, philosophy). Somewhere around the age of sixteen, a huge mass of children are ejected 'into production': these are the workers or small peasants.
>
> …
>
> Each mass ejected *en route* is practically provided with the ideology which suits the role it has to fulfil in class society: the role of the exploited (with a 'highly-developed' 'professional', 'ethical', 'civic', 'national' and a-political consciousness); the role of the agent of exploitation (ability to give the workers orders and speak to them : 'human relations'), of the agent of repression (ability to give orders and enforce obedience 'without discussion', or ability to manipulate the demagogy of a political leader's rhetoric), or of the professional ideologist (ability to treat consciousnesses with the respect, i.e. with the contempt, blackmail, and demagogy they deserve, adapted to the accents of Morality, of Virtue, of 'Transcendence', of the Nation, of France's World Role, etc.). (1971: 155–156)

Althusser's definition of the school's central role in the reproduction of the system of production in capitalist societies certainly applies to the conceptualisation of the educational system in *Marginais*. Despite being conjugated with the more visible effects of the repressive state apparatus, which will be analysed in more detail in Chapter 3, it is interesting to remark that the emphasis given to the often unperceived, yet determinant, part of the ideological state apparatus in the process of exclusion and marginalisation is the part that assures the prevalence of the system of exploitation. Encompassing one-third of the narrative, Sérgios' childhood and early adolescence's educational process within these institutions and on the streets of his neighbourhood will, to a large extent, determine his fate and deeds.

Nonetheless, Sérgio seems to be, at least by the time he writes his memoir, conscious of the educational system's influence in shaping society's hierarchical relations. This is noticeable in the way he recalls his time in school. About his confrontation with the school as a system of privilege, he writes:

> Na escola ou em qualquer lugar tínhamos um tratamento diferenciado em relação aos filhos dos engomados que exerciam cargo de destaque na zona do Aeroporto. No final do ano tínhamos notas mais baixas. Nós nascíamos com a marca da besta, carregando a sina do fracasso na escola. Não faltava alguém para nos lembrar da nossa condição e, bem cedo, comecei a odiar todos aqueles que feriam a minha integridade. A escola, tão apregoado centro de continuidade no processo da socialização, não passa de um centro autoritário, um campo de concentração que exerce a violência selectiva sobre os desfavorecidos e esquece que cada dia nas nossas vidas é um marco de sobrevivência. A escola ensinou-me que sou um indivíduo incapaz e predestinado a ser ruim. Os professores não fazem ideia do que é ir à escola de estômago vazio, de ter que aturar cinco aulas de bombardeamento de inutilidades, enquanto o estômago troveja, de ter que enfrentar uma turma de preconceituosos e bem comportados e de lutar contra o próprio pensamento que insiste em planear um furto para enganar a fome. (2010: 42)

> [At school or anywhere else, we were treated differently from the children of the poncy people who held prominent positions in the airport area. We got lower marks at the end of the year. We were born with the mark of the beast, carrying the fate of failure at school. There was no shortage of people to remind us of our condition and, very early on, I began to hate anyone who harmed my integrity. School, the much-vaunted centre of continuity in the socialisation process, is nothing more than an authoritarian centre, a concentration camp that exerts selective violence on the disadvantaged and forgets that every day of our lives is a milestone of survival. School taught me that I'm incapable and predestined to be bad. Teachers have no idea what it's like to go to school on an empty stomach, to have to endure five lessons of bombardment of uselessness while your stomach thunders, to have to face a class of prejudiced, well-behaved people and to fight against the very thought that insists on planning a theft to stave off hunger.]

In the same way, it is Sérgio's awareness of the structural inequality permeating his society that sparks his refusal to accept the route of exploitation as part of a cheap immigrant workforce that is laid out for him, as did his mother, who migrated to Europe to live up to hers. She wanted Sérgio to conform and to become a lawyer, but she knew way too well how closed that pathway in his class society was for him. Sérgio's non-conformity and his challenging spirit, which kept him from embodying the role of the exploited, did not save him from the entrapment of an underprivileged social fate. If by the age of sixteen he was not 'ejected into production', he was in any case homeless and on his own – 'Com quase dezesseis anos, eu estava entregue a mim mesmo' (2010: 76) ['At almost sixteen, I was left to my own devices']. Marginal to the legal side of the system, Sérgio was ready to be absorbed into its illegal mechanisms, into the underworld of global capitalism in the industry of tourism, where people like him would serve as livestock for human trafficking, defenceless and unwilling suppliers in the trade of human organs and tissues, or, more commonly, as the exploited workforce in drug trafficking or prostitution conveniently disguised as a booming 'industry of entertainment' – a site of entanglement between capitalism and culture.

Culture is portrayed in the novel as a redemptive horizon for Sérgio in his many attempts to escape the social determination of which he is a victim. His talent as a teenage amateur footballer almost had him hired by a Portuguese team, an attempt that failed due to his debilitating physical condition, which was collateral damage to his life in poverty. Similarly, his later endeavour in the world of music, as a singer at bars and restaurants entertaining the tourists of the island, falls through just before he had the chance to make his first record due to an arrest related to his earlier involvement in drug trafficking. As talented as Sérgio and his friends were, culture too is an organisation of social life that they are forbidden to join, as his remarks concerning the literary potential of a friend indicate:

> Lela foi o maior poeta marginal dessas ilhas! É pena que os jornais não publiquem seus poemas. Os jornais estão cheios de parvoíces que os editores, numa hipocrisia deslavada e gananciosa, destacam de uma forma leviana. É ministro-poeta versando mediocridades, é militante-contador-de-histórias que escreve antologias de ignorância e é levado para a televisão para falar de cultura. (2010: 199)

> [Lela was the greatest marginal poet on these islands! It's a shame that the newspapers don't publish his poems. The newspapers are full of rubbish that the editors, in a

blatant and greedy hypocrisy, highlight in a frivolous manner. There are minister-poets spouting mediocrity, militant storytellers who write anthologies of ignorance and are put on television to talk about culture.]

The cultural industry, however, is represented in the novel as just another institution belonging to the ideological state apparatus. It functions as a resource at the service of the ex-revolutionary bourgeoisie, who are in control of state power. It promotes the values of the class that retains the available political and economic means to successfully reproduce, at the cultural level, the system of production based on the invisibility of exploitation. By turning its back on the artistic manifestation of those deprived of power, the cultural industry makes them invisible to the same extent that, by preventing any competing aesthetics from surfacing, it plays its role in maintaining the status quo.

Another institution belonging to the ideological state apparatus that is extensively present throughout the novel is the legal system. Although, as Althusser indicates, the law also belongs to the repressive state apparatus, the legal system in *Marginais* is written as a set of rules and laws that, conjugated with politics, are made not only to exclude the poor but to marginalise every aspect of the lives that they are pushed into living (1971: 143). Law and politics in the novel, united by the character of Sérgio's antagonist, the reputable lawyer, politician and family man Dr Apolinário, are projected as ideological institutions of exclusion and dehumanisation guaranteeing just the right amount of injustice to, on the one hand, keep the rich's wealth and influence and, on the other hand, keep the poor helpless enough to serve as a labour hand to the rich's dirty business – 'Nesta terra, só vai para a cadeia ladão de galinha e filho de pobre' (Rocha 2010: 206) ['In this land, only chicken thieves and poor people's children go to jail'].

As law and politics are not there to promote justice, Sérgio finds his own ways to get even. Resistance is then projected into the character's small acts of civil disobedience, performed either alone or in a group with his gang, the Pitboys, a pun on the word 'pitbull'. Sérgio's vengeful and non-lethal attempts against the various humiliations imposed by Dr Apolinário serve as micro-cathartic opportunities necessary for the protagonist and his friends to have the strength to go on. His sympathies for other marginalised groups, such as prostitutes, gamblers, mad people and thieves, underline a sense of relative solidarity needed to compensate for the social justice that politicians are not willing to promote.

Even though it is right to conclude that *Marginais* denounces the human costs of social determinism in capitalist societies, even by those run by a class of governors who like to call each other 'comrades', the novel is also a narrative of resistance. Aside from the story's emphasis on the systematic nature of economic and social exclusion, promoted not only by the public set of institutions composing the repressive state apparatus but also by the various organisations belonging to civil society that comprise the ideological state apparatus, and despite the protagonist's premature death, his trajectory is still permeated by small initiatives of resistance that call our attention to the difference one can make. His tragic fate does not stop the reach of his narrative, which reverberates already within the diegetic sphere as it moves the engineer who receives his accounts enough to publish them. More than just locating the state within class struggle, Rocha's novel brings up the voice of those marginalised by the system. By doing so, Rocha indicates how marginality, precisely by being outside or just beyond and therefore out of the control exerted by state institutions, is empowered in its real function within the system. In its opposition to state institutions, the margin constitutes a meaningful site of resistance.

From national to political and social conscience – a pursuit for justice

This chapter has shown how contemporary novelistic production in Portuguese-speaking Africa registers a literary shift away from the national and towards the political and social aspects of each respective postcolonial space and time. Evidencing the relevance that local and global historical change has for literary registration, we have seen how contingent historical transitions owing to post-independence developments push the fictional representation of the nation away from the previous romantic paradigm of nation-building. By turning projects of nation-building into the very historical base of their fictional material, each novel

points to a further state in their postcoloniality that is yet to be understood as such by critics in the field.

 Aurélia de Vento actualises this transitional moment through the
parallelism of the characters of Minister Ventura and San Labeca, the
mother of the minister's assistant. Further into São Tomé and Principe's
post-independence period, San Labeca's nationalism is described as fanatic and her manners as authoritarian. In her stubbornness, she is incapable of connecting with a younger generation capable of more nuanced
approaches to problems inherent to the postcolonial condition of the
country. Antagonising the political orientation of the protagonist of the
story but lacking the flexibility underlying Minister Ventura's political
skills, San Labeca's death in the story becomes a necessary development to
match the hopeful tone of a narrative where even the state cannot escape
the rightful power of justice through law.

 Similarly, characters who fail to abandon the Manichean logic of an
'us versus them' characteristic of an initial moment of postcoloniality in
Teoria Geral do Esquecimento and *Campo de Trânsito* are also sacrificed.
In *Teoria,* Monte's death at the end of the novel liquidates the existence of
the only character who fails to liberate himself and to be reborn through
the cathartic moment that closes the narrative. Meanwhile, in *Campo*, the
death of the Director eliminates the one character who misappropriates,
on behalf of the state, the nation-building discursive devices of collectivity
and belonging. Although both novels relate to the history of their countries
in quite diverse ways – Agualusa makes direct allusions to it while Coelho
systematically avoids them – the deaths in both narratives do not seem to
refer to a fall of the state as such, since in both stories the state goes on un-
harmed. We should not forget that, despite the Director's embodiment of
the state in *Campo*, it is actually Mungau's decision to remain a prisoner at
the end of the novel that asserts the permanence of the state, showing the
continuation of that ideological apparatus as the real problem. What the
deaths of San Labeca, Monte and the Director seem to indicate, though, is
a transition away from practices connected to nationalist ideology, namely
the use of the national interest as an excuse to violate any individual rights
that would constitute an obstacle to the ambitions of those holding political and economic power.

Despite the differences in the ways *Tiara* and *Marginais* seem to bring about this shift in consciousness, they still relate to each other as much as to the other three narratives comprised in this study. The diametric oppositions between the situations of Tiara and Sérgio in the societies they belong to set them at opposite ends of the same continuum. Even though Tiara is educated, materially comfortable and healthy – three conditions Sérgio does not share – both narratives are told from the point of view of the underprivileged, as their respective protagonists are portrayed as social outcasts. Tiara is a foreign, woman of mixed ethnic heritage engaged in a traditional, racist and sexist anticolonial nationalist movement. Sérgio is a poor Black, outraged young man inserted into a heavily unequal and unfair post-independence society. Tiara's narrative is concerned with an earlier stage of her society's postcoloniality and is centred on a sensitive analysis of the anticolonial nationalist movement, its struggle and its takeover of power after independence. Sérgio's story, on the other hand, focuses on the aftermath of independence in a similarly postcolonial country, as he was born in 1977, hence his country's independence. He provides us with a complementary picture of the outcomes of the exclusionary practices put in place by the revolutionary elite who appropriated national discourse to monopolise the steering and the resources of the country, such as Dr Apolinário's crusade against the interests of the poor and the state's overall neglect of its poor population, leaving them vulnerable to the exploitation of the tourism industry.

> Sal é hoje, por excelência a ilha do turismo. Todos os dias nasce mais um restaurante ou um hotel … .
>
> Emprego como este não será difícil de encontrar. O safado do patrão queria que eu fosse para a cama com ele … . É isso o que acontece numa boa parte dos restaurantes e casas nocturnas desta ilha, disse Mirna com olhos inchados de porrada e afogados num mar de lágrimas. (Rocha 2010:88;91)
>
> [Sal is today the island of tourism par excellence. Every day another restaurant or hotel is born … .
>
> Jobs like this won't be hard to find. That bastard of a boss wanted me to go to bed with him … .
>
> That's what happens in most of the restaurants and nightclubs on this island, said Mirna with eyes swollen from the beating and drowning in a sea of tears.]

Less positive in tone compared to the other three narratives analysed –
as, by the end of their respective stories, Sérgio dies and Tiara is forced
to abandon a lifelong political and social project – although *Tiara* and
Marginais do not point, at a diegetic level, to a transition away from the
misuse of national discourse, they show an earlier stage of the process in
its unfolding, from establishment to outcomes. *Tiara* describes the details
of the misappropriation of national discourse within the transition of the
anticolonial nationalistic movement into a state party. *Marginais* offers
an account of the legacy of social injustice and human calamity brought
about by revolutionary governments in the aftermath of socialist single-
party state regimes. While in these two novels the shift from national to
political and social consciousness seems not to be shared by many in the
societies they portray, as can be seen in *Aurélia de Vento*, *Campo de Trânsito*
and *Teoria Geral do Esquecimento*, this awareness is the very standpoint
from which the characters of Sérgio and Tiara embark on their respective
narratives, marking the literary shift from national to political and social
consciousness in the African literatures in Portuguese.

Another aspect that links these five novels and which underscores
their turn from national to political and social consciousness is their the-
matisation of justice, law and the relation between the two – something
that John L. Comaroff and Jean Comaroff have called 'the fetishism of the
law' in the postcolony – a place in which '[t]he court has become a utopic
institutional site to which human agency may turn for a medium in which
to achieve its ends' (2006: 33). It is interesting to note how, in three of the
five novels analysed, the court is regarded as the site of justice against the
misdeeds of the state.

In *Aurélia de Vento*, the reader follows the development of the court
case of Santos against the state. We witness justice unfolding as the farmer
wins the dispute. His rightful ownership of the farm is secured, and he is
protected by justice from state abuse. It is this legal apparatus that Sérgio's
mother seeks when she reaches out to the local lawyer for help to denounce
the sexual violence perpetrated by the police – the state repressive apparatus – against her son and his friend. However, although in the Santomean
Aurélia, the best lawyer in town picks the side of the weak by refusing to
represent the state against the farmer, in the Cape Verdean *Marginais*, the

lawyer in question denies Sergio's mother any help and humiliates Sérgio, forcing his mother to file a complaint directly to the courthouse, which is never further investigated. Comparing these two projections of the court-room into fiction, we see that while the attainment of justice in *Aurélia* adds an important note of hope to a narrative whose conclusion signals the establishment of a social order permeated by justice and law, its denial in *Marginais* marks the turning moment in which Sérgio embraces being an outlaw and marginality:

> Infelizmente, o advogado recusou abrir-nos a porta para não sujar a sua alcatifa e disse à mamãe que fosse no dia seguinte apresentar queixa ao juiz. Ao passar debaixo da janela da casa do doutor fui atingido por um escarro quente no pescoço. Olhei para cima e vi seu rosto cínico num riso amarelo e insultuoso a fechar as persianas. Até hoje sinto uma queimadura de repugnância no pescoço por aquele malvado. A cuspidela foi uma ferida aberta na minha honra que só haveria de curar com vingança. A minha revolta contra a prepotência daquele homem desalmado e mal agradecido aumentava de uma forma assustadora. *Aquele momento marcou uma viragem radical na minha vida.* ... Mamãe apresentou queixa no tribunal. Ela, de tempos em tempos, aparecia no tribunal e voltava sempre com a promessa de que tudo se resolveria a favor das vítimas. *Decididamente, isolei-me do mundo e procurei refúgio entre os marginais.* (Rocha 2010: 61–62, emphasis added)

> [Unfortunately, the lawyer refused to open the door for us so as not to dirty his carpet and told Mum to go to the judge the next day. As I passed under the window of the doctor's house, I was hit by hot spit on the neck. I looked up and saw his cynical face in a yellow, insulting smile, closing the shutters. To this day I feel a burn of disgust in my neck for that evil man. The spat was an open wound in my honour that would only heal with revenge. My anger at the arrogance of that soulless, ungrateful man grew to a frightening level. *That moment marked a radical turning point in my life.* ... Mum filed a complaint with the court. She appeared in court from time to time and always returned with the promise that everything would be resolved in favour of the victims. I decided to isolate myself from the world and sought refuge among the outcasts.]

The next novel that mentions a formal resort to the legal system in the pursuit of justice is *Tiara*. Despite its reduced prominence, the courtroom is still regarded as the last resort in the protagonist's quest to obtain justice. Tiara chooses not to go to court against the state to fight the racism of which she is a victim because she is convinced that the complicity between politics and the legal system will prevent any attainment of justice for her. This perception clearly foregrounds the entanglement between the political and the legal, which is latent in both *Aurélia de Vento* and *Marginais*. It is a relation that is further thematised in *Campo de Trânsito* and *Teoria Geral do Esquecimento*.

Returnung to Comaroff and Comaroff, a reading of the courtroom as a resource of hope for the weak in the postcolony has to be understood in terms of the displacement of the political into the legal at a time in which the nation-state is moving away from the idea of homogeneous unity towards a politics of cultural difference undercut by wealth inequality. They argue that in situations such as these, legal instruments offer 'a repertoire of more or less standardized terms and practices that permit the negotiations of values, beliefs, ideals, and interests across otherwise-impermeable lines of cleavage' (2006: 32) within a society. Even though the matter is certainly connected to an ongoing process of change that pushes for the pluralisation of the notion of the nation-state that is traditionally conceived as a single, ethnical and culturally cohesive imagined community, and as the White ex-settler Santos' triumph in court against the state in *Aurélia* shows, one could additionally propose that the rise of the court in postcolonial fictional projections, at least in terms of Portuguese-speaking postcolonial Africa, is rooted at a more fundamental level.

Justice was certainly one of the most moving motifs of the anticolonial nationalist movement that shook Portuguese dominance in Africa. The pursuit of the right to sovereignty and self-determination in the political and economic realm by armed independence movements was also a pursuit of justice through law. As an expert on public law, Martin Loughlin puts it:

> [s]overeignty expresses the principle of external independence, internal authority, and ultimate legal supremacy of the State. A people occupying a defined territory and equipped with institutional self-rule presents itself as a sovereign entity, signifying independence from subjection to any higher authority. (2013: 44)

Sovereignty, thus, is the political and legal condition that allows the postcolonies to exist as equally independent countries in the international arena. Furthermore, it is the acquisition of this right that allows a postcolonial state to govern through law since '[t]here can be no limitations on a [sovereign] State's authority to rule by the means of law' (Loughlin 2013: 44). Law, then, presents itself as one of the tools for the making of the state through which it ratifies its existence towards other states, instituting it as such and, at the same time, constituting the means by which it can legislate and govern its people. This explains why the courtroom would be the place where one could imagine coming to terms with justice in this type of postcolony. If the achievement of justice is directly connected with the application of the law, and the law is what defines the sovereign state, to deny the law's justice-making authority is to deny the very possibility of legitimacy and recognition of the state.

The greatest commonality between the Mozambican novel *Campo de Trânsito* and the Angolan *Teoria Geral do Esquecimento* is certainly the state of exception underlying both their histories and their fiction. *Campo de Trânsito* – set in a camp, the space of exception *par excellence* – brings to attention the gruesome implications of the subordination of law to political power that allows the distortion of justice. The discursive nature of the actualisation of the state is especially visible when we consider that both state sovereignty and state governability are enacted through the manipulation and deployment of the law, that is, discourse. As Agamben claims:

> This is why in the camp the *quaestio iuris* is, if we look carefully, no longer strictly distinguishable from the *quaestio focti*, and in this sense every question concerning the legality or illegality of what happened there simply makes no sense. *The camp is a hybrid of law and fact in which the two terms have become indistinguishable.* (1998: 170)

While the archetypical structure of *Campo* compels us to ponder the implications of the inherent possibilities of slippage of an Idea(l)-state into a totalitarian state of exception, the approach of *Teoria Geral do Esquecimento* to the theme of attaining justice through law is certainly more concrete. As Agualusa's novel is set against the background of almost three decades of civil war – that point of imbalance between public law and political fact, which is the same point of imbalance that institutes the state of exception (Agamben 1998: 1) – justice is impossible in the realm where the law is being held hostage by the sovereign state power. It is for this reason that justice in *Teoria* never finds its way into a courtroom. Rather, it is found in the hallway of an apartment building, where judgement, verdict and sentence are enacted and reconciliation is achieved through dramatic catharsis.

Each of the five novels discussed gives way to social projections in which the pursuit of justice through law is thematised and skilfully elaborated. Whereas *Aurélia de Vento*, *Tiara* and *Marginais* propose a reflection of established and operating postcolonial legal systems, *Campo de Trânsito* and *Teoria Geral do Esquecimento* lead us to ponder the implications of the establishment of such a legal system. Together, these narratives point to the subordination of the law to political power and, with it, question the very possibility of attaining justice. It is a relationship that, as we are reminded by Comaroff and Comaroff, has been defined by Walter Benjamin as intrinsic and generative of violence: 'Lawmaking is power making and, to that extent, an immediate manifestation of violence' (Benjamin 1986: 295). Violence, thus, constitutes the next aspect of these contemporary postcolonial societies that this study will analyse.

The Weapon of Violence

Force is the midwife of every old society which is pregnant with a new one. It is itself an economic power.

— Karl Marx, *Capital Volume 1* (1990: 916)

If we accept the principle that the national liberation struggle is a revolution, and that it is not over at the moment when the flag is hoisted and the national anthem is played, we shall find that there is and there can be no national liberation without the use of liberating violence, on the part of the nationalist forces, in answer to the criminal violence of the agents of imperialism.

— Amílcar Cabral, 'The Weapon of Theory' (1979: 134)

Anyone studying African postcolonial societies knows Fanon's *The Wretched of the Earth's* opening line: 'decolonization is always a violent phenomenon' (2001: 27). More than an ideological positioning, history has shown that the adoption of violence constituted a concrete means for anticolonial nationalistic movements throughout the continent. Nonetheless, even though the independence of the African countries that faced Portuguese colonialism was deeply marked by an armed conflict in which thousands of lives were lost, the most renowned work of one of its greatest articulators and theoreticians, Cabral, is characterised by a concern with the role of local culture that has set the pace for local literary production as much as for postcolonial criticisms of it.

The celebration of Cabral's idea of 'The Weapon of Theory', often reinforces the culturalist aspect of the anticolonial revolutionary movements active in Portuguese-speaking Africa.[1] While it is true that Cabral's

---

[1]   The text was first delivered as a speech on the occasion of the First Conference of Solidarity of the Peoples of Africa, Asia and Latin America in Havana in January of 1966. Its original title is 'Fundamentos e objectivos da libertação nacional em relação com a estrutura social' (Cabral, 1979: 119).

ground-breaking statement that 'national liberation and social revolutions are not exportable commodities. They are (and increasingly so
every day) a local, national product' (1979: 122) condenses the view of
anticolonial revolutionary struggle that underlies his later works, such
as 'National liberation and culture' (1972), but his work is not restricted
to it. It is important to recall that, in the same 'The weapon of theory',
Cabral wrote an important section on the role of violence where he affirms that 'the only effective way of completely and definitively fulfilling
the aspirations of peoples for national liberation is by armed struggle'
(1979: 134).

Yet, accounts such as the one by Young (2001: 283–292), which imply
a connection of the thought of Fanon with violence and of the thought of
Cabral with culture, mask the role of violence in the revolutionary parties
in Portuguese-speaking Africa, along with its lingering use in the aftermath of independence. Therefore, in an attempt to understand how the
development of violence unfolds from anticolonial struggle to the contemporary postcolonial setting, this chapter parts with this view, which is
a recurring and misleading position in the field. While the recognition of
the importance of violence in Fanon's writings reiterates the violent nature
of the French colonial enterprise in Algeria, the downplaying of this aspect
of Cabral's writings runs the risk of abiding by the same lusotopicalist discourse deployed as a cultural logic of dominance in the late days of the
Portuguese colonial enterprise.

Hence the proposal in the book is, following the advice of Robert
Blackey (1974), to understand the work of both intellectuals as complementary not only when it comes to theories of African revolutions but
mainly when it comes to the understanding of the central role that violence
has in them. This epistemological option addresses the relative absence of
studies dedicated to the analysis of the structural role of violence in the
field, which, when conceived, tends to be limited to the acknowledgement
of violence as a topical circumstance or historical fact. Given the understanding of the postcolonial as a relationship in the *longue durée* of history,
the focus here rests on the *weapon of violence*, a tool without which no
theory seems to have been able to account for the postcolonial condition
in Portuguese-speaking Africa.

Due to the relevance of history in the contexts surrounding this corpus of novels, still very much influenced by the power of dominant classes that ascended in the aftermath of colonialism, the chosen starting point for the analysis of the representation of violence in the literatures of contemporary Portuguese-speaking Africa is at the time of the independence struggles. Driven by the violence inherent to colonialism itself, the resort to armed struggle became an unavoidable historical necessity for the anticolonial nationalist enterprise. As Fanon lengthily demonstrates in 'Concerning Violence', anticolonial violence was deeply rooted in the dehumanising Manichean logic of racism that comprised the main colonial weapon of conquest and subjugation, mediating the relation between colonised and coloniser. 'Their first encounter was marked by violence and their exist-ence together – that is to say the material exploitation of the native by the settler – was carried on by dint of a great array of bayonets and cannon', therefore those who decide to stand up for the end of their exploitation '[are]is ready for violence at all times. From birth it is clear for [them] that this narrow [colonial] world, strewn with prohibitions, can only be called in question by absolute violence.' (2001: 29). For that reason, the resort to violence by anticolonial nationalistic movements in Africa after almost five centuries of colonialism is understandable, though not necessarily legit-imate. Like action and reaction, colonising and emancipating endeavours relied on the same violent opposition that cannot simply be assumed to have stopped at the time independence was declared.

Acknowledging the overarching importance of violence as a structuring feature of post-independence societies encompassed by this study is in itself not a new initiative. The calamities caused by the civil wars that plagued Angola (1975–2002) and Mozambique (1977–1992) and the permanent state of civil unrest in the politically unstable Guinea-Bissau are all too vis-ible to allow anyone the optimistic belief that with political independence would, necessarily, come immediate peace. In the tripartite world order that followed World War II, no political system in the so-called Third World could hold without securing its choice of economic doctrine. However, the use of violence in these post-independence societies was not only cir-cumscribed to a local unfolding of the conflicts between capitalist and socialist superpowers at the global level that armed and financed the civil

wars within these two countries. As the historian Coelho reminds us in
relation to the violent post-independence orders in Angola, Guinea-Bissau
and Mozambique – the three ex-colonies in which the actual battles of the
liberation struggles were fought – among the determining circumstances for
these conflicts were the radical substitution of an extremely authoritarian
colonial state by authoritarian independent states (2003:176). Coelho's inquiry, which traced the historical roots of the contemporary use of violence
in Portuguese-speaking postcolonial Africa to the legacy of militarisation
present in these three societies during the period of anticolonial struggle,
shows that the clue to understanding contemporary African societies may
very well be in the observation of the postcolonial lingering of, rather than
the ruptures with, colonial mentalities and practices. Here, we might find
a way to renew our understanding of violence in the postcolony.

Authoritarianism: The legacy of people's war

The chain of violence from colonial to anticolonial did not cease to influence the fate of Portuguese-speaking African countries after their independence. As was largely debated in the 1980s, the success of those
newborn nation-states in creating societies that largely diverged from
the colonial forms of exploitation from which they had just emerged
derived from these countries' nationalist armed struggles' performances
as the *people's war*. Understood as 'the form of a guerilla war in which
the indigenous nationalist movement has sought to mobilise the lar-
gest possible section of the predominantly rural population to challenge
and eventually eliminate foreign political and military control' (Chabal
1983: 110), people's war was the actual means through which nationalist
movements confronted Portuguese colonialism in Africa. Contemplating
the five Portuguese-speaking countries that fought on the three distinct
fronts throughout the continent through their respective local nationalist
movements, the people's war was seen by scholars of its time such as Basil
Davidson (1974) and John Saul (1979) as a gateway to a social, political
and economic revolution unachieved by any African country until then.

Many believed that the experience of people's war was not only essential for defeating colonialism, but that it also played an important role in the construction of the new socialist societies that these revolutionary movements sought to establish after independence. As Chabal says, it was thought that '[p]eople's war would succeed, where constitutional decolonization had failed, in bringing revolution to Africa and thus in laying the foundations for a non neo-colonial path to development: a transition to socialism' (1983: 105).

Although not as constructively as predicted by those sympathetic to the idea of successful socialism in Africa, the relationship between people's war and socialist experimentation can be verified across the five Portuguese-speaking countries. Dividing them into two groups, separating the aforementioned three continental countries in which people's war actually took place from the two in which such mobilisation did not happen – the archipelago states of Cape Verde and São Tomé e Príncipe – shows the different ways in which the advent of war marked the role of violence in each society.

Much in line with the plans drawn by Cabral in 'Resistência Armada' (2008), it was thought that the mobilisation involved in a people's war of independence would prepare these countries for the installation of socialism because it would disrupt colonial practices and institutions, allowing the newly independent states to start anew. This type of war requires, at its core, an ideologically grounded vanguard party to achieve political mobilisation in urban and rural areas so as to secure the continuous supply of human and material resources. As a result of that, new national ideologies would be formed through the alliance of the revolutionary elites and the rural masses. New material conditions would also be developed, though mostly in the liberated zones. War would push for the development of more advanced and effective local agricultural production, breaking the (ultra-) colonial Portuguese cycle of production based on large-scale agricultural export production through forced labour, considered by some to be the most backward in colonial Africa (Anderson 1962: 97–100).

Reality, though, was less optimistic than the expectations of those who viewed the combination of national liberation and socialist revolution favourably. Already in 1983, Chabal noted that despite the success of the people's war in securing independence, the 'nationalists were not in any position to mobilise the population on the basis of economic and social grievances which have been paramount in most twentieth-century revolutions' (121). The lack of revolutionary preconditions, he argues, impeded the alliance between the revolutionary bourgeoisie and the peasantry from going beyond a joint opposition to the ex-coloniser, towards a new society directed at modernisation of modes of production and industrialisation. The ex-colonies' state of extreme economic and social underdevelopment, in which they were kept by Portugal, meant that agricultural production had never reached self-sufficient levels. Besides that, the various forced labour methods in place failed to engage the peasantry in large-scale productive processes. As soon as the authoritarian figure of the coloniser disappeared, the peasantry felt free to return to more traditional modes of production, which were clearly at odds with the modernisation process envisaged by the revolutionary project. The economic situation was also aggravated by the destruction caused by the liberation war and by the mass departure of the already scarcely qualified labour workforce – composed mainly of Portuguese. In this conjuncture, the large-scale production necessary to the planning of the economy, at the heart of Marxist-Leninist-oriented socialism as a mode of production, was virtually unattainable.

Regardless of these setbacks preventing the people's war from fulfilling its role in paving the way for a complete revolution, socialism was still the socio-economic system adopted by each of the five Portuguese-speaking countries in the first fifteen years after the end of the liberation struggle. As important as it was, the lack of infrastructure by itself did not account for the unfeasibility of the construction of prosperous socialist societies in these countries. The failure to promote political mobilisation through ideology can be seen as one of the main reasons why peasants did not seem willing to embrace the changes necessary for revolutionary practice. As Chabal observes, '[i]n most instances, anti-colonial sentiments in the village amounted to a desire for a return to "traditional" socio-political institutions rather than for integration into a modern socialist party organization' (1983: 119).

The experience of the people's war nonetheless fundamentally influenced the way in which the nationalistic movements, converted after independence into revolutionary state parties, organised the new socialist states. The causal relation between political ideology *and* violence, which was key for the mobilisation against colonial troops during the liberation war, was transformed into political ideology *through* violence. Once 'ideological orientation determined the main political, social and economic policies adopted [...] by the Lusophone African regimes' (Chabal 2002: 65–66), ideology needed to be enforced.

Ideological orthodoxy, thus, shaped much of the structural violence in the social fabric of socialist Angola and Mozambique. While these societies did unite – albeit to diverse extents – to expel the coloniser, the consolidation of the socialist revolution was still endangered by each country's civil war – largely financed by international interests due to the potential impact of the eventual success of African socialism during the Cold War and Apartheid in neighbouring South Africa. The continued state of war in each of these countries greatly favoured the enforcement of authoritarianism through the widespread use of violence by the single-party state. In Angola, the failed attempt at a coup by the MPLA dissidents under the alleged command of Nito Alves in 1977 led to the hardening of the regime through its use of constant political persecution. Due to the state of emergency inherent in times of war, the MPLA's Stalinist-style administration made room for corruption, economic deterioration and massive impoverishment of the population (Chabal 2002:117). While projects in the agricultural realm were impracticable due to the impact of years of war, both prior and subsequent to independence, the exploitation of the country's many mineral resources, such as oil and diamonds, through state-run companies was not enough to sustain the population, the war and the pockets of corrupt government officials. 'Socialism in Angola, for all the idealism which genuinely moved a large proportion of the party militants at independence, turned out in the end to have been the eminently practical instrument for an intense neo-patrimonial and economically unproductive authoritarianism' (Chabal 2002: 66).

Authoritarianism during Frelimo's rule was less iron-fisted than in Angola. Since the country's mineral wealth was not a the core economic industry at the time, agriculture through communal farms constituted one of the main economic attempts of the single-party state to both integrate and economically develop the country. Different from developments in Angola, the hardening of the Mozambican regime happened as the forced villagisation of the country came with the need to transform traditionally minded peasants into the 'New Man/New Woman', a process that gave way to the creation of re-education camps (Cabaço 2007: 410–417). While the mood that prevailed in Angola was one of political witch-hunting, the Mozambican regime directed its repressive force against traditional forms of social organisation, labelling them as obscurantism and enforcing ideological modernisation. Notwithstanding the appearance of a traditional religious-based 'witch/wizard hunt', Frelimo's eagerness to dismantle customary or traditional organisations was very political, as parts of the system of traditional authority had been co-opted by the Portuguese colonial administration as a way to control territories it could not penetrate.

Meanwhile, Guinea-Bissau did not really face a long-lasting civil war after independence, but the political fragmentation to which it fell victim – as foreshadowed by the assassination of Cabral in 1973 by members of his own party – assured the continuation of violence throughout its socialist years and beyond. The state-authoritarianism instituted by paranoid presidents was grounded in *de facto* political fragmentation, verifiable by the persistence of ethnic-oriented precolonial and colonial forms of local organisation in rural areas. The regimes' attempt to maintain their positions through factionalisation and personalification of political power' (Forrest 2002: 262) only increased the levels of political instability that crippled the country. Although promising, Guinea-Bissau's experience with people's war and political organisation – PAIGC managed to hold elections to establish independent regional councils even before independence – did not lead to a transformed post-independence society. Collecting a history of coups, political instability, civil war (1998–1999), and economic underdevelopment, what the country's post-independence history has inherited from the nationalist cause seems to be limited to the struggle.

Violence after revolutionary ideology

The situation of Cape Verde and São Tomé and Príncipe was, as one can expect, quite different from the aforementioned three continental African countries. Given that these two countries did not undergo the experience of people's war, ideological orthodoxy was not enforced. Nevertheless, for reasons that also relate to each country's political constitution, violence is still part of everyday life in these societies. If, as Thaler (2013) argues, strictly ideology-based violence tends to be more targeted and restrained – as shown by the cases of Frelimo and MPLA – in societies where ideology is not one of the main drivers of conflict, we find widespread, diffused and pervasive practices of violence, as can be seen in São Tomé and Príncipe and Cape Verde.

Much in line with Marx and Engels' conceptualisation of ideology (1970: 42) as a form of consciousness which, to be revolutionary, should be in tune with the material conditions of the societies within which it arises – or else it constitutes a false consciousness – Cabral's statement that 'ideological deficiency, not to say the total lack of ideology, on the part of the national liberation movements – which is basically explained by the ignorance of historical reality that these movements aspire to transform – constitutes one of the greatest weaknesses, if not the greatest weakness, of our struggle against imperialism' (1979: 122) anticipated some of the main problems of São Tomé and Príncipe and Cape Verde post-independence. The lack of ideological cohesion of a party like the Santomean MLSTP not only inscribed divisiveness as its main characteristic but also consolidated the country's political culture as one of protection of the private rather than of the public through the installation of clientelism, patronage and the institutionalisation of personal loyalties. Formed abroad by educated members of the elite in the diaspora who were barely known by the country's population from its foundation in the 1960s until after the Portuguese Carnation Revolution in 1974 (Seibert 1995; Nascimento 2010), the MLSTP bourgeois leadership lacked the revolutionary consciousness it could have acquired from a more direct involvement with the peasantry that never really happened.[2] This situation gave rise to a deeply atomised

---

2   The political agitation the country witnessed before independence was paved by the work of the components of the Pro-MLSTP Civic Association (*Cívica*), composed mainly by students from Lisbon who went back to São Tomé and Príncipe to spread ideas such as pan-Africanism, Black power, Marxism and Maoism (Seibert 1995: 242). This association, known for the radicalism of some of its components, was later dissolved for having opposed certain decisions of the MLSTP.

society in which access to resources – usually public ones – is directly proportional to the calibre of personal connections. A generalised disbelief in the public commitment of those in government gave rise to a type of utilitarian violence that targeted individuals that 'passou a ser um crivo da afirmação de poder pessoal e grupal' (Nascimento 2007: 55) ['has become a sieve for the assertion of personal and group power'].

Likewise, the 'particularistic political culture' (Pina 2010: 8) of Cape Verde is an important aspect of the country's complex social formation. It sets off a similar process of social atomisation that can greatly contribute to the spread of violence. While the undisturbed functioning of the country's bipartisan political system, with power alternation, causes international observers to see Cape Verde as a 'success story' (African Development Bank and African Development Fund 2012), more detailed inquiry provides less optimistic pictures of the country's internal situation. Understanding the establishment of a healthy democratic milieu in much more detail than is perceived by big international financial institutions, therefore going beyond the dichotomy of the presence versus absence of recognisably authoritarian political institutions, Leão Jesus de Pina (2010) offers a deeper analysis of the contemporary political climate in the country.

Departing from the acknowledgement of the importance of the principle of *morabeza* in Cape Verdean society, Pina sets out to verify the extent to which this trait is verifiable in the current political culture of the country. Constituting one of the pillars of the country's national identity, the word *morabeza* denotes a way of life that is inherently cordial, affable, sociable, receptive and, therefore, good for life in society, as its drive for peaceful living would make Cape Verdeans more prone to democratic interests and less inclined to conflict and violence. Nevertheless, the study concludes that the general climate of distrust caused by the country's atomised political culture points towards a general tendency of estrangement between citizens and the public arena, entailing a preference for the private sphere and withdrawal from a more active and solidary political role that goes against the *morabeza* principle.

The privileging of the private over the public, which is part of the archipelago's way of life, is deeply associated with the country's postindependence and post-revolutionary embrace of social democracy instead of socialism (Chabal 2002: 71). It can be argued that the country's economy, based on remittances from émigrés and foreign aid due to its harsh climatic conditions and lack of natural resources and infrastructure, has pushed it more quickly into a culture of capital and individualism without the material experience and collective consciousness raised by the performance of organised industrial labour. Such a culture of labour, which is pretty much at odds with the revolutionary ideals at the time of the struggle for independence but in tune with the liberal ideals of the developed world – mainly the United States and Western Europe, whence the majority of the remittances and international financial aid came – has led to an increase in youth violence in the country.

This leads researchers like Roque and Cardoso to question the apparent success story of countries like Cape Verde by showing how the rampant levels of youth involvement in crime – both as victims and perpetrators – are intrinsically connected with a 'projecto ou modelo de paz liberal … através da insistência na despolitização e burocratização da política … e no esvaziamento das funções sociais do Estado' (2010: 5) ['project or model of liberal peace … through the insistence on the depoliticisation and bureaucratisation of politics … and the emptying of the state's social functions']. The authors show that the level of youth marginalisation is directly linked with the structural and symbolic violence to which young people are exposed. While the government works to protect the elite's interests and investments, it abandons the marginalised youth that

> convivem com todos os níveis de violência o que torna fácil a sua utilização, principalmente quando se encontram em situações adversas e o uso da violência surge como reacção. Ela aparece na família – violência doméstica, irresponsabilidade paternal e precariedade habitacional –, na rua contra grupos rivais e, ultimamente, contra a polícia … . Não é estranho afirmar que a violência entra no processo de socialização. (Lima 2010: 12)

> [They live with all levels of violence, which makes it easy to use, especially when they find themselves in adverse situations and the use of violence comes as a reaction. It appears in the family – domestic violence, irresponsible parenting and precarious housing – in the street against rival groups and, lately, against the police … . It's not strange to say that violence is part of the socialisation process.]

It is on these grounds that violence has come to constitute one of the most important drives of the historical processes in Portuguese-speaking Africa.

Employed as a tool for subjugation and as a weapon of freedom – serving to reinforce socialism and to sediment liberalism, or to generate and usurp power and wealth – violence has been the means to a vast array of ends, and it is certainly an important part of these societies' processes of socialisation.

However, as it is important not to forget, the logic of 'violence begets violence' is not exclusively a Cape Verdean, African or even postcolonial endowment. If the treatment of violence here is circumscribed by its representation in the literatures of Portuguese-speaking Africa, it is because this is the purview of our case studies, and it should not, in any hypothesis, imply that it is their exclusive malaise. What this chapter aims to show is how violence constitutes a particularly structural feature in the Portuguese-speaking African postcolony and thus deserves more nuanced analysis. As our incursion into history shows and as fiction registers, violence is ingrained in the everyday life of these post-independence societies, being experienced and performed in a vast array of ways that, likewise, happen due to a variety of causes.

In what follows, three major ways in which violence is portrayed in each of the five novels analysed will be discussed: state violence, gender violence and memory violence. The comparative analysis employed highlights major commonalities and differences between how violence organises the subject's relationship with the state, its organisation in terms of gender and the way it permeates memory sediments. While the subsequent three analytical subsections will look at the significance of violence to each of the three aforementioned particular realms of life in society, the fourth and last section of this chapter will summarise and contrast the analytical findings to provide elements from which to draw a larger picture of the pervasiveness of violence in the fiction of contemporary literature in Portuguese-speaking Africa.

State violence

The strong tie connecting state and violence has become a given to the extent that the monopoly on violence itself constitutes one of the main components that defines the concept of state. In the field of sociology, Max Weber's definition of the state as a 'human community that success-fully claims the monopoly of the legitimate use of physical force within a given territory' (2009: 78) has set the pace for later conceptualisations of the term. Despite disagreeing with Weber's prominent positioning of violence in his definition of the state, Anthony Giddens still recognises its importance in defining the state. As he puts it, '[a] state can be defined as a political organization whose rule is territorially ordered and which is able to mobilize the means of violence to sustain that rule' (1985: 20). Even Gianfranco Poggi, whose monographic volume on the state sees it as a 'phenomenon principally and emphatically located within the sphere of political power', cannot avoid mentioning the state's intricate relation with violence, addressing it early in his opening chapter as 'the role of co-ercion' (1990: 4).

In a paradigmatic example of this intimate relationship, *Campo de Trânsito*'s mapping of an image of the state onto the material site of the internment camp suggests that these two spheres of society are inherently interlinked. It is a narrative consubstantiation between state and coercion that echoes a classic Marxist view of the state *conceived as* repressive appar-atus (Althusser 1971: 137). Seen this way, *Campo*'s close look at the camp's microphysics of violence constitutes a language through which one can read the state. By choosing the camp as the setting for his narrative, Coelho evokes a state that is, necessarily, a state of exception and, therefore, a site of violence *par excellence*. As Giorgio Agamben puts it

> [t]*he camp is the space that is opened when the state of exception begins to become the rule.* In the camp, the state of exception, which was essentially a temporary suspension of the rule of law on the basis of a factual state of danger, is now given a permanent spatial arrangement, which as such nevertheless remains outside the normal order. (1998: 168–169, emphasis in the original).

In the enclosed space of the camp, the lives of its unfortunate inhabit-ants can be stripped of any political status and reduced to *bare life*. The camp, therefore, is juridical and materially designed as the 'most absolute biopolitical space ever to have been realized, in which power confronts nothing but pure life, without any mediation' (Agamben 1998: 171). It is the anatomy of this place and its functioning that constitute the core of *Campo de Trânsito*, a repressive machine designed to discipline and punish.

Campo de Trânsito's detailed fictionalisation of the *modus operandi* of the camp bears similarities with Michel Foucault's elaborations in the field, whose work, according to Agamben, is characterised by 'its decisive abandonment of the traditional approach to the problem of power, which is based on juridico-institutional models (the definition of sovereignty, the theory of the State), in favor of a unprejudiced analysis of the concrete ways in which power penetrates subjects' very bodies and forms of life' (1998: 5). In so doing, one notices that Coelho's novel does not focus on the state of exception that gives way to the existence of the camp, which is portrayed as a given. What the novel underlines is that power institutions, such as the state, have to *simultaneously* subjugate body and mind. By so doing, the narrative strips away some of the hidden structures behind organic-looking, yet deeply coercive, initiatives for social management available to and at the disposal of any state. The following passage, portraying Mungau's moment of arrest, is an example of the narrative's emphasis on the concrete nature of the state's coercive power rather than on its juridico-institutional aspect:

'J. Mungau?'

'Sim, sou eu', responde.

'Estás detido!'

[...]

'Por ordem de quem?'

'Vá, vai vestir-te se não queres acompanhar-nos nesse estado', diz o que falou, que parece ser quem ali manda. Fá-lo numa voz monocórdica, tão sem sobressaltos quanto a avenida lá fora.

É maciço, um tudo-nada gordo até, pescoço taurino, cabeça rapada. Bexigoso. Mas o que verdadeiramente impressiona nele são os olhos. Não têm cor, quase brancos, incluindo as pupilas. Nunca viu umas pupilas assim. Duvida até que ele possa ver alguma coisa com aquilo. Levanta os braços para argumentar mas aquelas pupilas brancas travam-lhe o gesto a meio. Baixa-os, suspira resignado e vira-lhe as costas, voltando ao quarto. (Borges Coelho 2007: 10–11)

['J. Mungau?

'Yes, it's me,' he replies.'

'You're under arrest!'

[...]

'On whose orders?'

'Go on, get dressed if you don't want to accompany us in this state,' says the one who spoke, who seems to be in charge. He does it in a monotone voice, as smooth as the avenue outside.

He's massive, even fat, with a taurine neck and a shaved head. He's pockmarked. But what's really striking about him are his eyes. They're colourless, almost white, including the pupils. You've never seen pupils like that. You even doubt that he can see anything with them. He raises his arms to argue, but those white pupils stop him halfway. He lowers them, sighs resignedly and turns away, heading back to his room.]

The lack of elaboration of the juridical grounds on which Mungau's arrest is made is in itself a trace of the state of exception, which is skilfully translated into narrative tension. In the first direct address, the apparatus establishes its hierarchical position by addressing Mungau as 'tu', the second-person singular subjective pronoun (implicit in the conjugation of the verb 'to be', *'estás'*). However, it is worth noting that in European and Mozambican Portuguese, this can have a disrespectful connotation when used among strangers, as it involves either a familiar or friendly setting, which is not the case in this passage, or an address marked by an accepted hierarchy where the speaker is known to occupy a position that is higher than the interlocutor's. This is a typical way in which adults speak to children, for example, marking the implied superiority of the adult. Equally, the ease with which the representative of the police dismisses Mungau's enquiry implies a situation of entitlement that is clearly founded – although not expressed – on the reduction of Mungau's own political rights. Power is represented not in terms of legal entitlement but by the concrete physical characteristics of its representative. Its weight is materialised in the massive bull-like body of Mungau's interlocutor. Disfigured by pockmarks – in Portuguese, *Bexigoso* – and possessing colourless eyes, the embodiment of this apparatus is characterised by its bulkiness, its sickness and the appearance if his lack of sight. All this is enough to keep Mungau from trying to defend himself.

In the same way that power is inscribed on the body and in the language of the representative of the repressive apparatus, powerlessness is expressed in the bodies and minds of those it suppresses. In this sense, the analysis of Coelho's fine architecture of coercive power can identify a number of structures noted by Foucault in his study of the mechanisms underlying Western penal systems: *discipline and punish*. In the section of his study dedicated to the scrutiny of the disciplinary tools integrated in the penal systems, Foucault highlights that, in order to discipline, the system of power that is in charge has to produce 'Docile Bodies' (1995: 135–169) to be distributed and controlled. The distribution of bodies in enclosed spaces, he argues, is necessary to further divide people and destroy any sense of community that is contrary to the will of those in power. Added to this process of atomisation is the control of the activities of the subject through time-tabling, the imposition of activities aimed at the integration of the body with its designated objects of work, and exhaustion, through which the completely alienated, barely living subject can be put together with other equally tamed subjects and articulated as a collective mass of workers.

The next structure analysed by Foucault is 'The Means of Correct Training' (1995: 170–194), where he details how hierarchical observation – that is, surveillance, allied to normalising judgement, as the process of inculcating an idea of normality that makes it easy to detect and to neutralise through shame any display of individual difference – and examination work together to train and dispose of the docile body. These structures detected by Foucault's historical research are the pillars onto which the three-camp complex of *Campo de Trânsito* is built. As its name suggests, the Transit Camp is the first stop for those admitted into the camp complex – 'Este é um campo de Trânsito, o que significa que cedo ou tarde quem cá está acabará por ser transferido' (Coelho 2007: 83) ['This is a transit camp, which means that sooner or later those who are here will end up being transferred']. Enclosed by incarceration, divided by separation into individually numbered sleeping cubicles, after which they come to be identified, and time-tabled by rigorously set meal times, in the Transit

Camp, inmates are coercively trained by undergoing the processes of enclosure, division and time-tabling mentioned by Foucault.

As we see later in the novel, the enforcement of activities more directly connected to productive labour takes place both in the Old and New camps, where docile bodies are actively exploited – a process that will be detailed in Chapter 4. Still, despite the split of the mechanisms of body coercion among the complex of camps, the Foucauldian training devices, or the more intellectual part of the reprograming projects of disciplinary institutions, are present in different ways across the whole of the prison complex. The narrative also shows how the Foucauldian principles of hierarchical observation, normalising judgement and their combination in examination (1995: 170) are essential for the success of the disciplinary power. Hierarchical tasks are duly performed by the administrative structure in place. At the top of the pyramid, the Director is the representative of the state, commanding the police and the army, embodied by Bexigoso and his soldiers, as well as being superior to other figures of authority such as the Teacher of the Transit Camp and the Village Chief, who is in charge both of the Old and the New camps, respectively. In addition to this visible set of observers, the Director also has a set of informants, such as The Tea Seller, who intoxicates inmates with hallucinogenic tea to extract information, and Mungau himself, whose precious ability to read and write makes him valuable to the established informal surveillance system. Mungau's co-optation into the organisation of the camp is a rich example of what Foucault called the normalising judgement technique. Achieved through the installation of a gratification-punishment structure designed to inculcate the camp's standards of appropriate behaviour in the inmates, normalisation prepares for examination, the very role given to Mungau as he is asked to produce a secret written report of the state of affairs in the Old and New camps for the Director's evaluation of the administrative performance of the Village Chief.

Campo de Trânsito's approach to state violence, thus, denounces it as structural and concrete, physical and psychological, as well as concrete and ideological. In this sense, the final scene of the narrative is emblematic. After the death of the Director and the threat of the Transit Camp's invasion by mutineering prisoners from both the Old and New camps,

Mungau's voluntary continuation as a prisoner not only points towards a continuation of the state but also points to the continuation of the state, *specifically through* the survival of its coercive apparatus.

> 'Prepara-te', diz [Bexigoso], com a voz entaramelada. 'Está tudo pronto, vamos partir.'
>
> 'Vamos partir pra onde?', pergunta Mungau.
>
> 'Não te esqueças do teu estatuto de prisioneiro. Não te cabe fazer perguntas!', diz severamente o Bexigoso, antes de soltar uma gargalhada. (Borges Coelho 2007: 208).
>
> ['Get ready,' says [Bexigoso], hesitantly. 'Everything's ready, we're leaving.'
>
> 'Where are we going?' asks Mungau.
>
> 'Don't forget your status as a prisoner. It's not your place to ask questions!' says Bexigoso sternly, before letting out a laugh.]

Emulating the opening scene of the novel, its final moments, which are also centred on a power-marked dialogue between Bexigoso and Mungau, reassert the effectiveness of the prisoner's reprograming. Achieved through the submission of his now docile body and the training of his mind, the successful disciplining of Mungau is such that he does not attempt to escape his captor even when nobody is watching him. Moreover, due to his transformation, this time he is the one helping Bexigoso on their hurried departure before the confrontation of the prisoners in revolt with the army forces sent to neutralise them – ' "Vá, ajuda-me a transportar este saco de evidências para o camião!" ' (2007: 208) [' "Come on, help me carry this bag of evidence to the lorry!" ']. Mungau does this despite the possibility of the evidence being used to incriminate him for the death of the Director. Notwithstanding this instance of conditioning, the next and final act of the protagonist in the novel consists of a gesture that echoes the director's distribution of small favours, so characteristic of the normalisation process of which Mungau himself had been a victim. Just as the Director, who used to give out spoons to those from whom he wanted small favours – spoons purposefully not provided to the inmates who only had access to a plate to eat their meals in the camp –, Mungau 'atira furtivamente as colheres que tem no bolso para os desacordados prisioneiros, como se as semeasse. Para se ver livre delas e para que eles possam enfrentar as papas do futuro – se as houver – de colher na mão' (2007: 209) ['he furtively throws the spoons he has in his pocket at the unconscious prisoners, as if he were sowing them. To get rid of them and so that they can face the porridge of the future – if there is any – spoon in hand']. At the end of the novel, the apex of the protagonist's journey of learning, which could give way to a grim interpretation of a straight-up cyclical repetition as Mungau chooses to maintain his status as prisoner, gives way to a slight opening for transformation as he indiscriminately distributes – or gets rid of – the scarce resources represented by the spoons, to unconscious prisoners as if with it giving them an actual tool with which to change their future.

While Mungau's furtive distribution of the spoons to his unconscious fellow inmates can be read as an allegory of the relatively minor nature of the process of postcolonial change in the *longue dureé*, his ultimate embodiment of the inmate indentity, attesting to the success of his coercion, illustrates the intimate relation between coercive state apparatus and state ideology. In it, the role of the apparatus is to inculcate the ideology of the state into the subject's mind through manipulation of their body and the framing of their will. In this sense, it can be argued that the narrative's detailed picture of Mungau's trajectory in *Campo de Trânsito* brings forward precisely this constitutive relation between the physical and the political through which power can be assured by its representation in the form of ideology. Defined in Althusserian terms as 'an imaginary relation to real relations' (1971: 167), ideology is seen as an abstraction of the power dynamics in place – based on the primacy of exploitation of a large number of men by a small number of men – that is made into the code of conduct of a certain society through the use of violence as a device. Therefore, according to Althusser, ideology has both an imaginary aspect that determines how ideologies are described in the form of codes, rules and doctrines and a material form that is deeply enmeshed through its conscious performance by subjects. Where a subject 'is concerned, the existence of the ideas of his belief is material in that *his ideas are his material actions inserted into material practices governed by material rituals which are themselves defined by the material ideological apparatus from which derive the ideas of that subject*' (1971: 169; emphasis in the original). Thus, ideology can only exist in the dialectics between form and content – or concretel and abstract – that, in the case of the state, are set in motion by the force of violence, which is represented in *Campo de Trânsito* in an extreme form by the functioning of its coercive apparatus in the circumscribed and utterly meaningful space of the camp.

Campo de Trânsito's approach to violence follows a narrative structure that goes from the performance of violence to the idea or ideology of the state. It establishes a relationship of complementarity with *Teoria Geral do Esquecimento*, whose historical background suggests the opposite direction as it seems to depart from state ideology to the pervasiveness and performance of violence. Locked within the small space of the camp, the angle privileged by *Campo* explores the inner functioning of structured violent ideological disciplining that highlights its systemic nature as suggested by the inevitability of its continuation, regardless of any sporadic uprisings it might encounter or small-scale changes implemented. *Teoria*, in its turn, offers a wider and greatly fragmented picture in terms of diegetic space, time and point of view of a trajectory of violence. This trajectory comes from conscious state-oriented ideological practices rooted on a performance of violence that bears its own seeds for change, as we have seen through the analysis of the novel's representation of the state. Following the moves of Angolan history, in Agualusa's novel, the relationship between violence and state ideology is the departure point.

> Benjamim afundou o rosto nos joelhos, sem conseguir controlar o choro. Jeremias empurrou-o com o ombro, incomodado:
>
> Acalma-te. És um soldado português.
>
> Monte interveio:
>
> Deixe o miúdo tranquilo. Não o deviam ter trazido. Quanto ao senhor, não passa de um prostituto a soldo do imperialismo americano. Devia ter vergonha.
>
> E os cubanos, esses não são mercenários?
>
> Os companheiros cubanos não vieram até Angola por dinheiro. Vieram por convicções.
>
> Eu fiquei em Angola por convicções. Combato pela civilização ocidental, contra o imperialismo soviético. Combato pela sobrevivência de Portugal.
>
> Tretas. Eu não acredito nisso. Você não acredita nisso, a sua mãe não acredita nisso.
>
> ...

Monte desamarrou os dois mercenários. Endireitou-se:

Capitão Jeremias Carrasco. Suponho que Carrasco seja alcunha. O senhor é culpado de atrocidades sem fim. Torturou e assassinou dezenas de nacionalistas angolanos. Alguns camaradas nossos gostariam de o ver num tribunal. Eu acho que não devemos perder tempo com julgamentos. O povo já o condenou.

...

Monte regressou ao carro. Os soldados empurraram os portugueses até ao muro. Afastaram-se alguns metros. Um deles tirou uma pistola da cintura e, num gesto quase distraído, quase de enfado, apontou-a, e disparou três vezes. Jeremias Carrasco ficou estendido de costas. Viu aves a voarem no céu alto. Reparou numa inscrição, a tinta vermelha, no muro manchado de sangue, picado de balas:

O luto continua. (Agualusa 2012: 32–34, emphasis in the original).

[Benjamin dropped his head between his knees, unable to hold back the tears. Jeremias was annoyed, and nudged him with his shoulder:

'Take it easy. You're a Portuguese soldier.'

Monte butted in:

'Leave the kid alone. You shouldn't have brought him to our country. As for you, sir, you are no more than a whore in the pay of American imperialism. You ought to be ashamed.'

'And what about the Cubans? Aren't they mercenaries, too?'

'Our Cuban companions didn't come to Angola for the money. They came because of their convictions.'

'And I stayed in Angola because of my convictions. I'm fighting for Western civilisation, against Soviet imperialism. I'm fighting for Portugal's survival.'

'Bullshit. I don't believe that. You don't believe that, even your mother wouldn't believe that.

...

He straightened up.

'Captain Jeremias Carrasco… Carrasco, as in "executioner"? Well, I'm assuming that's got to be a nickname… You are guilty of countless atrocities. You tortured and murdered dozens of Angolan nationalists. Some of our comrades would like to see you in a courtroom. But I don't think we ought to be wasting our time with trials. The people have found you guilty already.'

...

Monte walked over to the car. The soldiers pushed the Portuguese men up against the wall. They took a few steps back. One of them pulled a pistol from his belt, and in a movement that was almost absent-minded, almost annoyed, he pointed it and fired three times. Jeremias Carrasco was lying on his back. He saw the birds flying high in the sky. He noticed an inscription in red ink on the bloodstained, bullet-pocked wall:

The struggle continues.] (Agualusa 2015: 25–27, emphasis in the original)

This section vividly illustrates the ideological colours of state violence in *Teoria Geral do Esquecimento*. Although it is not the only kind of violence experienced in the novel, ideologically laden state violence – not colonial violence – is represented as the core from which a culture of violence spreads through all the layers of Angolan society. The scene portrays the encounter between the Angolan Monte and his nationalist soldiers and the Portuguese Jeremias Carrasco and his fellow demobilised colleague, Benjamin, who decided to stay in the country despite Portugal's withdrawal of its troops. The encounter happens by chance, and regardless of the official end of hostilities between both parties, the direct confrontation between these enemies is unavoidable. At the dawn of an independent Angola, Monte is the closest to a repressive state apparatus there is – a role that will become clearer as a pathway to the character later in the novel. As such, his very first description highlights Monte's confidence and a position of power that is reinforced by the attention drawn to the benevolent politeness shown to his would-be victims. Regardless of their differences, Monte and Jeremias establish a relationship of mutual recognition of their status or positions, as evidenced by their use of the second-person personal pronouns *você* and *senhor* to address each other, signalling respect. The same does not happen with their address to Benjamin, treated as *tu*, given his youth and implied lower military rank. As the scene proceeds, the mirror effect between Monte and Jeremias becomes clearer, as they both fight for diametrically, hence interconnected, opposing causes. The almost distracted and bored way in which Jeremias and Benjamin's execution is performed indicates the banality of violence that is in place in the country's evident state of exception that empowers Monte as captor, jury, judge and executor of the law in the name of the people. A state whose dark *devenir* is predicted by the inscription on the bullet-perforated and blood-stained execution wall in which one reads the punning rendering of the famous catchphrase *A luta continua!* [The struggle continues!], as *O luto continua* [Grief continues].

The Angola of *Teoria Geral do Esquecimento* is one in which the state of grief (*luto*) that is concomitant with the struggle for independence passes on to the independent society, as death continues to be the main currency for power in an unstable country that has been long shaken by a lasting civil war (*luta*). In such a conjuncture, even when the country has never declared a state of war, siege or emergency that conditions the eventual suspension of citizen rights as secured by all three versions of the country's constitution to date, the novel portrays a de facto state of exception that seems deeply connected with the political tensions that are put forward by the civil war. Yet, the novel does not concentrate on the violence directly generated by the conflict between the state and its antagonists (MPLA vs. UNITA). It dwells on a yet more intimate level of the conflict: the fractionalisation within the state-party itself, which leads to the liminal position of ideological paranoia materialised by a situation in which 'os angolanos se matassem uns aos outros como cães raivosos' (2012: 71). [Angolans […] kill one another like rabid dogs.] (2015: 70).

As a consequence, the state violence that wrapped the country in the years of fear that followed independence is portrayed as 'slippages of reason' (2015: 61), since the narrative purposefully blurs the difference between colonial and independent-state coercion. The mirroring of Monte and Jeremias that frames how both characters are introduced in the plot is reiterated later on, when we get to know that what attracted Monte's wife to him were precisely the features he had in common with her father, a fanatic Portuguese (born in Angola) who was an eager supporter of the colonial enterprise and fiercely opposed revolutionary nationalism. The novel also indicates that the relationship between Monte and Horácio is similarly based on an interesting level of mutual respect. If Monte has silently prevented his father-in-law's being arrested many times, his father-in-law was the one crying the loudest during Monte's funeral (2012: 215). Moreover, the description of Horácio's routine after the death of Monte further reinforces the connection between old-time ideological enemies, as he spends his afternoons in a bar discussing politics and ideology with old men like himself (2012: 216).

The necessary connection this novel makes between state violence and a certain generation of subjects shows state violence to be mainly ideologically oriented and, hence, historically situated and progressive. It substantially differs from the circularity and inescapability that are found in *Campo de Trânsito*. *Teoria Geral do Esquecimento*'s focus on ideology as a pivotal element for the development of state violence is, at the same time, critical and hopeful. It is critical to the extent that it approaches ideology – both colonial and Marxist-Leninist – as a false consciousness, interpellating subjects to consciously accept and practice it, thus making it concretely real (Althusser 1971: 182). Nevertheless, Agualusa's approach is hopeful insofar as it projects Monte as a State agent capable of exercising subjectivity in its twofold sense of submissive being and autonomous entity.

The connection between ideology and violence and subjective will is visible in the way the novel repetitively underlines Monte's adhesion to a Marxist view of society that demands his support of the revolutionary state and that he acts violently. The passage in which Jeremias is executed shows Monte's unshakable commitment to the revolutionary cause. The next mention of him clarifies how torture-induced interrogations carried out by the agent were deemed 'excesses' necessary to preserve the socialist revolution (Agualusa 2012: 65). Later on in the novel, we discover that Monte's reason for leaving his job as a 'public servant' is the realisation of, as he clandestinely buries an innocent man assassinated by the regime as the result of a foolish mistake, how the state had betrayed the ideals it vouched for three decades earlier: 'Tantos anos decorridos, e ali estava, a cantarolar o *Funeral de um Lavrador*, enquanto sepultava, em terra incógnita, um escritor sem sorte' (2012: 156, emphasis in the original) [So many years had gone by, and there he was, humming 'The Labourer's Funeral' while he buried, in an unmarked grave, a writer who hadn't had luck on his side.] (2015: 160).[3]

---

3   *Funeral de um Lavrador* is a song by the Brazilian writer, songwriter and singer Chico Buarque de Hollanda. The song is part of the artist's album that turned the poem *Morte e Vida Severina* by the Brazilian poet João Cabral de Melo Neto (partially translated by Elizabeth Bishop into English as "The Death and Life of a Severino") into music. This song brings to mind a part of the poem in which the

Monte's performative awakening regarding the state's abandonment of the socialist ethos leads him to leave its coercive apparatus. The state has become a '"machine" of repression, which enables the ruling classes […] to ensure their domination over the working class, thus enabling the former to subject the latter to the process of surplus-value extortion (i.e. to capitalist exploitation)' (Althusser 1971: 137).

Campo de Trânsito and *Teoria Geral do Esquecimento* craft fictional worlds that reaffirm the centrality of violence to state ideology both systemically and historically. Despite not being foregrounded to the same extent as it is in the Angolan and Mozambican novels analysed, violence is also seen as constitutive of the state in *Tiara*, *Aurélia de Vento* and *Marginais*. Similar to *Teoria*, *Tiara* is a novel in which we see revolutionary violence employed as a means of internal oppression to secure political power for an ex-revolutionary bourgeoisie who are eager to establish socialism without democracy. In such a context, the novel gives more prominence to the pervasive violence in the cultures of independent societies that have successfully engaged in the struggle for independence. Its feminine perspective portrays the various forms of gender oppression in place, whereas cultural clash comes to the fore as the negotiation of postcolonial difference becomes key to the construction of independent societies.

Tiara's writing of violence registers a moment of transition from ideologically oriented organised war to a postcoloniality of political abuse by the state in the name of ideology. As the narrative advances, the violence represented gradually moves from the physical type to give way to cultural, abstract and diffused modes of violence that are shown to be essential for

---

migrant peasant, on his journey from the arid backlands to the city, witnesses the burial of another peasant worker. In Agualusa's novel, Monte sings the following verses: 'Esta cova em que estás/ com palmos medida/ é a conta menor que tiraste em vida/ é de bom tamanho/ nem largo nem fundo/ é a parte que te cabe deste latifúndio. ... É uma cova grande/ para teu corpo defunto/ mas estarás mais ancho/ que estavas no mundo.' (Agualusa 2012:156) [This grave where you lie/ measured out by hands/ is the smallest expense you ever claimed from the land / the grave is a good size/ not to deep a foundation/ it's the part that falls to you in this whole plantation. ...The grave is very large/ for your corpse off its bier/ but you'll be a bigger man/ than you ever were here.] (Agualusa 2015: 159).

the assurance of political power in times of peace. Consequently, violence is no longer portrayed as a weapon used exclusively by the belligerent sides of a declared armed conflict. In this sense, *Tiara* portrays the state laying down its firearms only to start violating the country's citizens with the weapon of bureaucracy that victimises the protagonist of the novel. The single-party state of *Tiara* starts its sovereign history by making political use of the administrative apparatus 'by emphasising ideological as against managerial criteria of action' (Poggi 1990: 163), thus costing Tiara the possibility of a professional career in the novel. This transition from physical to political and administrative violence by the state is shown in its more finished form in the fictional São Tomé and Príncipe of *Aurélia de Vento*.

Set at a subsequent postcolonial moment in relation to what we find in *Tiara*, *Aurélia de Vento* depicts a state in the aftermath of a struggle for independence fought in the political rather than in the armed arena. As noted in the analysis of the novel's representation of the state, the fervour of nationalist militancy in the story is limited to the memory of the late San Labeca. As a consequence, state violence in this novel happens through political misuse of power as Minister Ventura tries to appropriate land legally – and rightfully – owned by the protagonist's father. While also giving way to the portrayal of other forms of violence, such as misogyny, *Aurélia* still focuses on the fictionalisation of a state whose apparatus seems to be passing through a further historical transition. The novel's portrayal of the relationship of the state with the law clearly indicates the transformation of a single-party state into a liberal-democratic one in which the governmental attempt to manipulate the law is interrupted by a judiciary system committed to legality and justice. Poggi states that 'when contrasted with liberal-democratic systems, laws in Soviet-type party-states allow much greater discretion to state agents, or more freely refer to non-legal considerations' (1990: 161). Seen through this lens, the state in *Aurélia de Vento* is one that is transitioning away from an ideology-laden single-party system into the liberal-democratic mode that has thrived in market economies around the world. The impact of this transition is best exemplified by its fictional rendition in Rocha's *Marginais* from Cape Verde.

Interestingly enough, *Marginais*' stake on state violence establishes a historical continuum with the *Tiara* and *Aurélia de Vento*. The protagonist,

Sérgio Pitboy, is born after independence and lives his troubled adolescence in the 1990s, a time during which Cape Verde's postcoloniality has already abandoned the single-party state socialist experiment and plunged into a market economy under the flag of a multiparty democracy strongly reliant on the exploitative tourism industry. In tune with the liberal turn, the state Sérgio describes in his memoir is an absent one. As he puts it:

> A pior violência é não se importar com os outros, com aqueles que vivem em condições sub-humanas. A indiferença dói mais que um murro no estômago e neste sentido as autoridades da ilha emergem como os mais violentos. A minha vida tem sido um circo romano, abandonado na arena de atrocidades, de roubos, de tráficos, da violência num salve-se quem puder. (Rocha 2010: 159)

> [The worst violence is not caring about others, about those who live in subhuman conditions. Indifference hurts more than a punch in the stomach and in this sense the island's authorities emerge as the most violent. My life has been a Roman circus, abandoned in the arena of atrocities, robberies, trafficking, violence and anyone who can save themselves.]

Negligence is the most systemic and effective way through which the state, via the authorities of the island, violates its citizens. In addition to rape, beatings and other coercive activities by the police, neglect seems to be the most effective and widely deployed way through which the state violates the island's inhabitants. Basic rights such as housing, healthcare, clean drinking water and sanitation are denied to those condemned to live on the margins of society. The state of indigence in which Sérgio and his neighbours are found reflects a lack of civil rights that turns them into easy prey for private investors in the legal and illegal sectors of the economy who are eager to maximise their profits through the exploitation of these people's semi-slave labour. Along with economic violence, the marginalisation of the poor portrayed in *Marginais* gives way, as discussed in the next sections of this chapter, to many other forms of violence that derive from state indifference.

When compared, these five novels furnish the reader with a prismatic, yet complementary, view of state violence in late postcolonial Portuguese-speaking Africa. *Campo de Trânsito*'s allegorical narrative details the functioning of an integral relationship between state coercive apparatus and state ideology that is relevant to each of the five countries at some point in their post-independence history. *Teoria Geral do*

Esquecimento, in its turn, builds on history to show a state rendering of ideology into violence in the postcolonial *durée*. Agualusa's view of the relationship between state ideology and civilian coercion supplements Coelho's as it sets the narrative against a background of historical effects of that relationship on civil society across nearly three decades, instead of in the universalisable microcosms of the camp chosen by the Mozambican author. In contrast with the systemic views of the relations between state and violence offered by these two novels, the Guinean, Santomean and Cape Verdean narratives illustrate more specific cases. Despite registering an important change in terms of emphasis, capturing a historical shift from the state as a focal point of societal violence to the gradual spread of violence throughout civil society, the three narratives still emphasise the importance of postcolonial state violence. As each novel concentrates on a specific and successive period in the shared history of the five countries, they record the gradual abandonment and the combination of state infliction of violence on the civilian body – as we see in the camps of *Campo* and in the tortures of *Teoria*. Their picture of state violence, therefore, includes the development of other non-physical forms of equally harmful civil coercion, such as political coercion, abuse of law and the denial of elemental infrastructure and protection. In the remaining sections of this chapter, attention will be given to the literary representation of other prominent modes of violence that, combined with state violence, haunt the contemporary fiction of Portuguese-speaking Africa.

(En)Gender(ing) violence

Gender violence is a worldwide phenomenon of major relevance in the societies of Portuguese-speaking Africa. Seen largely through the scope of violence against women and girls 'because it derives in part from women's subordinate status in society' (Rose 2014: 4), contemporary views of gender violence are not circumscribed to violence against those sexed female at birth. Shelah S. Bloom defines gender violence as:

the general term used to capture violence that occurs as a result of the normative role expectations associated with each gender, along with the unequal power relationships between the two [or more] genders, within the context of a specific society. VAW/G [violence against women and girls] constitutes a part of GBV [gender-based violence]. Men and boys can also be victims of GBV. For example, homosexuality in many communities is considered an aberration from the expectations of how men should behave. Men who have sex with men in these communities experience everything from discrimination in the health and legal sectors to physical attacks in the community because they are deviating from expectations around masculinity. Men may also experience GBV from their intimate partners, other family members as children, and peers. (2008: 14)

The fundamental aspect of gender, sexuality and gender violence for the comprehension of the challenge faced by contemporary postcolonies has been gaining visibility as studies become more critical of the unfulfilled promises of freedom and equality in post-independence face the acknowledgement of the intrinsic connection between colonialism (and its legacy) and the regulation of gender and sexuality (Lugones 2007). Decades after the success of the wave of revolutionary nationalisms that freed the African continent from direct European colonialism, critics who are now very aware of the many ways in which colonialism was gendered turn to postcolonial governments and revised nationalist projects, asking the same questions once posed to colonial states concerning gender.

Despite the many advances brought about by revolutionary nationalisms in the field of gender equality across the continent, the fact that gender and sexuality cannot be detached from nation or state, now fully acknowledged for at least the last three decades (Connell 1987; Mosse 1995; McClintock 1995; Yuval-Davis 1997), raises important questions about gender in postcolonial states. According to Raewyn Connell, a scholar widely known for her work on 'hegemonic masculinities', the state's management of gender derives from its legitimising power over essential gendered aspects of civil life such as marriage, parental rights, pre- and post-natal policies and natality control, among many others. 'It can hardly be denied that the state is deeply implicated in the social relations of gender', she states (Connell 1987: 126). Nira Yuval-Davis, whose work on gender and nation is canonic, reminds us of the inherently gendered character of the nation given its constitutive dependence on activities such as 'national reproduction, national culture and national citizenship as well as national conflicts and wars' (1997: 3), which are all gendered. However, while the material weight of everyday life makes the gendered nature of the nation-state unquestionable, the gendered nature of nationalism, especially of revolutionary nationalism, has only recently been challenged in the realm of postcolonial studies.

Anne McClintock closes the main body of her *Imperial Leather* with a chapter on nationalism, gender and race, where she states that '[a]ll nationalisms are gendered, all are invented and all are dangerous – dangerous not in Eric Hobsbawm's sense of having to be opposed, but in the sense that they represent relations to political power and to the technologies of violence' (1995: 352). Being a determinant tool for armed revolutionary nationalisms, violence, as we have seen, permeated the anticolonial and postcolonial structures that followed the colonial enterprise in our contexts. With that in mind, it is impossible not to think that the gendering of nationalism was articulated without resorting to the gender violence that was inscribed in the postcolonial societies it helped to create. As McClintock proceeds with her argument concerning the obliviousness to gender of mainstream theories on nationalism (Gellner 2006 [1983]; Anderson 1991 [1983]), and finding a sketch of gender agency only amidst the ambivalences of Fanon (she looks into his views of gender in 'Algeria Unveiled' [1965]), we understand that an appreciation of the links between gender and nationalism is more likely to happen in the context of the former colonies than in the context of the former metropoles. While theoreticians of European nationalism managed to ignore the differences of gender, those theorising – geographically or epistemologically – from the colonies cannot afford to do so.

In this particular field of analysis, one can be sure that scholars concerned with the literatures of Portuguese-speaking Africa have been quite busy with matters of gender and sexuality that extrapolate on the representation of women alone. Many of the essays concerning gender in these literatures that can be found spread throughout the various edited volumes of literary critique, especially over the last twenty years. In terms of single-authored volumes, some highlights are Phillip Rothwell's *A Postmodern Nationalist: Truth, Orality, and Gender in the Work of Mia*

Couto (2004), Hillary Owen's *Mother Africa, Father Marx: Women's Writing of Mozambique 1948–2002* (2007), Ana Margarida Dias Martins's *Magic Stones and Flying Snakes: Gender and the Postcolonial Exotic in the Work of Paulina Chiziane and Lídia Jorge* (2012), Eleanor K. Jones' *Battleground Bodies. Gender and Sexuality in Mozambican Literature* (2017) and Maria Tavares' *No Country for Nonconforming Women: Feminine Conceptions of Lusophone Africa* (2018). When it comes to edited volumes, some relevant works are Susan Canty Quinlan and Fernando Arenas' *Lusosex: Gender and Sexuality in the Portuguese-Speaking World* (2002), Hilary Owen and Phillip Rothwell's *Sexual/Textual Empires: Gender and Marginality in Lusophone African Literature* (2004), Inocência Mata e Laura Padilha's *Mulher em África: Vozes de uma margem sempre presente* (2007), Hilary Owen and Anna M. Klobucka's *Gender, Empire, and Postcolony: Luso-Afro-Brazilian Intersections* (2014) and Paulo Pepe and Ana Raquel Fernandes' *Beyond Binaries. Sex, Sexualities and Gender in the Lusophone World* (2019).

These numbers speak not only of the scholarly robustness of the work dedicated to this particular area in the field but also of the unevenness in the production and circulation of the book as a research output, where publications edited in the Global North, mainly in English, are made more accessible. This number of interventions will be multiplied many times over if expanded to include the growing number of doctoral theses and master dissertations in course or approved in the various universities across the globe, especially in the countries of the Portuguese-speaking world located in the Global South.

Although different in their particular enquiries, studies in the field seem to univocally state the inescapable relevance of the comprehension of any given gender struggle in the field in the *long durée* of pre-colonial, colonial and postcolonial gender and sexual oppression. By examining the continuations of gender violence throughout different times of a society's history, a gender-oriented critique of African literatures in Portuguese interrupts the process of a critical reification of nationalism that proliferates in the field, predominantly among studies that focus on the close relationship between literature and national identity. In its call for differentiation after the achievement and assurance of sovereignty with national independence, the gender-oriented critic continues the vital calling for social change that is preconised by the revolutionary ethos that oriented the very anticolonial struggle.

In this spirit, scholarship tends to highlight the bizarre connections between gender roles and sexual morality that were preached by the revolutionary nationalist movements and the colonial moralism imposed by the Portuguese *Estado Novo* (1933–1974) regime under the autocracy of António Oliveira Salazar. As Hilary Owen (2007) explains in detail, the ways in which gender was conceived by the Portuguese *Estado Novo* deeply impacted how gender roles were conceived in the colonies. Drawing from Ana Paula Ferreira's study of femininity propaganda during Salazar's rule (1996), Owen observes that the regime's stress on family ideology limited women to the domestic sphere, which was converted into the site of patriarchy. Equally, the model of hegemonic masculinity set by the regime stressed the White man's civilising mission, which is embroiled in paternalism. These models, later coupled by Salazar's political use of Lusotropicalist theory as developed by the Brazilian sociologist Gilberto Freyre in his canonic *Casa Grande & Senzala* (2003 [1933]), were fundamental in a post-World War II scenario in which Portugal was under pressure by the United Nations to let its African colonies go.

The Lusotropical argument was based on the premise of '[u]ma singular predisposição do português para a colonização híbrida e escravocrata dos trópicos' ['[a] singular predisposition of the Portuguese to the hybrid and slave colonisation of the tropics'] due to its 'passado cultural étnico, ou antes, cultural de povo indefinido entre a Europa e a África' ['ethnic cultural past, or rather the cultural past of an undefined people between Europe and Africa'] (Freyre 2003: 66). The bi-continental character of the Portuguese, thus, would make him – always a heterosexual cis man – 'naturally' adaptable to the heat of the tropics and, conveniently, both sexually voracious – due to his half-Africanness – allowing him to mingle through the (ab)use of the colonised black female body – and civilization-prone given the 'righteousness' conferred on him by his Europeanness. These characteristics, highlighted to support the argument of the innate Portuguese talent to be a 'mild' coloniser, separating him from the forms of British and French colonisation that were deemed violent and segregationist, were the prerequisites to defend a colonial enterprise that, based on racial mixture as it was, could not be labelled as racist and exploitative. Freyre's outrageously softened description of the widespread practice of sexual abuse by Portuguese men in the colonies, despite its sympathetic tone, did not hide the fact that colonisation did not only pass through the violation of the female Black body; it depended on it:

> [O português f]oi misturando-se gostosamente com mulheres de cor logo no primeiro contato e multiplicando-se em filhos mestiços que uns milhares apenas de machos atrevidos conseguiram firmar-se na posse de terras vastíssimas e competir com povos grandes e numerosos na extensão de domínio colonial e na eficácia da ação colonizadora. A miscibilidade, mais do que a mobilidade, foi o processo pelo qual os portugueses compensaram-se da deficiência em massa ou volume humano para a colonização em larga escala e sobre áreas extensíssimas. (2003: 70–71)

> [From their first contact with women of color, they [Portuguese] mingled with them and procreated mestizo sons; and the result is that a few thousand daring males succeeding in establishing themselves firmly in possession of a vast territory and were able to complete with great and numerous peoples in the extension of their colonial domain and in the efficiency of their colonial activity. Miscibility rather than mobility was the process by which the Portuguese made up for the deficiency in human mass in or volume in the large-scale colonization of extensive areas.] (1986: 11)

Hence, as Owen rightly points out, informed by the work of Boaventura de Sousa Santos and Miguel Vale de Almeida, hybridisation in the context of the Portuguese colonial enterprise was rather a tool for oppression than a weapon of liberation, contrary to established views of hybridisation such as the one developed by Bhabha (1994). In such a conjecture, '[p]hysical hybridity thus has more to do with the affirmation of the Portuguese empire than its deconstruction' (Owen 2007: 31). In the specific context of Mozambique, whose project of national identity was deeply grounded in an idea of *moçambicanidade* (Mozambicanness), '[i] nsofar as Marxist-Leninist national unification fell heir to a Portuguese colonial version of national homogeneity, the image of an all-inclusive "racial melting pot" could continue to gloss racist and sexist exclusions in practice' (2007: 28).

Despite its local colours, the problem Owen describes in Mozambique also affected the progression towards gender equality throughout the rest of Portuguese-speaking Africa, whose impact in their national literatures from independence to the beginning of this century has been deeply explored in the studies by Jones (2017) and Tavares (2018). Not only were all five countries subjected to the same colonial principles regarding gender policy, but they were also united in their pursuit of a transformed socialist and postcolonial future under the banner of an adapted Marxism-Leninism. Notwithstanding the visible desire, at least to a certain extent, to address issues of gender equality within the nationalist movement that can be found in the surviving writings of Cabral, Samora Machel and Agostinho Neto, the actual result may have liberated men and women from colonialism but not from the chains of patriarchy.

Surviving the nation's independence either due to the maintenance of certain traditional practices or due to the drive for modernisation, patriarchy found its way into the new societies that the nationalist movements struggled to shape. It was among the reasons that led progressive parties such as Frelimo, for example, to dismantle matrilinear social networks and practices in certain northern parts of Mozambique, 'effectively promoting more patriarchal social structures in the name of progress' (Owen 2007: 35). Regarding Angola, Margarida Paredes' analysis of the journals left by the female combatant and martyr of the anticolonial war, Deolinda Rodrigues, leads her to state that '[e]m nome da unidade Neto esbatia as diferenças regionais, étnicas, raciais, de género, geração e classe. Em nome da unidade impunha o chapéu da ideologia socialista, a hegemonia não religiosa e uma nova moral revolucionária' (2011: 4) [in the name of unity Neto minimised differences in the order of regional, ethnic, race, gender, generation and class. In the name of unity he imposed the socialist ideology, a non-religious hegemony and a new revolutionary morals]. Similarly, Aliou Ly's study of the role of women in the armed struggle in Guinea-Bissau shows that 'when Amílcar Cabral and the PAIGC fought for independence, what independence meant to them was freedom from the colonisers and social justice for Guinea-Bissau's citizens. But the outcome of independence is a society that remains divided and unjust along gender and ethnic lines' (2014: 25–26). As these three sites were the ones in which the existence of people's war could constitute the laboratory of social change, their relative failure in bringing about significant emancipation in the realm of gender corroborates Owen's assertion that the Marxist-Leninist classic productive view of liberation was not enough to bring about a complete revolution. She remarks that the project 'notoriously lacked a theory of gender struggle, with which to critique the patriarchal practices of men within the liberation movement itself' (2007: 33).

The pervasiveness of colonial gender norms in the revolutionary movements and in postcoloniality was, however, not limited to the oppression of women. bell hooks defines patriarchy as a 'political-social system that insists that males are inherently dominating, superior to everything and everyone deemed weak, especially females, and endowed with the right to dominate and rule over the weak and to maintain that dominance through various forms of psychological terrorism and violence' (2004: 29). This domination, though, is enforced in those sexed males at birth as much as in those sexed females, and forms of masculinity are held hostage to hegemonic forms widespread in their respective cultures.

When it comes to Portuguese-speaking Africa, Mário Lugarinho, in line with Owen's argument, points out the continuities permeating the construction of masculinities in the colonial and postcolonial times of Portuguese-speaking Africa. He draws attention to the binary opposition linking the nationalist definition of Homen Novo [New Man] – which, although emerging at different moments, was essential to the nationalism of PAIGC, Frelimo and MPLA – to the Salazarist one.[4] According to Lugarinho, while the Portuguese New Man was intimately connected with 'um modelo de masculinidade que emergia [nos momentos de ruptura com o Antigo Regime], identificado pelos valores que garantiriam a estabilidade da sociedade burguesa: a nação, a família e a propriedade' (2012: 99) [a masculinity model that emerged [at the moment of rupture with the Ancient Regime], identified by the values that assured the values of bourgeois society: the nation, family and property], the model of New Man privileged by these specific forms of African nationalism, despite relating to a Soviet

4   Lugarinho's account of the variation between the three forms of New Man posed by PAIGC, Frelimo and MPLA emphasises their differences in terms of times and conditions of emergence rather than any substantial dissimilarity in content. He states that, while Cabral's views on the matter are part of his theoretical formulation

conceptualisation of the term, worked similarly to what it sought to counter. As he concludes: '[o]s regimes de força, tanto à direita, identificados ou não com a burguesia nacional, quanto à esquerda, na efetivação de seus objetivos regeneradores e reformadores, também se ocuparam de colocar à margem os indivíduos que não se adequassem ao pretendido modelo [de gênero] hegemônico' (2012: 101) [[t]he regimes of force, either to the right, related not to the national bourgeoisie, or to the left, in the actualization of their regenerative and reformative objectives, have also marginalized the individuals that did not match the intended hegemonic model [of gender]. A nationalist model that, still according to Lugarinho, replaced the colonial ethos of a virile white heterosexual male, a modern civiliser inheriting from the Portuguese 'sea heroes' of their so-called Age of Discoveries, zealous of family and property, with a virile Black heterosexual man, a modern proletarian inheriting from the local 'national martyrs' of their independence struggle, zealous of the common good and of the socialist revolution.

Emphasised femininity

Speaking from a perspective informed by an analysis of Mozambican literary writing of gender and sexuality, specifically from the paradigmatic relevance of the work by José Craveirinha for the literature of his country, Jones explains that 'the objectification of black femininity and reinforcement of the hierarchical gender binary' is the dangerous 'flipside' of the 'consolidation of black masculinity' (2017: 177) in contexts such as the ones described by Lugarinho. Having had their bodies programmatically used as vessels in which both the colonial empire and the independent country were gestated, women have been symbolically represented according to the ideology of the day. As Owen rightfully demonstrates when analysing the case of Mozambique, despite being an essential rhetorical

---

on the struggle prior to its success, essential to the revolutionary movement and for the implementation of the state – that he did not live to see independence – the New Man of the MPLA was developed in historical documents after the success of the nationalist struggle, and the version of Frelimo was moulded during and by the struggle. (2012: 109).

trope to the colonial Lusotropicalist project, women were impeded from featuring in it. As time went on, the few Mozambican women writers who managed to publish had to work 'simultaneously within, and against the allegorical manicheisms of African nationalism and socialist revolutionary struggle that reduce[d] women's perspectives to a single, fetishistic uniformity' (2007: 214). Drawing from the work of Maria Nazareth Fonseca (2007) and Laura Padilha (2002), Tavares explains that when it comes to the rise of the literatures of Angola, Mozambique, São Tomé and Príncipe and Cape Verde that found their first expressions rather in poetry than in prose, 'indeed, very few female poets were allowed into the literary canons'. The most significant of these women were 'those who were actively involved in the anti-colonial struggle through their participation in the bulletin *Mensagem*, published between 1948 and 1964 by the CEI (Casa dos Estudantes do Império) in Lisbon' (2018: 6). Nowadays, though, being marketed as 'Postcolonial Exotic' (Huggan 2001; Martins 2012), 'women must also resist being simply recast as the symbolic (and redemptive) national "interior" that Mozambican male writers set out to rediscover' (Owen 2007: 221).

In such a conjuncture, one is both surprised and suspicious upon encountering a corpus in which the majority of protagonists are female, as is the case in this study. Of the five novels analysed, three have women as their protagonists, although only one is authored by a woman. While, at first glance, this slight predominance might suggest an increase of female protagonists in the contemporary literatures of Portuguese-speaking Africa, which could indicate an interesting movement towards a wider variety of gender representation, a rigorous approach towards these narratives might alert to the modesty of this supposed progress.

Tiara, Aurélia and Ludo are the three women featured, respectively, in the Guinean *Tiara,* the Santomean *Aurélia de Vento* and the Angolan *Teoria Geral do Esquecimento. Tiara*'s narrative portrays the trajectory of an exceptionally beautiful, righteous and fearless young woman of mixed ethnic heritage into maturity amidst challenges such as racial persecution, exile, love, marriage, involvement with an African nationalist movement in the struggle for independence, pregnancy, miscarriage, rejection by traditional sectors of society, betrayal by the nationalist movement, betrayal by her husband, divorce, withdrawal, and finally exile with the possibility of finding love again. *Aurélia de Vento* gives us a protagonist who, like Tiara, is also an exceptionally beautiful, righteous and fearless young woman of mixed ethnic heritage. Given that the five years in which Bragança's novel extends itself is a significantly shorter span than that of Embaló's novel's two decades, we have only a realist portrait of Aurélia, rather than a *Bildungsroman*. Nevertheless, she is also wronged by those who envy her and is despised by a female character who embodies the African traditional and non-modern world. The novel also features a miscarriage as its ending, although not Aurelia's but her stepmothers'. It diverges from the Guinean novel given that Aurélia rises from her adversities stronger than the protagonist in *Tiara*. Ludo, in her turn, is not easily described. The almost three-decade span of this postmodern novel's diegesis shows a fragile White Portuguese middle-aged woman suffering from a psychiatric condition, whose symptoms are close to agoraphobia, who is still strong enough to kill a man, bury him, build a wall separating her apartment from the rest of the building and live an isolated and barely self-sufficient life in blindness and malnutrition for twenty-eight years. As an attentive reading of these three novels shows, despite the similarities between their protagonists, an interesting variation of intensity in two key aspects can be found between them: centrality and agency.

Comparing the three narratives, it is noticeable that, despite having women as their protagonists, or the central referential core around which the discursive universe of the narrative is constructed (Woloch 2003: 18), these three women are not necessarily central to the development of their stories. Another evident feature is the interesting correlation between the centrality of the female protagonist and the author's biography, as the centrality of each protagonist within its respective narrative seems to be higher to the degree that its protagonist shares more biographical parallels with the author of its narrative. In this way, Tiara's centrality to her narrative is indisputable. One can chart important parallels between Tiara and Embaló, an African woman who experienced migration between African countries herself. Aurélia, on the other hand, seems to be less central to her own eponymous narrative since the novel disproportionately focuses on her father, Santos. Correspondingly, the resemblance between Aurélia and Bragança is more distant than the one between Tiara and Embaló, as Aurélia and Bragança share culture and nationality but are different in terms of gender and generation, while notably, these two characteristics are shared between Bragança and Santos. On the other side of the spectrum – in comparison to the correspondence between protagonist and author as found in Tiara – Ludo, whose centrality to a multifaceted and fragmented narrative such as *Teoria Geral do Esquecimento* reflects its postmodern contours, is, at the same time, the least central of the three protagonists as well as the one who is most distant from her narrative author's biography. Ludo does not share with Agualusa either gender, nationality, ethnicity or generation and her centrality is rather reduced to the privileged point of view from which the story is told.

If compared in terms of agency, we notice a slight difference in the ranking between the three protagonists. While Tiara keeps the undisputed top position, we find a clear exchange of places between Aurélia and Ludo. Interestingly, Ludo is portrayed as a much more active protagonist despite her three decades of loneliness and isolation than Aurélia, who is portrayed as a fully functioning member of society. This difference gets even more prominent when we consider the aesthetic choices of both novels. *Teoria*'s use of a decentralised narrative structure relieves Ludo of the necessity of agency, as agency itself is often an issue that postmodern aesthetics seeks to deconstruct rather than reiterate. As a result of that, the novel provides us with a protagonist who is not necessarily the referential core around which the story develops but rather an estranged point of view from which the reader – also estranged from the diegesis – can access the story. Offering, at times, an eyewitness account that complements the omniscient narrator's, Ludo is more of a strategic point of reference from which to observe Angolan history in development than a character who is an active subject within the society portrayed. In contrast, *Aurélia*'s realist aesthetics should give way to a more active protagonist, since, as posited by Antonio Candido 'a personagem pareça o que há de mais *vivo* no romance' (Candido 2005: 54; emphasis in the original) [the character seems to be that which is the most *lively* in the novel]. The difference in terms of agency between Aurélia and Ludo, therefore, points to a lack of coherence in the way in which the Santomean protagonist is represented in the context of the aesthetics of her novel, which, when associated with the analysis of the centrality of these three narratives, shows an interesting pattern in terms of representation of the women as protagonists in the early twenty-first-century African novel in Portuguese.

The coupling of centrality and agency in these three narratives draws attention to the telling relevance of the character space as an index for the analysis of gender relations in narrative fiction. If we follow Alex Woloch, who in his *The One vs. the Many: Minor Characters and the Space of the Protagonist in the Novel* (2003), sees the character space as 'the *intersection* of an implied human personality – that is, as Dostoevsky says, "infinitely" complex – with the definitely circumscribed form as a narrative', which is directly proportional to the level of centrality of a given character, since 'our sense of human figure (*as* implied person) is inseparable from the space that he or she implies within the narrative totality' (13, emphasis in the original), we see that the more space a character occupies – either explicitly or implicitly in their texts – the more real, the more lively their personalities, their feelings and their causes are to the reader. In this sense, both the centrality of Tiara and the marginality of Aurélia, when held against the aesthetics of their own narratives inserted in their own societies, point to the tendency of the circumscription of African women to the realm of emphasised femininity even when they are conceived as protagonists.

In her foundational book *Gender and Power* (1987), Connell devised the concepts of hegemonic masculinity and emphasised femininity, which can help conceptualise these gender relations. Essential to her study of hegemonic masculinities, the term 'emphasised femininity' refers to the central role that compliance with male hegemony plays in patriarchal gender dynamics where women are subordinated to men. It epitomises the idea of a model of femininity that entails, necessarily, any form of submission to the hegemonic masculinities in place, which puts them in a relation of constitutive opposition to one another. Although specific configurations of emphasised femininity will depend, at least on the most basic level, on cultural specificities that are very local, it usually involves representations of women privileging the 'display of sociability rather than technical competence, fragility in mating scenes, compliance with man's desire for titillation and ego-stroking in office relationships, acceptance of marriage and childcare as a response to labour-market discrimination against women' (1987: 185). And most importantly, it is a normative model of gender held in place by the maintenance of a 'practice that prevents other models of femininity gaining cultural articulation' (1987: 188), such as the literary representation found in the characterisation of the protagonists of *Tiara*, *Aurélia de Vento* and *Teoria Geral do Esquecimento*.

The emphasised femininity found in *Tiara* is part of the aesthetics of her *Bildungsroman*, as it is the set of qualities that defines her as an exceptional woman that turns her into a heroine. As is widely known, the rise of the *Bildungsroman* in Germany as a narrative of maturation is closely connected to the emergence of Germany as a nation-state. No wonder, as McWilliams remarks, that 'the genre underwent, in the first instance, a (highly regrettable) rebirth in the context of Nazi Germany, where the genre's close association with nation-building was given a new and sinister dimension' (2009: 7). Another example is the importance of the *Bildungsroman* or *romance de formação* for the literature of a recently independent country from colonial rule, as Candido observes in Brazil, a place where the genre became extremely popular in the late nineteenth century, as the vehicle for a set of stories privileging local colours, flavours and rhythms, mostly instituted as one of Brazil's literary cornerstones, such as José de Alencar's *O Guarani* (1857). While the almost two centuries separating the emergence of the *Bildungsroman* from the context in which it appeared both in Europe and Brazil make *Tiara* a narrative substantially different from the ones found then, this form is clearly preferred to tell a story of personal maturation at the dawn of an independent country born through the violence of the liberation struggle.

Tiara is, therefore, a heroine who is in tune with her epic time of transition into postcoloniality, a time for the utopic transition between colonial past and independent future; between traditional local heritage and modernity. Lisa Downward evokes the thoughts of Bakthin that define the *Bildungsroman* hero as one that:

> emerges *along with the world* and [s/]he reflects the historical emergence of the world itself. [S/]He is no longer within an epoch, but on the border between two epochs, at the transition point from one to the other. This transition is accomplished in [her/]him and through [her/]him. [S/]He is forced to become a new, unprecedented

type of human being. What is happening here is precisely the emergence of a new [wo/]man. The organizing force held by the future is therefore extremely great here- and this is not, of course, the private biographical future, but the historical future. (2010: 111; emphasis in the original)

However, while Tiara's embodiment of the heroism of her time would certainly inspire a model of femininity that could be dissociated from any patriarchy-endorsing kind of emphasised femininity, her final sense of failure and consequent exile, in opposition to the journey of progress and development the form usually implies, show the impossibility of a woman matching the hero's intrinsic ability to overcome great obstacles. Tiara is, therefore, crushed by the weight of the patriarchal society within which she is written, whose model of femininity clearly entails a certain ethnic background and behaviour constantly forced upon her.

Despite being disguised by the affable tone of the narrative and by Tiara's excessive righteousness, supposedly justifying her quiet acceptance of adversities, an attentive reading reveals the violent way in which very specific gender roles are imposed on her. She is forced to let her first boy- friend go so that he can 'fulfil his duties' by marrying an ex-girlfriend who is found to be pregnant. Forcing Tiara to take this decision is the certainty that, if unmarried, the pregnant young woman, who was a young profes- sional of means, would certainly be marginalised by a highly sexist society. Later, when meeting her future husband, Kenun, Tiara has no doubts that she is the one to leave everything behind and follow him, just as her mother followed her father. The connection between her fiancé's condi- tions and the country's struggle for independence, since he is part of it, adds extra pressure to her abnegation. Once it is implied that she would be serving both her husband and the nationalist cause, her acceptance seems doubly inescapable. In order to live her love, she has to accept the physical struggle of the war and the social struggle to adapt – 'entre tu e o Kenum estarão sempre presents as suas obrigações para com o país e o peso das tradições familiares. Kenum é um patriota e porá certamente os interesses do seu país acima dos seus, para não dizer em detrimento destes' (Embaló 1999: 83) ['Between you and Kenum there will always be your obligations to the country and the weight of family traditions. Kenum is a patriot and will certainly put his country's interests above his own, not to say to their detriment']. The situation leaves little room for doubt: Tiara's conquests in life depend on hard work and submission. Her ability to face material and social hardships and to take the risk of falling victim to physical and psychological violence is what makes her an exemplary woman, the heroine. As a female friend of Tiara says to her fiancé in order to guarantee that his wife-to-be will surely accept all the challenges the relationship would impose on her: 'O Suevo tem razão, não podias encontrar uma melhor companheira. Nunca conheci alguém como ela! *Tem todas as qualidades que se exigem a uma mulher*' (Embaló 1999: 93; emphasis added) ['Suevo's right, you couldn't find a better partner. I've never met anyone like her! She has all the qualities a woman needs'].

These qualities also include Tiara's constantly refusal to fight back. The appraisal of Tiara's enduring qualities is used to keep her in a place of relative disadvantage in society for being foreign and for being a foreign woman: 'Quem pensas que és tu? Não é por teres andado na Luta, que te tornaste uma verdadeira Muritiana!' (Embaló 1999: 195) ['Who do you think you are? It's not because you've been in the Struggle that you've become a true Muritian!']. Tiara's most remarkable characteristics are rendered into the omens of her defeat: her defiance of racist ideologies by marrying a man from another racial background and another country is converted into the reason for her matrimonial failure; her rejection of the home as the only space for female agency and her active role in the struggle for independence become the reasons for her miscarriage and the loss of her ability to conceive; her inquisition of traditional practices becomes the reason for her failure to integrate with her husband's culture and her insubordinate character causes her to be ostracised by the national party after independence.

While Tiara's own decision to distance herself from the party, her husband and a culture that does not accept her could be interpreted as an act of protest or a coming-of-age process of self-valuation at the end of a journey of extreme social self-donation, one should not skip the melancholy involved in her decision:

> Chegou finalmente o último dia de trabalho no Instituto. Tiara sentia um certo nervosismo. Era também o último dia de mais uma etapa da sua vida. Mais uma que terminava e, como há vinte e quatro anos atrás, de forma trágica, e com ruptura.

Agora com uma dupla ruptura. Com a sua profissão e com o marido. No entanto
não se arrependia da sua trajectória. Kenum e o Muriti foram fundamentais na sua
existência. Com eles conheceu os verdadeiros valores da vida. Viveu momentos
extraordinários com o marido, que a sua decepção presente não poderia apagar das
suas recordações. (Embaló 1999: 253–254)

The last day of work at the Institute finally arrived. Tiara felt a certain nervousness.
It was also the last day of another stage in his life. Another one that ended and, like
twenty-four years ago, tragically, and with rupture. Now with a double rupture.
With her profession and with her husband. However, she did not regret this path.
Kenum and Muriti were fundamental in her life. With them she learned the true
values of life. She lived extraordinary moments with her husband, which her present
disappointment could not erase from her memories.

Sadness and resignation, followed by a quick act of self-consolation,
neutralising any emotional escalation to anger or revolt, mark Tiara's acceptance of her defeat. She loses the battle in the public arena of heroes
and exiles herself to a small village where, long ago, her marriage had been
happy. Her withdrawal from the public sphere to the domesticity of the
private environment, where Tiara is violently pushed into by all those who
did not accept her, such as her mother-in-law and members of the party,
is crowned by the consolation prize, à la *Deus ex machina*, of finding love
once again in the arms of her forgotten first love, now conveniently free
and ready to catch up with what their relationship could have been. If
there is one lesson to be learned from Tiara's coming-of-age story, published at the outset of the twenty-first century, it is that although women
can help men destroy colonialism, they can hardly defeat patriarchy and
definitely need to be in relationships with men to live a happy life.

Tiara's role as a protagonist and her centrality to the story, therefore, do not amount to a celebration of liberation and empowerment of
women, but constitute a first-hand feminine account of the undeniable
weight of male hegemony encrusted in tradition as well as in nationalist
modernity, from which she, as a woman and because a woman, seems unable to escape. Tiara's struggle is one that is against the violent methods
of exclusion to which she is constantly subjected as a foreign woman. Her
subalternity is doubled because she cannot fulfil the role of cultural repro-
ducer that is assigned to the local women, nor is she allowed to act freely
in the public sphere. The social tension detected in the textual fabric is

translated into the novel's aesthetic to the extent that we see a romantic heroine fail in her social goals and retreat from public life. The novel's inherent commitment to history leaves no room for a female heroine to win, registering a pattern of submission to the inevitable persistence of a patriarchy kept in place by men and women and by a nationalism that depends on the role of women as biological and cultural gatekeepers of the nation (Yuval-Davis 1995).

In a related manner, Aurélia's failure to constitute the actual centre of convergence in the realist *Aurélia de Vento* attests to the weight of social conventions. The result is a story in which she is written as an admirable, beautiful and complacent example of emphasised femininity. Aurélia is a character seen from the outside by an omniscient narrator who keeps her almost voiceless. It is not until page 65 of a short novel of 150 pages that we have the first segment of direct speech by Aurélia, which happens in the context of her meeting with a friend and lawyer to obtain advice regarding her father's property dispute with the state:

> — O que é que aconteceu para ter hoje à minha frente a mulher mais inteligente e mais popular desta cidade? …
>
> — Obrigada, doutor Altino. Mas o que o senhor diz é um exagero que não posso aceitar como verdade. Se o fizesse, estaria a ofender as mulheres verdadeiramente inteligentes e famosas da capital… Aceito que não sejam assim tantas, mas, em todo o caso, creio não pertencer ao grupo… – Riu-se também e Altino pôde aperceber-se melhor da beleza daquela mulher que quase toda a cidade admirava. Sim, sem quaisquer sofismas, Aurélia era bela e muita razão tinha o despachante de a tratar com o desvelo que o fazia, pois não era fácil ter a ocasião de partilhar o destino como alguém como ela.
>
> Invadiu-o, por momentos, uma incomum sensação de inveja de João Lourenço, mas logo se recompôs e, dirigindo-se para o centro da sala que servia de antecâmara ao gabinete, convidou-a a sentar. (Bragança 2011: 65)

> ['What happened for me to have the most intelligent and most popular woman in this city in front of me today?' …
>
> 'Thank you, Doctor Altino. But what you say is an exaggeration that I cannot accept as true. If I did that, I would be offending the truly intelligent and famous women in the capital… I accept that there aren't that many, but, in any case, I don't think I belong to the group'… She also laughed and Altino could tell better of the beauty of that woman that almost the entire city admired. Yes, without any quibbles, Aurélia

was beautiful and the attorney had every reason to treat her with the care he did, as it was not easy to have the opportunity to share a lifetime with someone like her.

For a moment, an unusual feeling of envy towards João Lourenço invaded him, but he soon recovered and, going to the center of the room that served as an antechamber to the office, invited her to take a seat.]

The quote offers an example of Aurélia's characterisation in the narrative. Utterly admired or envied, the character is constantly evoked using open declarations of her exemplary qualities: her beauty, sense of social duty and justice, intelligence and many others. Upon her first segment of direct speech in the narrative, the first quality Aurélia demonstrates is some inflated sense of modesty that is followed not by an expansion of her interior dimension but by a description of the impression she makes on her male interlocutor, which, again, is constituted solely of praises. Next, before the conversation between both characters could continue in the scene, a small segment speaking of the instant jealousy the lawyer had of Aurélia's husband refocused on her meaning to the men around her rather than on the character herself. Here, even in a fragment where Aurélia's voice can be heard in the narrative, what we have is a description of how, almost inevitably, she can only be an object of desire, an example of the modern woman, and emphasises femininity.

Aurélia's lack of agency and centrality in the novel becomes evident when we look at the space given to her as a character. Of the seventeen parts of the story, Aurélia's voice is heard in no more than four of them. Her interventions, though, are written in the style of the quote above: brief sections of direct speech followed by the addition of little to no psychological expansion. These, when they exist, are disproportionally attributed to male characters. Together, these narrative choices dislodge Aurélia from her purported central position, not only in the novel but also in the segments describing her actions. The two examples are the section in which she visits the lawyer Castro to have him intervene in her father's court case against the state (Chapter V, cited earlier) and the anniversary celebration of the association that she manages (Chapter IX). While in the first instance, Aurélia's presence ends up emphasising the legitimacy of her father's claim, in the second, she is the magnetic persona around which all the influential people of the city gravitate. Again, the whole scene seems to serve a different purpose than to draw our attention to developments connected to the life of Aurélia. Instead, it highlights her father's worthiness as he poses a key question to the guest lecturer of the night, showing Santos' abomination of the institution of slavery that reinforces the righteousness of his character that transcends the racist legacy associated with his skin colour.

Always mentioned but never really the centre of the narrative, we can say that Aurélia's character is the embodiment of a number of important qualities in Santomean society. Her function is to serve as a reagent, written as a device to reveal the nature and intention of the characters with whom she reacts. For this reason, she speaks less than she is spoken about, as it is against her example of unshakable virtue, which is the embodiment of emphasised femininity, that the vices of the Santomean society are revealed. The latent violence of this process of reaction is expressed through the narrative, as we not only witness how Aurélia's exemplary virtuosity is constantly policed but also how the revelation of other characters' flaws or virtues depends on how they interact with her. The narrative starts with her husband's decision to investigate accusations of his wife's infidelity, even when they were made by a relative who is known to be unreliable, and ends around where she almost falls victim to an assassination attempt that was ordered by her jealous stepmother. If anything, it is clear that Aurélia's excellence in performing her role of emphasised femininity is the very source of her potential ruin, as her flawlessness seems to threaten both non-hegemonic masculinities and other forms of femininity.

While the ways in which the protagonists of *Tiara* and *Aurélia de Vento* are written point to a rather similar pattern that highlights how impossible it is for these women to achieve success and recognition through their actions, the seeming difference between them and the case of Ludovica Fernandes Mano might be just superficial. It is true that *Teoria Geral do Esquecimento*'s postmodern features move away from the aesthetics of the grand narrative, opting for a prismatic structure of multiple voices and perspectives that does not promise the story of a righteous and exemplary woman. Nonetheless, Ludo still manages to have agency, to have her own voice, to develop and grow as a person by undergoing a deep transformation and to overcome her fears. It is also true that the space given to Ludo in the narrative is large enough to sustain her role as a pivotal character in the story, even despite the introduction of a significant number of characters and their own subplots. Yet, in a way that relates to the roles of Tiara and Aurélia, Ludo is not made into the main human material, whose successful development is the central point of the narrative. Her point of view is privileged by the symbolism of her ex-centric position and by her estrangement as an unsuccessful White Portuguese spinster who suffers from mental health and trauma. From her marginal position and failing vision, one can see the contradictions of both the colonial and post-independence systems in Angola.

This way, akin to what happens with Tiara and Aurélia, the centrality of Ludo is not the symbol of female resistance, development and empowerment that is necessary if one is willing to counter the predominance of narrative models that emphasise female subservience. Her character construction as a protagonist, on the contrary, may reinforce the existing sexist structure by reiterating it and by not offering a way out for Ludo. Being the only one amongst our three female protagonists who clearly defies certain aspects of emphasised femininity – as she is not depicted as beautiful, pleasant, motherly or necessarily kind, as she shoots a man dead and prefers the company of a dog called Phantom – Ludo is the most marginalised of the three. Her isolation develops to the extreme of physical separation when she erects a brick wall that cuts her off from the outside world.

The only one among our three protagonists who is shown in terms of her actions and commitment to changing the status quo, notwithstanding her failure to do so, is Tiara, a character in a novel written by a woman. As the present reading of these novels has shown, male portraits of femininity in the literatures of Portuguese-speaking Africa are still reproducers of a very stable model of femininity, in line with an idealised woman who is relatively submissive to the men in power, and work more like a surface onto which male action is reflected than as fully fledged characters endowed with agency. Women who do not conform to a model of sexualised femininity are depicted as unattractive, such as Ludo or Madalena in *Teoria* and the Teacher's Wife in *Campo*. Women depicted as candid and virtuous are also usually described as beautiful and young, which is not only the case with Tiara and Aurélia but also of the Village Chief's daughter in *Campo*, of Ludo's sister, Odete, and of young Madalena in *Teoria*.

Moreover, intellectual achievement and detachment from the African traditional world are seen as highly praised elements of these novels' local models of emphasised femininity. Tiara, who excels at everything, is constantly applauded for her two bachelors (law and history), and, notwithstanding her respect for the traditional world, she keeps a fairly critical distance from it. Aurélia is often referred to as 'doctor', a title usually given to someone who has attended university, not only to a medic or doctor of philosophy. She is praised for her Christian devotion, which suggests her distance from other traditional African religious beliefs. Even Ludo, despite her ex-centricity, spends almost thirty years alone with books and paintings, thus showing an intimate relationship with the written word in an European language. Additionally, Ludo's neighbours mistake her accidental interventions for divine providence, as they take her noise as manifestations of the local deity, also conveys a degree of distanced critical commentary in the story. Contrastingly, the female antagonists in *Tiara* and *Aurélia* are enmeshed in a world described as one of African traditional beliefs and a lack of formal education. They include Kenum's mother, who ruined Tiara's marriage; Clotilde, who commissioned the attempt against her stepdaughter's life during Aurélia's participation at a Catholic function and San Labeca, the Santomean nationalist committed to ruining the marriage of her daughter, Aidy, in *Aurélia de Vento*. These women, who are openly associated with non-Christian spiritual tradition and a mode of living that is customary rather than intellectualised, in terms of the European standards of what is considered modern, are seen in an ambivalent way by the men surrounding them. When facing these two antagonistic models of femininity, the educated, logical, righteous and revolutionary men populating these novels show a double allegiance. If their revolutionary minds make them love, desire and admire modern educated and critical 'new women', such as Aurélia and Tiara, their nationalistic commitment to tradition makes them inert, fearful and respectful of women such as Kenum's mother, Clotilde or San Labeca, all three committed to the destruction of our heroines' marriages. Here, too, the nationalist ambivalences make themselves visible, and it becomes clear that the destruction of patriarchy is perceived as incompatible with the praxis of a revolutionary nationalism that relies on local difference to erect a national rhetoric deemed by them capable of uniting their population towards the common goal of defeating colonialism.

Furthermore, the novels where femininity is not represented in terms of oppositional models such as *Tiara* and *Aurélia de Vento* draw pictures of femininity that are both greatly distanced from any notion of gender norm and where women are continuously targeted by sexual violence. This is openly the case not only in terms of the Teacher's Wife in *Campo*, Ludo in *Teoria* and Mirna in *Marginais*, who are victims of sexual violence, but it is also the case of the Village Chief's daughter in *Campo* and the vast number of women violated throughout the course of *Marginais*. It is striking to notice the pivotal role that rape and sexual exploitation play in these three narratives, in which it is difficult to locate a coherent model of emphasised femininity. In *Teoria*, Ludo's rape is a well-kept secret throughout the story. However, as we learn in the last parts of the narrative, it was the mix of her rape by a stranger coupled with heavy shaming by her father that caused Ludo to cut herself off from society. The scene, narrated in the first person, brings to light the physical and emotional scale of the gendered violence that will scar Ludo through life:

> Rasgou-me o vestido, arrancou-me as calcinhas e penetrou-me. Lembro-me do cheiro. Das mãos, ásperas, duras, apertando-me os seios. Gritei. Bateu-me no rosto, pancadas fortes, sincopadas, não com ódio, não com fúria, como se estivesse a divertir-se. Calei-me. Cheguei a casa aos soluços, o vestido rasgado, cheio de sangue, o rosto inchado. O meu pai compreendeu tudo. Perdeu a cabeça. Esbofeteou-me. Enquanto me açoitava, com o cinto, gritava comigo, puta, vadia, desgraçada. Ainda hoje o ouço: Puta! Puta! ...
>
> A vergonha é que me impedia de sair de casa. O meu pai morreu sem nunca mais me dirigir a palavra. Eu entrava na sala e ele levantava-se e ia-se embora. ...
>
> Nunca mais consegui sair à rua sem experimentar uma vergonha profunda. (Agualusa 2012: 226–227)
>
> [He tore my dress, ripped my knickers, and penetrated me. I remember the smell. And his hands, rough, hard, squeezing my breasts. I screamed. He slapped my face, hard, rhythmic blows, not with hatred, not angrily, as though he were enjoying himself. I fell silent. I arrived home sobbing, my dress torn, covered in blood, my face swollen. My father understood everything. He went out of his mind. He slapped me. As he lashed me, with his belt, he screamed at me. Whore, tramp, wretch! I can still hear him today. Whore! Whore! ...

The shame. The shame is what stopped me leaving the house. My father died without ever addressing another word to me. I would go into the living room and he'd get up and leave.

...

I was never again able to go out without feeling a profound shame.] (Agualusa 2015: 234–235)

In a related way, subjugation of women through sexual violence is the key ritual through which men seem to solidify their power in the oppressive structure of the camp in *Campo de Trânsito*. The Teacher's Wife is herself an object whose possession is an indication of power in the camp. By being a nominal possession of the Teacher, the Teacher's Wife reflects the power her husband holds in the camp. This direct connection between the level of physical intimacy with the Teacher's Wife and male power can be verified both by the lack of a description of intimacy between her and the Teacher and by the repeated description of her being raped by the Director, the man with the most power in the camp. Henceforth, it is by raping her that Mungau legitimates his recently acquired power in the hierarchy of the camp.

Mungau não faz o menor esforço para suavizar as intenções. Chega perto, agarra o vulto tenso, tira-lhe a enxada da estranha mão e deita-a por terra.

A origem do cheiro é indistinta, vem da terra ferida ou do corpo molhado do esforço, do suor de outono, e do trabalho; acres, um e outro. O som é agora um gemido que vem de dentro pois que a boca se mantém cerrada. Há ainda um movimento ritmado como o do rio ondulando a espinha para poder descer seu curso, chegar à foz e expulsar no oceano as águas que carrega. E, finalmente, dois dedos tacteando como antenas de uma formiga, numa deriva diligente. Tudo isso mais o escuro, que agora é pesado e envolvente. (Borges Coelho, 2007: 85)

[Mungau makes no effort to soften his intentions. He gets close, grabs the tense figure, takes the hoe from the strange hand and throws it on the ground.

The source of the smell is indistinct, it comes from the wounded earth or the body wet from effort, autumn sweat, and work; acres, one and the other. The sound is now a moan that comes from inside as the mouth remains closed. There is also a rhythmic movement like that of the river undulating its spine so that it can descend its course, reach the mouth and expel the waters it carries into the ocean. And finally, two fingers groping like an ant's antennae, in a diligent drift. All this plus the dark, which is now heavy and enveloping.]

Although the rape of women in *Marginais* is often seen in the light of forced consent as a bargaining chip for survival, the same kind of subjugation is at stake in the other three novels. Seen in relation to each other, these three works offer me a panorama of how gender violence in the form of sexual abuse takes place in three key realms of life in society. While in the case of Ludo, sexual violence is amplified by its repercussions within the intimacy of the family environment, for the Teacher's Wife, rape mediates her connection with the institution of the state and its representatives, and for Mirna, abuse is inflicted as another form of economic oppression:

> O Calvário dela começou quando o gerente de um *snack-bar* lhe disse que com um corpo bonito como o dela podia ganhar muito. Servia os clientes de *top less*, levava palmadinhas nas nádegas e, como o salário era insignificante, saía com alguns que a presenteavam com roupas caras. ... Trabalhamos como escravas, mas o aumento de salário ou paga, por exemplo, de um copo quebrado, inadvertidamente, é sempre discutido em cima da cama. Se quiseres ganhar mais tens de abrir as pernas aos filhos da mãe e fazer-lhes festinhas. Todo o patrão gosta de festinhas. (Rocha 2010: 90–91).

> [Her ordeal began when the manager of a snack bar told her that with a beautiful body like hers, she could earn a lot. She served customers topless, she was patted on the buttocks and, as the salary was insignificant, she went out with some who presented her with expensive clothes. ... We work like slaves, but the salary increase or payment, for example, for a broken glass, inadvertently, is always discussed in bed. If you want to earn more, you have to open your legs to the bastards and pet them. Every boss likes being pleased.]

What these three passages of abuse have in common is the fact that these women were already in marginal positions before being assaulted. Ludo was already an outcast when she was young, compared to other girls her age, as she lived an *almost* normal life (Agualusa 2012: 225). The Teacher's Wife is an isolated and voiceless woman in a prison camp run by men, and Mirna is exposed to the extreme poverty that threatens her survival. Next, we have these women's objectification by men. In the case of Ludo, the violence of rape is amplified by the reaction of her father, who blames her for spoiling the virginity that he sees as his possession. As Ludo clearly puts it, more than the trauma of rape, what makes her withdraw from society is the shame inflicted on her by her own father. This assertion of male power through the subjugation of women's bodies shows parallels with what happens in *Campo,* where the rape of the Teacher's Wife completes a rite of passage for Mungau's investiture of power. The skilfully written scene suggests that the possession of the Teacher's Wife ratifies and completes his upgrade in the hierarchy of the camp. The reference to the volume found when Mungau palpates his trousers and feels the volumes of the objects gifted by the Director, effectively changing his status, denotes the double sexual and literal meaning of possession preceding the rape, the righteousness of which seems undeniable to the point that he does not even bother to disguise his intentions. The imagery involving earth, the act of sowing and the fluvial metaphor that implies the rapist's ejaculation talks back to the camp's own distorted view of the philosophical role of labour and the modification of nature to subjective development described in Chapter 2. Just after the rape scene, the narrator states that '[p]assado um tempo a Mulher do Professor serena e cobre-se. *É agora muito mais humana'* (Borges Coelho 2007: 85; my emphasis) [after a while the Teacher's Wife calms down and covers herself. *She is now much more human*]. In the sick logic of the camp, the rape humanises the victim as if what is enacted on her body is the sublation achieved through an androcentric dialectic of labour, to which women relate as a resource of nature that is to be modified and worked upon.

The idea of women as the commodities of men in the realm of labour relations under patriarchy, which in *Campo* is painted in allegory, gains concrete contours in *Marginais.* The naturalistic aesthetics of this Cape Verdean novel leaves little room for doubt when it comes to the economic importance of patriarchal culture in subjugating women. 'A fome faz com que as mulheres, que não tiveram oportunidade de estudar, que viveram a vida inteira subordinadas ao culto do macho, se entreguem ao cuidado de um homem que seja trabalhador para sustenta-las' (Rocha 2010: 93) ['Hunger causes women, who have not had the opportunity to study, who have lived their entire lives subordinated to the cult of the male, to hand themselves over to the care of a working man to support them']. In a society where women have little opportunity, those who do not find relative protection in abusive relationships early enough are recruited by the sex industry. Hence, these three examples bring up the multiple levels of violence that mediate gender relations in the sample of this corpus. The clear connection between sexual violence and marginality casts light on the privileges separating the Teacher's Wife, Ludo and Mirna, and the two heroines embodying models of femininity, Aurélia and Tiara. While the two heroines enjoy social, economic, physical and psychological privilege, having been brought up with love, basic living conditions and access to education, their three less fortunate counterparts are drowned in a sea of ignorance and disabilities in terms of physical and mental health, as well as economic disadvantage. We should not forget that even Ludo, despite being a White woman in colonial Angola, is also dispossessed, living as a maid to her sister, who married a rich Angolan out of convenience, revealing the intersectional nature of women's oppression depicted in these narratives.

Despite the existence of female protagonists in contemporary African literature in Portuguese, this analysis has found that women are constantly represented in ways that rarely challenge the oppressive nature of the gender relations within which they are locked. When compared, these novels offer a rich picture of the intrinsically intersectional nature of the many levels of women's oppression. Showing the relevance of the combination of categories such as race, ethnicity, class, and privilege to the many forms of subordination of women by men, these narratives underline the intrinsically systemic character of inequality in postcolonial gender relations. While women of the elite, such as Tiara and Aurélia, are forced to adapt to subordinate models of emphasised femininity, women on the margins of society who cannot fit the rigorous requirements of normative femininity are left defenceless and vulnerable to all sorts of exploitation, often sexual in nature.

Despite the fair argument that these works play an important role in denouncing the precariousness of the position of women in their respective societies, it is important to highlight that by not offering any way out for their cast of female characters, these fictional projections can also perpetuate their subordinate status. The lack of justice and reparation for Mirna and Ludo and the non-recognition of the revolutionary potential of the Teacher's Wife's killing of her rapist, the Director of the camp, seem to ratify the inevitability of their disgraced fate as women and, consequently, underprivileged. Equally, the celebration of the heroism of women who, notwithstanding their somewhat privileged economic and social position, willingly accept subaltern positions in society seems to promote a model of femininity that is strong and capable but ultimately passive. Women, therefore, are held hostage to fictional representations that depict them as tropes, motifs and symbols rather than tridimensional agents capable of saving themselves and others. To the extent to which history imposes itself on these stories, the verisimilitude of the novel where the transgressive woman wins is still hard to achieve.

Hegemonic masculinity

Connell's study is clear when it defines hegemonic masculinity in relation to various subordinate masculinities as well as in relation to women's (1987: 183). Therefore, the assessment of the emphasised femininity done in the previous section is essential for the understanding of the dynamics between hegemonic and non-hegemonic masculinities. As inequality is translated in terms of subordination, attention to the constructions of emphasised femininities is vital for a clearer understanding of the forces that keep such structures in place. Henceforth, after our in-depth look into how femininities are written in the contemporary fiction of Portuguese-speaking Africa, we turn to the different models of masculinity that populate our fictional corpus to better grasp how these literatures register gender relations in the contemporary postcolony.

Before proceeding, however, it is important to emphasise that Connell's understanding of hegemonic masculinities does not only focus on the opposition between men and women but also equally stresses the importance of the role played by the myriad subordinate or non-hegemonic masculinities and different models of femininity that complete this intricate system of forces. Hence, she clarifies that ' "hegemony" does not mean total cultural dominance, or the obliteration of alternatives. It means ascendancy achieved within the balance of forces, that is, a state of play. Other patterns and groups are subordinated rather than eliminated' (1987: 184).

Additionally, force and violence constitute important components in this state of play, to which oppression is key:

> though 'hegemony' does not refer to ascendancy based on force, it is not incompatible with a system based on force. Indeed, it is common for the two to go together. Physical or economic violence backs up a dominant cultural pattern [...] or ideologies justify the holders of physical power ('law and order'). The connection between hegemonic masculinity and violence is close, though not simple. (Connell 1987: 184)

Therefore, given our understanding of the complex connection between gender roles and violence – be it physical, economic or social – since those roles are usually enforced on many levels, the analysis will map the models of masculinity that populate these fictional universes and understand how they relate to one another. With the intention of complementing the analysis on violence and to offer a more complete overview of the gender relations within the literatures this corpus represents, particular attention will be paid to the ways that masculinity is engendered by violence.

While three of the five novels analysed present female protagonists, the other two narratives invest in protagonists identified as male. However, where one notices the emergence of a relatively uniform model of desired femininity ascribed to the female protagonists, a clear picture of hegemonic masculinity cannot be ascribed to the two male protagonists. Interestingly, while *Campo de Trânsito* and *Marginais*, the two works with male protagonists, provide us with quite dissonant models of masculinity, it is in *Aurélia de Vento* and *Tiara* that a more clear-cut type of hegemonic masculinity seems to emerge.

The two examples of hegemonic masculinity offered by the Santomean and the Guinean novels are, respectively, Santos and Kenum. While this model appears in the two narratives in which the protagonists are women, a careful reading can easily illustrate the necessity of this model of hegemonic masculinity in relation to the construction of each narrative's exemplary heroines. Nevertheless, even these two exemplary models of masculinity in their righteousness, fairness and commitment to national causes seems to illustrate Lugarinho's point that '[e]spremido entre o presente da vida colonial e a utopia futura, o homem africano, tal qual as Literaturas das nações africanas de língua oficial portuguesa, já seria um indivíduo dotado de uma identidade de gênero em crise' (2012: 134) [squeezed between the colonial present and the utopic future, the African man, just as in the African Literatures in Portuguese, would already be a man with a gender identity in crisis]. This crisis, Lugarinho continues, comes from a maladjustment that is structural. If on the one hand 'foi preciso que as literaturas fossem construídas a partir de formações discursivas que instalassem identidades rigidamente calcadas no perfil épico de heróis que se nacionalizavam' (2012: 137–138) [it was necessary for literatures to be constructed from discursive formations that installed identities rigidly based on the epic profile of heroes who were nationalized], on the other hand, to the extent that these identities were built in reaction to the colonial way of life they were dependent on for their premises, any attempt to overcome them would erode the basis onto which these alternatives were built. It is for this reason that, as much as Santos and Kenum are the closest one can get in terms of hegemonic masculinities modelled after the image of the national hero consecrated through violent engagement with the national cause, neither of them can fully accomplish it. Santos' skin colour stops him from fully embodying the form of hegemonic masculinity, and in Kenum's case, this is attributed to his inability to fully transition from tradition to modernity. By falling for his mother's trap and taking a second marriage in the traditional mould, Kenum deviates from the model of New Man, whose refusal of African non-modern customs and traditions that do not match the socialist interpretation of progress is key to bringing about the revolution necessary to change the country after the achievement of independence.

Aurélia de Vento seems to build up a case in favour of Santos, while *Tiara* shows disappointment towards Kenum's failure to resist the lure of his mother. They indicate that the problem with these attempts to achieve hegemonic masculinities is their very impossibility. These characters' inability to meet a normative model of gender reflects the lack of verisimilitude of the romantic model of masculinity that is shaped after the canonisation of the national hero. Santos' and Kenum's slightly non-hegemonic masculinity mutually call into question the inflexibility of the model of the national hero that ought not to be of the same race as the coloniser. However, it is important to notice that while these characters' potential critique of their societies' hegemonic models of masculinities questions the kind of racial and cultural features chosen as distinctive of the 'national man', they fall short of challenging the legacy of violence subjacent to it. Inserted into the novels that successfully give life to archetypal female characters, the slight incompleteness of Santos and Kenum as successfully archetypal and matching male heroes evidences, as Lugarinho argues, a male identity in crisis (2012: 149). This crisis, at least when it comes to the central male characters of both narratives, does not indicate a break with the association of masculinity and the monopoly of violence – be it in private or in public – nor does it openly contest the masculine hegemony that is intrinsically linked to femininity.

If *Aurélia de Vento* and *Tiara* both understate their problematisation of enforced models of masculinity, *Campo de Trânsito* and *Teoria Geral do Esquecimento* critique those models in a much more open fashion. Surprisingly, these latter novels do not celebrate the embodiment of the model of hegemonic masculinity, as they also treat certain aspects commonly prescribed to hegemonic males in these post-independence societies in a way that inspires a critique of these models. Looking at *Campo de Trânsito* from this perspective shows the portrayal of a problematic social structure that is built upon the shaky pillars of patriarchy and the male quest for hegemony. The system is composed of three men in positions of power, whose power, as noticed already, is directly proportional to their possession of women. The Village Chief has a daughter, and the Teacher has a wife. However, as we observed in the case of the Teacher, the power of these two male characters is limited by their sexual dominance over their female assets. Real power, as becomes clear throughout the narrative, comes attached to monopolies on violence, sexual dominance and material accumulation, which is epitomised in the figure of a short, tiny and manipulative Director. The pure force of Bexigoso or the articulation of Mungau are insufficient for them to hold power, which must be exercised in the physical, sexual and material realms. Seen from this perspective, the fall of the Director is the fall of patriarchy and of its symbols:

> Só então e vira para trás, para o Director. Só então repara como ele é uma colina onde estão espetados dois paus de bandeira: numa das extremidades um pequeno pau de alumínio com um defeito de série; na outra tem as calças descaídas, enroladas em

volta dos tornozelos. Traindo um miserável acto interrompido, agora suspenso para todo o sempre. (Borges Coelho 2007: 206)

[Only then does he turn back to the Director. Only then he notices how it is a hill on which two flagpoles are stuck: at one end a small aluminum stick with a defect in it; on the other, the trousers are hanging down, wrapped around the ankles. Betraying a miserable interrupted act, now suspended forever.]

Only after the Teacher's Wife's visit to confirm the death of her rapist and to reclaim the murder weapon does Mungau notice the Director's naked penis out, 'suspended' for eternity. Resembling two flagpoles, the spoon that Mungau puts in his open mouth matches the phallus, which, amidst the unravelling order of the camp, is no longer a vehicle of power but a sad reminder of the vileness inherent to that kind of domination. In this commentary, the flagpole, the spoon and the penis openly evoke the camps' tripod of the state's monopoly on violence, economic resources and sex. If the revolution in the camp depended on mass disobedience from those confined to the labour fields, its chances of success are indebted to the death of the Director and to the gendered act of self-defence by the Teacher's Wife.

When it comes to the representation of masculinities, *Campo* provides a picture of the structural association between the state, violence, masculinity and subjugation of women, while *Teoria* invests in a more personal and subjective perspective on it. In *Teoria*, Monte is the closest we have to a model of masculinity in the story. Having embraced socialist ideals, he merges the models of the New Man and of the national hero, exposing how these types of masculinities' inherently contradict the very socialist view of societal progress and equality. The degree of proximity between Monte and his antagonist, Jeremias, in terms of sexism questions their professed opposition in terms of ideology. Despite the difference they express when it comes to each man's preferred mode of 'having' women – as Jeremias tries to bribe Monte with the opportunity to have 'many' women but faces his executioner's satisfaction in having 'only one' – both see women in the same objectified and oversexualised light:

A propósito, que diabos estavas a fazer no prédio da Rita? [Monte asks Jeremias]

Conheces a Rita?!

Rita Costa Reis? A Ritinha? Grandes pernas. As melhores pernas de Luanda.

Conversaram alegremente sobre as mulheres angolanas. Jeremias apreciava as luandenses. Contudo, acrescentou, nenhuma mulher do mundo igualava em tempero e destempero as mulatas benguelenses. Monte recordou então Riquita Baleuth, nascida no seio de uma das mais antigas famílias de Mossâmedes, eleita Miss Portugal em 1971. Jeremias capitulou. Riquita, sim, daria a vida para acordar uma manhã à luz daqueles olhos negros. (Agualusa 2012: 33)

[Talking of which, what were you doing in Rita's building?' [Monte asks Jeremias]

'Wait, you know Rita?'

'Rita Costa Reis? Ritinha? Great legs. Best legs in Luanda.' They chatted happily about Angolan women. Jeremias did fancy the Luandan ones, however, he added, there wasn't a woman in the world who could match the mulatta women of Benguela. Then Monte recalled Riquita Bauleth, born into one of the oldest families in Moçâmedes, named Miss Portugal in 1971. Jeremias concurred. Yes, Riquita – he would give his life just to be able to wake up one morning in the light of those dark eyes.] (Agualusa 2015: 25–26)

The dialogue stops abruptly as the men arrive where Jeremias' execution is set to take place. As a representative of colonialism in the story, Jeremias dies at the hands of the new political and economic system, but their shared sexism lives on. The same happens to the violence that continues beyond the rise of the newly independent country, as Monte is tasked with the perpetration of violence deemed necessary to secure the socialist revolution. In the narrative, Monte's insistence on trying to perform a type of masculinity in line with the moulds of the socialist New Man or the national hero is precisely what prevents him from reaching the dimension of redemption achieved by all the other characters – including Jeremias – at the end of the novel.

Rocha's *Marginais* differs from what we encountered in the other four novels discussed, given its option for painting a radically diverse portrait of its masculinities. Instead of focusing on the contradictory and virtually unachievable nature of the models of hegemonic masculinities circulating in independent Portuguese-speaking Africa, *Marginais* invests in the narrative of men who, at the margins of society, perform almost exclusively non-hegemonic or normative forms of masculinity. The impoverished Espargos neighbourhood of the Cape Verdean island of Sal is the stage on which characters like Sérgio,

Fusco and Valdomiro/Mirinha perform their non-conformity in a seemingly natural and symbiotic relationship with their inhospitable environment.

   One of the few scholars writing about this novel, Lugarinho, categorically states that in *Marginais*, violence is endemic (2012:173). Manifesting itself at all levels of the narrative, violence is a nodal factor for the development of these characters' gender and sexuality, as rape is the main initial contact with sex as experienced in the novel. In *Marginais*, rape is perpetrated by parents, police and strangers alike. It victimises and marks the lives of children and young people, regardless of their gender and sexuality. Many are the examples of girls who, like Mirna, started their lives as prostitutes due to a mix of economic deprivation and early sexual molestation. Boys, too, are early recruited by the sex industry, which supplies the tourism on the island with victims of sexual violence. Pianista, a character saved from being raped by police by Sérgio, later joins the sex industry by recruiting young girls into prostitution. Fusco, whose identification is varies in a spectrum ranging between gay man and trans woman, also went into prostitution after the economic ruin of his family caused by the arrest of his father, who is found to repetitively rape his onwn daughters.[5] Nevertheless, the novel does not seem to offer just a perspective locked into simple social determinism. Crossing gender, sexuality and class, the narrative suggests that not only *because* these characters are left over on the margins of society, they can live their own personal and non-conforming gender identity, but it is also *despite* that.

   The performance of non-normative gender identities by the characters of *Marginais* seems to be an open strategy of protest and recuperation of individual agency in a society of bourgeois values that systematically excludes them, constituting what Connell and Messerschmidt have called 'protest masculinities' (2005: 847). Vandalism, abuse of sex, drugs and all other practices condemned by the bourgeois morale of those in positions of power are the marginalised islanders' exercise of freedom. Hence, homosexuality is seen as a natural and accepted practice that is not dissociated

---

5   This study follows the pronominal choice made in the novel to speak of Fusco, which identifies the character as he/him. At no point in the narrative this choice is challenged by the character.

from or diminished in comparison to heterosexuality. Sérgio's own homosexual experiences are narrated with no harm to his masculinity:

> No fim da aula, encontrei Fusco com o bolso cheio de moedas de cinco escudos atrás
> da escola numa cantarola desenfreada, folheando uma revista pornô e disse-me que só
> partilhava comigo as moedas se eu lhe penetrasse. Apanhei mais um susto daqueles,
> Já vens com essa coisa de doido. Sabes que não posso, é pecado.

> Então deixa um gajo tocar-te punheta. Num riso apalermado e delinquente,
> contemplámos os pingos de esperma desaguados, em esguicho, como uma garrafa
> de champanhe nas festas de casamento.

> Eu tinha fome e o Fusco tinha dinheiro. (Rocha 2010: 49)

> [At the end of class, I found Fusco with a pocket full of five escudo coins behind the
> school, humming wildly, leafing through a porn magazine and told me that he only
> shared the coins with me if I penetrated him. I got another scare like that, You're
> already thinking this crazy thing. You know I can't, it's a sin.

> Then let a guy give you a handjob. With a stupid and delinquent laugh, we con-
> templated the drops of sperm released, squirting, like a bottle of champagne at
> wedding parties.

> I was hungry and Fusco had money.]

Later, during his homosexual relationship with Valdomiro/Mirinha,
Sérgio plainly establishes how his sexuality does not interfere with his masculinity. Represented as an extension of affection and as a much-needed
weapon to fight the injustice that victimises those that are dispossessed on
the island, sexuality here is seen as disconnected from gender identity. 'O
meu envolvimento com Valdomiro foi mais por compaixão, depois de saber
que ele tinha sido abusado por um grupo de delinquentes. Quis ajudá-lo
e perceber melhor o que levava um homem a escolher esse caminho. ... Eu
não amava Mirinha como jamais amaria ninguém.' (Rocha 2010:116) ['My
involvement with Valdomiro was more out of compassion, after learning
that he had been abused by a group of delinquents. I wanted to help him
and understand better what led a man to choose this path. ... I didn't love
Mirinha like I would never love anyone.']

Equally, Fusco's open performance of genderqueer is seen by Sérgio as
a defiant act of courage. For Sérgio, Fusco's feminine traits did not cancel
out the crucial points of his masculinity:

Eu admirava o comportamento de Fusco. Rebolava a polpa obstinadamente, mas era arrojado. ... Era como se tivesse transformado numa fera, um mutante que se libertava das peças de roupa feminina e da fragilidade de mulher para vestir a roupagem de uma fera ferida na sua dignidade.

...

Não acredito que ele fosse uma mulher num corpo de homem como ele gostava de afirmar. Acho que tudo começou com brincadeiras de menino, mas depois foi difícil contornar o vício. (Rocha 2010: 154–155)

[I admired Fusco's behavior. He shook his head obstinately, but he was bold. ... It was as if he had transformed into a beast, a mutant that freed himself from feminine clothing and the fragility of a woman to wear the clothes of a beast wounded in its dignity.

...

I don't believe he was a woman in a man's body as he liked to claim. I think it all started with boyish games, but then it was difficult to overcome the addiction.]

Sérgio's perception of genderqueer identity as courageous and transgressive underscores the ideological factors subjacent to the way in which the masculinities of the boys of the neighbourhood, grouped into the Pitboys gang, clearly contrast with their local example of hegemonic masculinity. Embodied by the wealthy, greedy, corrupt and snobbish Dr Apolinário, hegemonic masculinity seems to be experienced less as a gender identity than as a bourgeois value. For this reason, Apolinário's complete ruin is necessarily preceded by a sexual scandal that destroys his position as a hegemonic male. The tragicomic scene begins when the lawyer's wife, Dona Eufémia, decides to visit the office of her busy husband and finds him having sex with his driver. The scandal drove him crazy, and he died under unexplained circumstances (Rocha 2010: 213).

Marginais' treatment of masculinity complements and advances trends have already been made visible in this study. It is clear that each of the analysed novels contains major male characters unable to conform to norms of masculinity modelled after the socialist New Man or national hero. However, rather than jumping to the conclusion that the contestation of masculinities found is the result of a conscious effort of all five authors' commitment to deconstructing the idea of normative masculinities, we argue that the discussions of gender taking place in these narratives occur as an unavoidable effect of these novels' aesthetics. By subscribing to forms of realism that, notwithstanding their differences in terms of narrative technique, show a common concern with their respective postcolonial contexts under the sign of the nation-state, these novels need to balance elements of familiarity and of estrangement in relation to their own society. Therefore, given gender and sexuality's intrinsic importance to the very existence of the nation-state as both a cultural and political entity, their faithful expression in these narratives becomes an essential feature for verisimilitude, which works, collaterally, as a sign of issues with the very nation-state in question.

Consequently, despite gender not being the core issue of each of these novels, the extent to which central characters are forced to adhere to or deviate from their respective norms of masculinity maintains a close connection with each novel's own critical stance on its respective country. This way, Kenum's inability to move from tradition to modernity is crucial to *Tiara*'s view of issues faced by Guinea-Bissau. In *Aurélia de Vento*, Santos' heroism as man and citizen in defying the binary racial order put in place during colonialism shows the narrative's positive tone towards the postcolonial present and future of São Tomé and Príncipe. The violent exercise of hegemonic masculinities in *Campo de Trânsito* by the Director and Mungau's aspiration to it match the narrative's critical view of the structural and systemic nature of oppression in post-independence Mozambique. Similarly, the violence involved in Monte's attempted performance of hegemonic masculinity works as a critique of the very model of the New Man or national hero to which normative forms of masculinity are fundamental and which approximates it to colonialism much more than self-professed political ideologies would have it be. Finally, supplementing the critical portrait of masculinities within the boundaries of Portuguese-speaking African postcolonies, *Marginais*' choice to represent forms of masculinity that actively distance themselves from normative models matches the novel's focus on humanising and showing the agency of those who are excluded from the national system of privilege.

Rocha's novel abandonment of discussions centred on normative masculinities, consciously foregrounding the experiences of non-hegemonic males, radically changes the focus of the discourse and questions the overall validity of the model, as the example of Dr Apolinário indicates. Moreover, the novel expands on the links between hegemonic masculinity, violence and the national bourgeoisie, as suggested by the other works analysed, as it highlights the relevance of class and force in the gender equation. As such, *Marginais* naturalizes non-hegemonic forms of masculinity and denounces the reification of hegemonic masculinities, treating the latter as a trace of bourgeois morality necessary to the affirmation of the class's entitlement to the wealth and privileges it is denied to those it excludes to exploit.

Despite reaching high levels of explicitness in *Marginais*, the close association between hegemonic masculinity and violence – often sexual violence – as the means for subjugation of non-hegemonic masculinities and diverse forms of femininity is perceptible in each of the narratives analysed. As we have seen, gender violence is still deployed on an everyday basis as a weapon of subjugation that is shown to be as essential for the postcolonial status quo as it was in the colonial one. If in colonial times, gender norms coming from Portugal decisively influenced the possibilities of gender performance by people, the internationalisation inherent to the anticolonial movement that shaped the cultural practices of the revolutionary states pushed for the emergence of very palpable transnational gender hierarchical structures across Portuguese-speaking Africa. The societies imagined in each of the analysed works of fiction show that heavy control of female bodies keeps the national sense of race, ethnicity and culture in the places that are convenient for the dominant classes. Essential to this order too is women's subjugation in the public sphere, their confinement to the domestic space, or their controlled participation in the political one. The control over the sexuality of those living outside the framework of normative masculinity is also connected to the generation of wealth for the elites. These groups are easy prey for exploitative moulds of sex industry, benefiting those at the top of their respective pyramidal societies.

Notwithstanding these constraints, gender and sexuality in these narratives have also been shown to work as a site of empowerment, as their intrinsically performative nature entails a relationship with the body that favours levels of awareness essential for the process of affirmation of one's identity in the contemporary fiction of postcolonial Portuguese-speaking Africa. The transformative potential of the exercise of non-hegemonic masculinities, which, despite being often painful and difficult, sows the seeds of contestation that are so necessary for social change. Yet, the narrow extent to which this transformative potential is explored is an indication of its overarching patriarchal legacy. Its conceptualisation only in the plane of masculinities reveals that even the attempts at transformation are not yet strong enough to cross the gendered line, which works as an essential reminder that the possibilities of much-needed changes are still a long way ahead in these societies' postcoloniality.

Memories of violence

Another remarkable aspect of the novels included in this study is that the narrative of the most subaltern character takes the form of a memoir. *Marginais* is, before anything else, the first-person narrative of a wretched young man to whom none of the promises made by the anticolonial revolutionary movement came true. In a similar fashion, the stories of the marginalised protagonists of *Teoria Geral do Esquecimento* and of *Tiara* too are told from a very intimate, personal point of view that does not bear any pretence to totalisation. Through critical and situated accounts of their respective societies in the aftermath of independence, these novels desacralise an official discourse of national heroism surrounding those who assumed the political and economic steering of their countries. By doing so, these narratives promote a revisionist approach to official history, registering a violent battle also in the realms of memory. Therefore, in this section, we look into these novels' representation of the pervasion of violence in the fictionalisation of memory.

Given the widely known role of national literature in shaping identities and identities' intrinsic connection with memory, it is no surprise that memory has become quite an important topic for those concerned with the study of literature, mostly when the literature in question establishes ties with forms of nationalism. For this reason, when it comes to the study of the African literatures in Portuguese, memory is a recurrent topic. The relevance of memory in these works dates back to colonial domination, when the territories that today comprise the five countries of

Portuguese-speaking Africa were featured in literature almost exclusively by Portuguese authors committed to the racist regime of domination of their time. In line with Fanon, who, already in 1964, affirmed that colonial racism was heavily dependent on cultural devaluation (1967, 38–40), Mata locates the beginnings of a systematic fictionalisation of Africa in literatures in Portuguese in the second half of the nineteenth century, when, having lost Brazil, the Portuguese turned their attention to their African colonies. According to Mata, the cultural production about Africa by then had an essentially subalternising function, characterised by the representation of the continent's space-time as a hostile *locus horrendous* (2013: 64). As Mata explains in detail, such a negative constitution of the African people, culture and space was at the heart of the colonial literary project as envisaged by the metropole. By justifying the alleged inferiority of the colonised people and confirming the need for a civilising mission that constituted the façade of the colonial enterprise at that point, the first appearances of Africa in literary works in Portuguese were marked by a violence of form and content that mirrored the violent project of domination in whose bosom it emerged.

In light of this situation, it is clear why literary works produced in each of these five former African colonies during the struggle and in the immediate aftermath of their independence have taken a radically opposite direction from most colonial literature. As Chaves puts it with regards to Angolan literature, '[n]ão é de estranhar, portanto, que a idéia de libertação que marca o processo literário angolano seja assim atravessada por um desejo de resgate de um passado distante. Regressar no tempo seria também um modo de apostar numa identidade tecida na diferença.' (2004: 149) ['[It] is not surprising, therefore, that the idea of liberation that marks the Angolan literary process is thus crossed by a desire to rescue a distant past. Going back in time would also be a way of investing in an identity woven by difference.'] Conjoined with the identity project was the acute need to fill in the gaps left by colonial historiography and, at the same time, to accumulate material evidence of the cultural wealth of the countries in search of independence. That, according to Chaves and most scholars who look into the issue, has decisively contributed to making these literatures into some kind of supplementary anthropological and ideological material. As Fonseca (2005) has observed in a study concerned with the literary registration of orality, the preservation of many items of these countries' cultural memories has relied almost entirely on fictional memory. Offering an endogenous and more recent view on the matter, the Angolan writer Ondjaki also stated something along the same lines in an interview. According to him 'à falta de uma maior e qualitativamente relevante produção de ensaios históricos, é sobretudo no mundo da ficção – o que também engloba poesia – que a História está a ser escrita' (Leite et al., 2012: 105–106) ['in the absence of a greater and qualitatively relevant production of historical essays, it is mainly in the world of fiction – which also includes poetry – that History is being written'].

Not only circumscribed to Angola but also extending itself through the other four countries of Portuguese-speaking Africa (Calafate Ribeiro and Semedo 2011; Calafate Ribeiro and Jorge 2011; Leite et al., 2012), the establishment of fictional memory as a site of condensation of national histories is seen by critics nowadays as an inescapable fact in the cultures of this transnational region. However, due to the intrinsic relation between text and context, the modes of remembering displayed by these literatures in the aftermath of independence still carry the scars of societies that were enmeshed in violence. Just as colonial domination and anticolonial revolution counted on battles fought in the realms of cultural memory, these literatures point out that contemporary debates on the topic are grounded in the clash between the plurality of individual memory and the institution's national official histories.

Pierre Nora's understanding of memory as tradition, or lived experience often brought to the present via the performance of repetition and embodiment, and of history as the 'reconstruction ... of what is no longer' (1989: 8), suggests that the fictional consubstantiation of history and memory in these literatures might be most accurately perceived as a process of turning memory into history. Although this process, as the critical essay by Fonseca shows, shares some of the anxiety underlining Nora's conceptualisation of *lieux de mémoire* – whose existence is tied to the belief that a socially engrained memory is effectively lost (1989: 7) – it highlights literature's crucial position when it comes to national collective memories. At the same time that it prevents the total loss of certain traditional stories, modes of narrative, or registers that have been endangered by the succession of new beginnings that so deeply marked the histories of these postcolonial societies, literature too is a material site of condensation of new *lieux de mémoire*.

Notwithstanding its transferability as a concept, we should not forget that following Nora's usage of the term, to state that something constitutes a *lieu de mémoire* implies that the given object or subject no longer takes part in a *milieu de mémoire*, which, according to the historian, constitutes 'real environments of memory' (1989:7). Criticised by scholars such as Michael Rothberg, who alerts to the method's 'linear and binarized account of history and memory' (2010: 4), Nora's rather rigid approach to the relationship between memory and history is certainly indebted to the historian's place of enunciation: the post-imperial *milieu* of late twentieth-century France. While Nora's binary and linear logic is hardly enough to explain the multiplicity that characterises postcolonial societies and their cultures – probably one of the reasons why postcolonial France was absent in his monumental multivolume work *Realms of Memory* (Rothberg 2010: 6) – his conceptualisation can still be useful to focus not on the linear way in which he sees history taking over memory but instead choose to concentrate on the intrinsic relationship that the theoretician sees between *lieu, milieu de mémoire* and experience.

Nora's understanding of the emptied, inorganic and disembodied nature of the site (*lieu*) of memory in contrast with its embodied, live and performative mode of experimentation in an environment (*milieu*) of memory calls attention to the process by which certain memories are cherished as history. Echoing Walter Benjamin's (2007) interrelated view of memory and communicable experience, Nora notices, for example, that in the case of France, history and memory have only been united under the same *milieu* when put in service of the nation during the Third Republic. He explains that throughout this period 'the relationships between history, memory, and the nation were characterized as more than natural currency: they were shown to involve a reciprocal circularity, a symbiosis at every level – scientific and pedagogical, theoretical and practical. This national definition of the present imperiously demanded justification through the illumination of the past' (1989: 10). The break of this synthesis between history and memory happened in France, according to Nora, during the crisis that the country faced in the 1930s, 'when the coupling of state and nation was gradually replaced by the coupling of state and society' (1989: 11). After this disintegration,

> the three terms [nation, history, and memory] regain their autonomy. No longer a cause, the nation has become a given; history is now a social science, memory a purely private phenomenon. The memory-nation was thus the last incarnation of the unification of memory and history (1989: 11).

Distanced from the everyday experience, the memory of the nation needs reification, which leads Nora to state that in the age of the *lieux de mémoire*, '[w]e no longer celebrate the nation, but we study the nation's celebrations' (1996: 7).

In its relevance to this study, Nora's view of the memorialisation of the nation raises questions concerning the role played by contemporary African literatures in Portuguese in their respective national processes. If we agree with Anthony Smith, who, echoing Ernst Renan, affirms that '[t]he nation is built on shared memories of joy and suffering, and above all of collective sacrifices. Hence the importance of battles, defeats no less than victories, for mobilising and unifying ethnicities and nations' (1996: 382), we can easily understand the organic relationship established between memory and nation in the literary works produced in the 1960s, 1970s and 1980s. By then, the violence underlying the national project was taken as a creative force whose reflection in literature was positive, evidencing the national *milieu* of the memorialisation of the nation. However, when it comes to more contemporary works of fiction, conceived in a time of relative peace as the political integrity of the states backing these nations is no longer under immediate threat, it is worth asking whether the nation is represented as a communicable experience of living memory or as a distant historical fact. Does it constitute a *lieu* or *milieu de mémoire*? Also, given that the performance of the nation as living memory is crucial for the deliberation of its role as *lieu* or *milieu de mémoire,* how does it condensate in the aesthetics of the novel? And finally, what is the role played by violence in these fictional histories?

Memory as lieu

Addressing the establishment and functioning of collective memories such as national ones, *Campo de Trânsito* and *Aurélia de Vento* offer a more explicit discussion on the mechanisms behind the process of sedimentation of memories into national or collective histories. Despite approaching the theme in quite diverse ways, both narratives offer a critical account of the phenomenon by unveiling the unnatural, highly ideological, historically contingent and even violent nature of the condensation of memory into history.

The management of collective memory plays a fundamental part in the development of the plot of *Campo de Trânsito* since it is vital to the organisation of the activities developed by the state in the three-camp complex. While the concentration of the narrative focuses on the Transit Camp, which is the administrative core of the prison complex, the reader later finds out that the camp's main purpose is the triage of incoming prisoners. It is during their stay in the Transit Camp that it is decided to which of the other two camps each new inmate is suited. These two spaces – the Old and the New camps – are where the truly central activities of the prison complex take place. The collection of truffle mushrooms at the Old Camp and the extraction of naphtha in the New Camp are the economic activities that constitute the *raison d'être* of the prison complex as a whole. Moreover, vital to the undertaking of these activities by the captive labour force of the complex is the manipulation of individual and collective memory.

As the analysis of the novel's representation of state violence shows, the docilization of bodies is a performative action destined to also have an impact on the minds of inmates. Being the first stage of the prisoners' journey into de-subjectivization, the transit camp is the place where the major investment in terms of disciplining the body happens. While the deprivation of freedom, the separation of individuals and the routine fashion of basic activities such as eating and sleeping are consistently reinforced, the classes of the Teacher are not of compulsory attendance. The lessons are designed to attract prisoners more prone to intellectual activity, to whom the mere performance of body discipline lacks a strong correlation with the discipline of the mind. Those like Mungau are the ones who have to learn the ethos of the camp – an ethos of transformation, as the Teacher's best student puts it during the protagonist's first lesson in the camp.

The activities undertaken in the Transit Camp are, thus, only initial samples of what is adopted systematically in the Old and in the New camps. As the narrative advances, we understand that those who were successfully transformed into nameless parts of a collectivity go to the New Camp. They tend to be young, strong and alienated enough to focus on combining their forces exclusively to fulfil the tasks they are given. The Old Camp, in its turn, is the destination of prisoners who must pay for 'memory crimes'. The prisoners are old, have curved backs and need thick glasses to aid their tired vision. There, these men's ability to remember is put in service to the state and against their own interests. They are the ones in charge of going into the fields in search of truffles. Given the rudimentary way in which they are forced to execute their task, memory is a valuable asset. It allows them to precisely locate explored and unexplored areas and track truffles not yet ripe, which should be collected later. It is through the careful scrutiny of the earth and the collection of truffles, which to Mungau resemble 'little brains', that the prisoners lose their minds.

Moreover, as idleness at that stage can give way to insurrection, when prisoners are not engaged in the work designed by the Director, they have to follow the lead of the chief of the village, who is the administrator whose memory and sense of tradition direct the remaining hours of the men in archaeological excavations that search for the remains of an 'Original Chief'. As it happens, the place where the Old Camp was installed was obtained through the displacement of the village that used to be located at that site since time immemorial. The archaeological search, then, is a necessary act of reparation for the memory of the village, besides being a ploy to keep the prisoners' minds occupied. Underlying it all, there is the exploitative logic of the camps, which, transformed by the chief of the village, gets under the convenient cloak of tradition. The seemingly paradoxical nature of memory in the camp – as both crime and virtue – puzzles Mungau. The chief of the village then promptly offers the prisoner a clarification:

> "Tens de aprender a distinguir lembrança de tradição, Prisioneiro", diz. "Ambas dependem da memória mas são inteiramente diferentes. Enquanto a lembrança é um exercício individual e rebelde, fútil e pouco produtivo, a tradição é fruto da

ordem. Estes prisioneiros chegaram aqui com suas privadas e desprezíveis lembranças. Acusavam as autoridades de acontecimentos antigos, acontecimentos dispersos que hoje não fazem qualquer sentido. Aos poucos, contudo vão chegando à tradição, a este sentido supremo que é sabermos todos de onde vimos, esta certeza de virmos todos do mesmo lugar. E sobretudo, esta vontade de fazermos hoje como foi feito antigamente". (Borges Coelho, 2007: 102)

['You must learn to distinguish memory from tradition, Prisoner,' he says. 'Both depend on memory but they are entirely different. While remembrance is an individual and rebellious exercise, futile and not very productive, tradition is the fruit of order. These prisoners arrived here with their private and despicable memories. They accused the authorities of ancient events, scattered events that today make no sense. Little by little, however, they arrive at tradition, at this supreme meaning that is that we all know where we come from, this certainty that we all come from the same place. And above all, this desire to do today as it was done in the past.']

Spelt out in this quote is the importance of the ordination of memory into embodied tradition, for which the discarding of individual memories is vital. Tradition is shown in terms that are similar to the ones used by Nora, as it also relies on performance. Yet, the naturalised framing of tradition is deconstructed in the novel, for it is manipulated by the Village Chief first and foremost to answer his own agenda. The structural feature of this process is further explored as the narrative exposes how the manipulation of tradition is crafted by the camps' Director. As the reader comes to know later, it is the Director who, through the use of his network of spies, is the one in control of which archaeological remains will be found by the Chief's prisoners and which must remain hidden. Therefore, it is he, or the state he represents, that ultimately manipulates tradition in *Campo de Trânsito* – a cultural asset diligently used to serve state's interests.

Notwithstanding its critical approach to the manipulation of tradition, the manipulation of history in its written form is also important in *Campo de Trânsito*. The role of registration and archivization of the state is present early on in the novel when Mungau is exposed to the director's administrative folders even before meeting him in person. This is what leads the Director to entrust Mungau with the task of visiting both labour camps and to write down his interpretation of what he sees – 'Pretendemos um relatório escrito (uma versão inequívoca, portanto) dos problemas que surgem, das suas causas e dos seus efeitos' (Coelho, 2007:83) ['We want a written report (an unambiguous version, therefore) of the problems that arise, their causes and their effects']. As it is later revealed, the written and 'unequivocal' account of Mungau that the Director is aiming for consists of an interpretation of what he sees. Hence, Mungau's simple witness' account makes for a poor report: 'Falta aqui no relatório uma crença, um empenhamento sem o qual a procura de entendimento da realidade se torna num exercício fútil, diríamos mesmo perigoso!' ['The report lacks a belief, a commitment without which the search for understanding reality becomes a futile exercise, we would even say dangerous!']. Mungau still lacks the ideological commitment necessary to produce a piece of writing in tune with the openly fabricated mode of historicising used by the state. As the words of the Director evidence: '[n]ão há mal algum em manipular ideias. Pelo contrário, é para isso que elas servem!' ['[T]here is no harm in manipulating ideas. On the contrary, that's what they're for!'] (Coelho 2007: 147–148).

The manipulation of collective memory that is vital to the organisation of the society portrayed in *Campo de Trânsito* also shows its relevance in the Santomean *Aurélia de Vento*. Nonetheless, instead of developing an entirely allegorical basis for his discussion of memory, Albertino Bragança makes reference to the history of his country. In this particular passage, the farmer previously wronged by the state has already won the lawsuit over his land and is invited to join the jubilee of the association presided over by his daughter, Aurélia, who also invites a number of important political and social notables in the country (Bragança 2011: 93). As part of the festivities of the Association of Mutual Help, a celebratory lecture drawing from one of the most important foundational stories of the country is scheduled. The clash that will follow is already enunciated in the passage explaining how Aurélia managed to convince her father, a man unused to the company of the elite, to show up at the event:

> devia estar presente e usar mesmo da palavra, ele que incarnava, na sua opinião e na de muitos outros, o sentido de justiça, coragem e de defesa intransigente dos seus interesses, como acontecera ainda recentemente. Como recusar se estes eram os principais temas a serem abordados pelo famoso orador.
>
> ... "Yon Gato e a reivindicação social no S. Tomé e Príncipe do séc. XVI", matéria tanto mais aliciante quanto tão pouco se sabia dessa figura quase lendária, um cego à frente de uma revolta de proprietários em busca de poder político? (Bragança 2011: 95)

[He should be present and speak, as he embodied, in his opinion and that of many others, the sense of justice, courage and uncompromising defense of his interests, as had happened recently. How could he refuse if these were the main topics to be addressed by the famous speaker.

... 'Yon Gato and the social demand in S. Tomé and Príncipe in the 21st century. XVI', a subject all the more enticing as so little was known about this almost legendary figure, a blind man at the head of a revolt of landowners in search of political power?]

Delivered by an enticing professor with the suggestive name of Fausto Boaventura [Faust Fortunate], the lecture is designed to praise the spirit of social justice upon which the liberation movement has imagined the nation. The story of Yon Gato, as told by Bragança himself in his capacity as a researcher, is the following: 'Yannus (João) Ruiz "O Gato", vulgarmente apelidado "Yon Gato", fazendeiro mestiço que encabeçou, em 1553, um levantamento de proprietários nativos, em protesto contra o método de eleição de juízes à Câmara, os quais reclamavam para si o direito à respectiva candidatura e que para tal fortemente se armaram começaram a tomar a cidade' (Bragança 2013) ['Yannus (João) Ruiz "O Gato", commonly nicknamed "Yon Gato", a mestizo farmer who led, in 1553, a rising of native landowners, in protest against the method of electing judges to the Chamber, who claimed for themselves the right to their candidacy and that to this end they armed themselves strongly and began to take the city']. This revolt, in which locals attempted to take over political power from the hands of the White colonial elite, was reappropriated by the liberation movement and by the government that took over after the end of colonial dominance as one of the foundational stories inscribing the desire for independence at the very cultural basis of the young sovereign nation. Praised by the guest professor in *Aurélia*, this story – and by extension, the very idea of national mythology – is promptly criticised by Santos in its inherent contradiction as he asks: 'aqueles homens que o senhor gabou bastante, tinham ou não escravos? Porquê então elogiar tanto a revolta deles?' (Bragança 2011:101) ['Those men that you complimented a lot, did they have slaves or not? Why then praise their revolt so much?']

The scene, clearly designed to ratify Santos' sense of justice despite being White and raised in a family of colonial settlers, also exposes the fabricated nature of national memory-making in the country where the narrative is set. The professor and the elites surrounding him, including the very academy filled with its attested intellectuals with whom Fausto Boaventura would rather discuss, embody the institutions responsible for choosing and shaping the memories deserving of being elevated to the status of history that summon up the sense of nation filling up the hollow shell of a state built over the blueprint of a colony designed irrespectively of the cultural affiliations of its populations. In such a context, the critical intervention of Santos is amplified to reaffirm the character's position as the hero and de facto protagonist of the story. The vigour of his criticism is reassured precisely by his position as an outsider in terms of race as well as in terms of belonging to the country's official institutions and elites. This passage overtly denounces the complicity between the type of national memory celebrated through history and the interests of the ruling classes at the expense of the interests of the population at large. For this reason, Bragança, with his researcher's hat on, does not miss the opportunity to intervene in the history-making of his country. In his article 'Dia de Amador', the author recovers the history of Amador Vieira, whose 1595 uprising against slavery in the country still lacks diffusion to the wider population, despite being celebrated by the state after the achievement of independence, turning it into a 'símbolo artificialmente criado e só aparentemente tolerado' (2013) ['artificially created and only apparently tolerated symbol'] for the people of São Tomé and Príncipe.

Connecting these two novels in their consideration of memory is a critique of the processes surrounding the erection of collective memories, such as national myths and histories. They show that the very institutional effort necessary to authorise certain narratives already denounces the disembodied nature of the collective memories under construction in and by postcolonial states. In *Campo de Trânsito*, the distance between the state and the prisoners is so wide that it requires a whole project of memory reprograming so that the institution can make some sense for the inmates. In *Aurélia de Vento*, this distance comes to the fore in the denunciation of the bourgeois ideology behind the selection of what is to be celebrated as collective national memory, betraying the interests of the population. The much reinforced distance between what is represented as collective memory and the interests of those represented as collective in these two novels strongly suggests a distance between the project of national collective memories and a nation's peoples. It shows that national projects envisaged by the governing elites are very distant from those these elites are supposed to represent, which, in the terms carved out by Nora, would make these national memories into *lieux de mémoire* rather than *milieux de mémoire*.

The representation of national memory as a *lieu* or site rather than a *milieu* or environment evidences the incommunicability of the nationalist experience at this point in their country's postcoloniality. By constituting a *lieu*, national memory in these novels is exposed as 'extreme ideological, full of nationalism and far from being neutral or free of value judgements' (Boer 2008: 21). As such, this way of representing a national collective memory attests to the historicisation or disembodiment of nationalism itself. By portraying it as a manoeuvring tool to preserve political and economic power in the hands of self-serving elites, these novels' fictional rendering of the relationship between national memory and nationalism shows a mismatch that contrasts with what took place at the time of the rise of African literatures in Portuguese.

In these contemporary novels, memory is portrayed as something that has to be reclaimed from institutions and given back to the people. This is suggested in *Aurélia de Vento* as Fausto's dismissive answer to Santos, pulling the character even further away from the country's institutions. This passage, in fact, marks a turn in the story since what we have from that point onwards concerns Santos' family rather than his public life. The ensuing focus on the hostility of Clotilde towards Aurélia takes the novel to the terrain of the intimate and yet collective world of spirituality and tradition.

In a different way, this reclamation in *Campo de Trânsito* is tied to the notion of revolution. There, despite the efforts of the Director and his administrators, such as the Teacher and the Chief of the Village, the order in the complex of camps crumbles exactly because of manipulation. At the end of the narrative, the Director's decision to steal and hide the recently found skull of the Original Chief puts the workers of the Old Camp off-balance and prompts them to start a revolution that spreads through the whole prison complex. This way, it is possible to conclude that one of the most vital aspects of state-building in this novel by Coelho is not only the management of memory but also its key role in the antagonistic processes of domination and revolution, which is a way to conceive memory that is further explored by *Tiara, Marginais* and *Teoria Geral do Esquecimento*.

Towards a multidirectional memory

One of the most visible differences in terms of the role given to memory in *Tiara, Marginais* and *Teoria* from the one in *Aurélia* and *Campo* is these three novels' focus on individual memories. While the two previously analysed narratives problematise the constitution of collective memories, their Guinean, Cape Verdean and Angolan counterparts invest in the transformative potential of personal archives in collective memories. Such a focus adds an important dimension to the understanding of the dynamics of collective memory in the literatures of Portuguese-speaking Africa; this is because it uncovers the violence inherent to the clash between canonic and archival memory underlying the solidification of collective memories.

The concept of canonic and archival memory put forward by Aleida Assman can shed light on how these instances of personal memory interact with institutionalised vehicles of memory. In 'Canon and Archive', Assman draws attention to the fact that collective memories are largely composed by the active efforts of institutions such as the state which decides on the memories to canonise and the ones to keep out of public reach, often in the form of an archive. Drawing on the example of institutions like the museum, Assman concentrates on the material dimension of the archive as that which is concrete and stored away from public gaze, making it into 'a space that is located on the border between forgetting and remembering; its materials are preserved in a state of latency, in a space of intermediary storage (Zwischenspeicher)' (2008: 103). Seen as a concept rather than a strictly material artefact, the notion of archival memory can be useful for understanding the memory dynamics at stake in these three novels. As their analysis will demonstrate, by giving voice to characters who are marginalised in their respective societies, these narratives critically supplement mainstream heroic views of the nationalist movement as well as of the revolutionary bourgeoisie that seized power in these countries' aftermaths of independence.

One of the most striking differences in the representation of memory found in *Aurélia* and *Campo* from what is done in *Tiara*, *Marginais* and *Teoria* is that, in the latter group of novels, the perspective is almost exclusively that of characters victimised by the system, leaving very little space for the furthering of the psychological profile of members of the political and economic elites of the societies represented in each narrative. *Tiara* is the story of a woman who is denied the chance to participate in the construction of the country she helped to liberate; *Marginais* is the memoir of a young man who is systematically excluded from society and *Teoria* is a compound of stories that gives space mostly to the narratives of those who were victims of the colonial and post-independence political and economic systems. Even the two characters who had an active role in the oppressive systems to which they belonged, such as Monte and Jeremias, are portrayed, to quite a large degree, as victims themselves. They are constantly tormented by the gruesomeness of their past actions and can be seen as victims of their movements' respective ideologies.

In a supplementary relation to the treatment given to memory in *Campo de Trânsito* and *Aurélia de Vento*, where the focus rests on the relationship between collective memory and those in positions of power, these three novels' preference for the archival memory of the excluded deconstructs the process through which certain topics come to constitute *lieux de mémoire*. As it uncovers the fabricated, incomplete and ideology-laden nature of this condensation of memory, it exposes its inherently disembodied condition. Thus, in line with the argument by Assman, the relationship between canonic and archival memory in these five narratives is one in which the former represents a memory that is canonic because it is invested with aura and the latter, being archival, has the ability to destroy such aura (2008:102). This is evident in the comparison of the role ascribed to the skull of the Original Chief in *Campo* or to the narrative of Yon Gato in *Aurélia* with the way Tiara deals with her own memory. After tasting the bitterness of exclusion by her adoptive country, Muriti, the heroine decides to go back to her country of birth, where she had an idyllic childhood. The confrontation, though, is disappointing but enlightening: 'Tiara chegou, finalmente, à conclusão que o seu país era uma terra de sonho, situada algures num mundo imaginário desprovido de uma dimensão terrestre' (Embaló 1999: 214) ['Tiara finally came to the conclusion that her country was a dreamland, located somewhere in an imaginary world devoid of an earthly dimension']. Taking this reality shock as a therapeutic exercise, Tiara assertively disagrees with the suggestion she would have been better off not visiting her home country: 'Oh, não, pelo contrário! Ainda bem que fui. Era preciso! Eu tinha contas a ajustar com meu passado, agora está feito. Agora posso continuar a minha caminhada sem olhar para trás' (Embaló 1999: 215) ['Oh no, on the contrary! I'm glad I went. It was necessary! I had a score to settle with my past, now it's done. Now I can continue my journey without looking back'].

Tiara's revisionist approach to the postcolonial societies it portrays – Muriti as a metaphor for Guinea-Bissau and Porto Belo as a metaphor for Angola – ascribes an important role to memory as the protagonist journeys through mnemonic processes aimed at undoing the aura that protects sectioned national narratives from critique, historical scrutiny and institutional accountability. In a related manner, *Teoria Geral do Esquecimento*'s voicing of so many narratives of victimisation offers another dimension of Angola's history as it retells the first three decades post-independence from the perspective of the system's victims. While Agualusa's proposal of a theory of oblivion might seem contradictory at first, given the novel's heavy investment in acts of remembrance, a careful examination of the narrative's representation of the dynamic between active memory and forgetting in the arena of collective memory can certainly elucidate the pertinence of the title. Throughout the narrative, forgetting is a strategy deployed for the maintenance of the status quo. Perpetrators such as Monte were the ones willing to forget and to be forgotten:

> [Monte e]vita, inclusive, recordar os anos setenta, quando para preservar a revolução socialista, se permitiram, para utilizar um eufemismo grato aos agentes da polícia política, certos excessos.
>
> ...
>
> Certas pessoas padecem do medo de ser esquecidas. A essa patologia chama-se atazagorafobia. Com ele sucedia o oposto: vivia no terror de que nunca o esquecessem. Lá, no Delta do Okavango, sentira-se esquecido. Fora feliz. (Agualusa 2012: 65; 187)
>
> [[Monte]'d even avoided recalling the seventies, when in order to preserve the socialist revolution, certain excesses – to use a euphemism for which we're indebted to the agents of the political police – were permitted.

...

> There are some people who experience a fear of being forgotten. It's a pathology called athazagoraphobia. The opposite happened to him, he lived in terror that he would never be forgotten. There, on the Okavango Delta, he had felt forgotten. He had been happy.] (Agualusa 2015: 63; 184)

Forgetting, therefore, is an important aspect concerning content and context since its presence in the narrative emulates actual strategies used by real institutions to keep certain past actions away from public scrutiny. A device historically used given the position still occupied by its perpetrators in the elites of the country – mainly at the time of publication of this book when José Eduardo dos Santos was still serving as president during his thirty-eight-year-long mandate terminated in 2017. As Andreas Langenohl describes when observing the processes of memory and reconciliation in postauthoritarian societies, '[i]f perpetrators or their supporters still hold influential positions in society … the postauthoritarian government sees itself exposed to pressure to advocate impunity' (2008: 164). While not yet fitting into all the requirements for being called a postauthoritarian society, given that those in power during the hardest times of the regime are still part of the local political apparatus, the emergence of such a narrative in Angola certainly signals progress towards the breaking of this pattern. Notably, in the universe of the novel, the person who wants to forget the most is the only one among the core characters who dies. The message conveyed is communicated through the voice of the character, who was once a symbol of colonial oppression and violence. The former captain of the Portuguese army, now reborn as Jerónimo, chooses to remember as he confesses to being the murderer of Ludo's sister and brother-in-law:

> Não se atormente mais. Os erros nos corrigem. Talvez seja necessário esquecer. Devíamos praticar o esquecimento [disse Ludo].
>
> Jerónimo abanou a cabeça, irritado. Rabiscou mais umas palavras no caderno. Entregou-o ao filho:
>
> O pai não quer esquecer. Esquecer é morrer, diz ele. Esquecer é uma rendição. (Agualusa 2012: 221)
>
> [Don't torture yourself any more. Our mistakes correct us. Perhaps we need to forget. We should practise forgetting, reaching for oblivion [said Ludo].'

Jeremias shook his head, irritated. He scribbled a few more words in the little notebook. He handed it to his son.
'My father doesn't want to forget. Forgetting is dying, he says. Forgetting is surrender.] (Agualusa 2015: 229)

The attitude of Jeremias/Jerónimo clearly gestures towards a process of reconciliation between Angola and its violent Portuguese colonial past. Equally, Ludo's transformation and slow process of integration into the country are another indication that, in the realm of the novel, the trauma of colonisation is a wound in the course of healing to the extent in which it has a place in the country's collective memory. Ludo also remembers her sins, and, as the young Angolan boy who saved her life teaches, Ludo's remembrance will calm the dead. 'A minha mãe dizia que os mortos sofrem de amnesia. Sofrem mais ainda com a pouca memória dos vivos. Você se lembra dele [o jovem morto por Ludo] todos os dias, e isso é bom. Deveria se lembrar dele rindo, dançando. ... Conversar sossega os mortos.' (Agualusa 2012: 161) [My mum used to say that the dead suffer from amnesia. They suffer even more because of the poor memories of the living. You remember him every day, and that's good. You should laugh as you remember him, you should dance. ... Talking calms the dead.] (Agualusa 2015: 165). The clear contrast that Jeremias' and Ludo's acts of memory establish with how the traumatic events of the country's most recent past are treated indicates that, while one tries to reconcile the colonial past through memory, the same does not hold when it comes to the wrongdoings of the post-independence regime. In this context, the oblivion theorised in the story is the cement that, at the same time, binds society together while keeping it from moving forward towards a comprehensive postcolonial conciliation capable of placing the complexity of colonial and post-independence history into collective memory. It is a situation that allocates the systems' victims – both the dead and living – to the margins of memory, on the threshold of oblivion, the only place from which these societies' subalterns, such as Sérgio from *Marginais*, can speak.

The narrative of Sérgio, whose subtitle is *Apontamentos de um Vagabundo* [Notes from a Tramp], is a testimony to the lives of those who are successfully forgotten by his society. Furthering the narrative strategies seen in *Tiara* and *Teoria,* where we find a growing focus on the excluded, *Marginais* purposefully excludes any major elaboration of characters who are part of the privileged classes. Those, when represented, come in the heavily typified colours of stock characters, establishing an interesting contrast with the different levels of elaboration and depth ascribed to the characters of the lower strata of the represented society. Invested with a strength deeply connected with the strategy to feature solely those who are excluded from political and economic power, the novel reminds us that invisibility is directly linked to memory. For this reason, Sérgio is compelled to remember and to register in posterity not only his own story but also those of friends and neighbours whose lives were like his, a theatre of horrors and precarity (Rocha 2010: 62). Oblivious to the country's collective memory, these characters' only weapon against the invisibility that leaves them vulnerable to all sorts of abuse is to remember. As the narrator puts it when he gives his manuscript to a former classmate who, in the story, publishes it after Sérgio's suicide, to remember was the only way to keep alive: '[n]estas páginas consegui afogar muita mágoa e se não morri antes foi por estar com a mente ocupada nestas anotações.' (Rocha 2010: 13) ['[i]n these pages I managed to drown a lot of sorrow and if I didn't die sooner it was because my mind was occupied with these notes.']

It is through the material registration of their existence that Sérgio and his friends, the Pitboys gang, make themselves visible both in the public space and for the elites. It is striking to notice how much effort these characters put into voicing their existence, transforming their stubborn perseverance into resistance. In this context, graffiti and vandalism are the means through which the boys make themselves defiantly visible as they force the anger and dissent of the excluded in public and private spaces.

> imprimíamos nas paredes verdadeiras obras de arte depois de defecarmos. A habilidade dos dedos das mãos tomavam contornos de um pênis majestoso, a boca de um canto de *rap* se confundia com o sexo ameaçador da mulher; disposto à engolir o mundo a sua volta. O grafismo na parede parecia ter vida. Pichávamos as paredes dos homens grandes, dos coronéis e as impressões ficavam lá, pois ninguém podia mandar-nos ficar calados. Já não era necessário roer as unhas ou coçar a cabeça para aliviar a emoção glandular. Se estivesse deprimido, dava uma *cacada* de pedra à montra da loja e fugia. Há melhor terapia do que quebrar os vidros de uma montra num país

onde os filhos dos pobres são excluídos e a discriminação é estimulada? ... As paredes
das casas foram feitas para que pudéssemos desabafar a dor que nos atormentava a
alma. (Rocha 2010:39–40)

[we printed real works of art on the walls after we defecated. The skill of the fingers
took on the contours of a majestic penis, the mouth of a rap song was confused with
the woman's threatening sex; willing to swallow the world around it. The graphics
on the wall seemed alive. We spray-painted the walls of important men, the colonels
and our inprint remained there, as no one could tell us to remain silent. It was no
longer necessary to bite your fingernails or scratch your head to relieve glandular
emotions. If I were depressed, I would would throw a stone in the store window and
run away. Is there better therapy than breaking shop windows in a country where
the children of the poor are excluded and discrimination is encouraged? ... The walls
of the houses were made so that we could vent the pain that tormented our souls.]

Besides clearly staging aspects of local class struggle 'in an urban environment increasingly defined by the segregation and control of social space'
(Ferrell 1997: 78), the description of the role given to graffiti and vandalism
in the novel goes beyond the reclamation of public space for those systematically excluded from it, which frames much of the understanding of these
phenomena by scholarship. This quote also sums up the role ascribed to
memory in the novel since, as deployed by the Pitboys, graffiti and vandalism are no more acts of reclamation of space than vehicles for their voices,
which are violently imposed by them as retribution to the violence they
are subjected to as they are silenced by society. The process of inscription
that these manifestations represent turns the boys' tools of oppression into
weapons of resistance. Hence, the scatology forced upon the protagonist
and his equals on a daily basis is thrown back at the so-called respectable
members of the local bourgeoisie, a process in which faeces are transformed
into paint and explicit portrayals of genitalia are deemed appropriate for
public display. The calming effects of such a type of expression on Sérgio
and his friends also reiterate the protagonist's aforementioned view of
his memoir in the beginning of the story and reveal the psychologically
disturbing effects of their voicelessness. In this context, vandalism becomes
a form of social catharsis, a temporary relief needed for the excluded to
go on existing in the shadows. Yet, despite the relevance of the disruptive
potential of these acts of vandalism to the excluded social structure of the
island, it is important to emphasise that these manifestations also constitute

important acts of memory. Echoing Rothberg's assertion that 'memory is the past made present' (2009: 3), Sérgio and his friends' graffiti dialogues with the very premise of the memoir, which aims at presanctifying those who are absent from the social picture of their society.

Despite their contrast with *Campo* and *Aurélia*, *Tiara*, *Teoria* and *Marginais* dialogue with memory as a theme and a process in a complementary way. Together, these five novels offer a wide and rich panorama of memory in the twenty-first century narratives of Portuguese-speaking Africa that shows a critical engagement with national canonic history. The distancing of the point of view of the local bourgeoisies, represented only insofar as they constitute objects of critical scrutiny, indicates that in the face of the establishment of political independence, the critical impetus of these literatures has now turned to the postcolonial status quo. This movement reiterates the critical vigour and social commitment that have marked these literary histories as they carry on the tradition of contributing to social development by going against the grain. In the same way that the independence was achieved through complex processes of legitimisation of the nationalist claim led by the local elites with the support of the literary registration of social critique in the period around the anticolonial struggles, in contemporary postcoloniality, the newly established status quo is the object of critique in this socially committed literature. In its engagement with a colonial memory that saw Africa as a *locus horrendous*, literature works towards the construction of local memories based on the valuation of local cultures as well as political and economic claims. At a time in which the nationalist bourgeoisie manipulates history to glorify its own cause, literature gives voice to the narratives of those who question the single-sided national commemoration that leaves aside the (hi)stories of violence, dissent and inequality that constitute the complex fabric of postcoloniality.

Put alongside each other, we see that these novels' critique of the institutional manipulation of national memory uncovers its transit from *milieu de mémoire* to *lieu de mémoire*. These novels also contest mainstream versions of national memory by actively voicing the memories of those who had the courage to disagree with the local ruling classes and became victims of political isolation, repressive violence and social and economic exclusion. In their critical relationship with canonic versions of national memory, these novels embark on a struggle over memory as they recount history from the perspective of the underrepresented, using these archival testimonies to desacralise the aura and the canonicity of nationalistic movements and independent governments, preventing them from addressing their underlying contradictions. In this sense, while *Campo* and *Aurélia* question the fabricated nature of collective memories backed by institutional needs such as the state's, *Tiara* heavily critiques the nationalist bourgeoisie and deromanticises the years of socialist experiment, and *Marginais* denounces the catastrophic failures of the current neoliberal projects put in place in the aftermath of socialism. These novels highlight the violence underpinning the memory battles at stake. In *Campo,* the manipulation of memory is supported by the violence of a state apparatus in the form of a prison system. In *Aurélia,* the violence is manifested in the form of the ostracisation of those who disagree with official historical narratives. The same happens in *Tiara*, whose defeated protagonist falls victim to social exclusion, so that her narrative of dissent is silenced and the sanctity of the status quo protected. *Teoria* directly links acts of remembrance to social, economic and political resistance and reconciliation, while acts of oblivion are connected to oppression, exclusion and subjugation in all these domains. And finally, in *Marginais*, we have social invisibility as a mode of systemic violence. They are all depictions that, by focusing on the dissident content of these archives of memory well situated in terms of gender, sexuality, race and class, seem to push for the transformation of what can be perceived as current models of competitive memory into a complex whole of multidirectional memory.

Conceived by Michael Rothberg, multidirectional memory accounts for a way to conceptualise memory that 'considers a series of interventions through which social actors bring multiple traumatic pasts into an heterogeneous and changing post-World War II present' (2009: 4). Although Rothberg's theorisation is grounded in the study of remembrances of the Holocaust, the concept is very transferrable to the countries of contemporary postcolonial Portuguese-speaking Africa. In in his study, Rothberg uses the concept to support his hypothesis that Holocaust memories do not necessarily obliterate other kinds of human suffering and articulate with the remembrance of other genocides. Here, the proposition is useful to remind us that these novels' narratives of postcolonial distress do not go against the nationalist project but, on the contrary, enrich it. By denouncing the problems and contradictions faced by each respective society in the aftermath of independence, these narratives, to paraphrase Rothberg, consider a series of interventions through which social actors bring multiple traumatic pasts into a heterogeneous and changing *postcolonial* present. It is a project that, much in line with the literary traditions of the countries in question, is inclusive in nature and fundamentally necessary for an everlasting critical movement that is, in itself, for the sovereign nation, even when it is critical of the contemporary state.

Postcolonial violence – from physical to symbolic

Bruce Lawrence and Aisha Karim, in *On Violence*, affirm that '[t]here is no general theory of violence apart from its practices' (2007: 7). Henceforth, this chapter resorts to the anticolonial theorisation of violence in the work of Fanon and Cabral to understand what seems to be an intrinsic relationship between violence and postcoloniality. As discussed earlier, the violence permeating the postcolonial works of the African literatures in Portuguese cannot be dissociated from contextual revolutionary practices, nor can it be disconnected from the single-party socialist and democratic neoliberal practices that deeply transformed their postcolonialities.

This chapter's approach to the representation of violence in the contemporary fiction of Portuguese-speaking Africa has concentrated on three forms of violence found in the novels analysed. Emerging as a result of empirical comparison, state violence, gender violence and memory violence point to largely unexplored links between modes of violence and political practices in these literatures. Together, these novels suggest that literary registration of violence in Portuguese-speaking Africa gradually change their focus from physical to symbolic violence as postcoloniality develops and non-democratic forms of government lose their strength. The further from undemocratic forms of government these societies are in both diegetic and historic time, the more prominence is given to the symbolic, rather than physical, dimensions of violence. In the following paragraphs, attention will be given to how this transition is presented in the corpus with the view of assessing whether they point towards new articulations of violence that are inherent to their contemporary context of postcoloniality.

Symbolic violence is defined by Bourdieu and Wacquant as 'the violence of which one is both the subject and the object' (1992: 166). It is a violence in which 'social agents are knowing agents who, even when they are subjected to determinisms, contribute to producing the efficacy of that which determines them insofar as they structure what determines them' (1992: 167–168); it is a form of violence that is not necessarily physical but which can be so. As Bourdieu once acknowledged, 'even when based on naked force, that of arms or money, [violence] always has a symbolic dimension' (1992: 172). In relation to the sample of fiction analysed, Bourdieu's terminology can be useful, for it allows the identification of forms of violence that are more subtle than the kind of phenomena that critics tend to discuss when speaking of violence in these literatures. As a result, it enables a *longue durée* of violence to be noticed, contrary to what happens when the focus lays on physical violence, which is often seen as an episodic occurrence, often circumscribed to singular events of limited – even if prolonged – duration, such as the struggle for independence, civil wars or political persecution put in motion by a given political regime.

In *Campo de Trânsito*, *Teoria Geral do Esquecimento* and *Marginais*, explicit physical violence is symbolically laden and perpetrated almost exclusively by the coercive apparatus of a strong, authoritarian state or in reaction to it. The very setting of a camp administered by state representatives in *Campo* is illustrative of it. Physical violence in the story comes either in the form of arrests, isolation, forced labour and rape perpetrated by the state through its agents or in the form of an inmate's revolt against the state at the end of the narrative. In the case of *Teoria*, the concentration of physical violence rests in the hands of the state agent Monte, who becomes gradually more hesitant to fulfil his duties as the regime opens up politically and economically until he completely abandons his functions after the end of the Angolan civil war. Even in *Marginais*, where the diegesis is set long after independence, the police are shown to be the most violent in the first part of the narrative, when the protagonist and his friends mirror the youth of the newly independent country as they are portrayed in their early teenage years. Using the birth year of the protagonist (1977) to determine the approximate time of his arrest and sexual abuse by local police – which happened a little before he claimed to be sixteen years old – we are left with the approximate time stamp of 1992, a year that marks the democratic turn of the country as a new constitution ratifies the adoption of multiparty democracy. Therefore, the observation of these physically violent episodes shows that, despite being connected to modes of symbolic violence, the representation of physical abuse is episodic and portrayed as connected to finite political or social situations.

While such representations of violence in *Campo de Trânsito*, a narrative that is confined almost in entirety to the space of suspended time of the camp just like its inmates, the other four novels discussed cover expressive amounts of chronological and historic time. The Guinean narrative runs for twenty-four years between the struggle for independence and the consolidation of the political sovereignty of its fictional African country. The Cape Verdean novel covers the length of the lifetime of its protagonist, from 1977 to 1999. Although the span of the Santomean narrative is never revealed, its relatively short time span of a few years is often stretched by narrations of past events of relevance to the story. Providing the narratives with a perfect canvas onto which the long processes of change in their society can be painted, these long time spans are essential for showing the transition in focus from physical to symbolic violence.

In *Tiara*, the presence of physical violence is circumscribed to the part of the narrative where the struggle for independence is portrayed. Combined with it, and gradually taking more prominence in the oppression of the protagonist of the novel, we have instances of symbolic violence. They are occurrences where Tiara is both object and subject of violence, given that she is both victim of and complicit with the system sustaining that kind of violence up until her decision to part from it, retiring from the country's politically oppressive scene. Similarly, although practiced on a larger scale given the scope of the narrative, *Teoria Geral do Esquecimento* stages a change in terms of the predominance of modes of violence from the physical to the symbolic. As the analysis of the novel's representation of gender relations has shown, in the beginning of the story, both modes of violence are very much intertwined. Whereas the death of Jeremias Carrasco opens the novel with a single scene mashing together revolutionary violence and gender violence, it ends with a notable absence of physical violence, whose apex is in the metaphorical nature of Monte's staged assassination.

Marginais and *Aurélia de Vento*, on the other hand, show more nuanced renderings of this phenomenon. Even though the presence of physical violence does not disappear completely from the Cape Verdean novel, after the episode where policemen rape a boy, we observe a change in the way this mode of violence is represented. Physical abuse is no longer portrayed as a prerogative of the state's coercive apparatus but rather as a widespread practice throughout civil society. Along with it, the emphasis on the pervasiveness of symbolic violence in that society is increased as it comes to constitute the most extensive mode of violence deployed in the rest of the narrative. Finally, the post-independence and seemingly democratic environment of *Aurélia* simply does not depict instances of physical violence, with the exception of the failed attempt against the life of the protagonist ordered by her stepmother. Yet, the whole narrative is permeated by symbolic forms of violence perpetrated mostly against Aurélia and her father – a woman and a foreigner.

Put alongside each other, the novels constituting this fictional corpus point towards a consistent trend when it comes to the representation of violence in the Portuguese-speaking African postcolony. The novels that explicitly portray or suggest a setting similar to the early days of sovereignty of their respective postcolonies, such as *Tiara, Teoria Geral do Esquecimento* and *Campo de Trânsito*, tend to emphasise a predominance of physical over symbolic violence that is often concentrated in the hands of the state. The narratives whose internal time span is long enough to reach the last decade of the twentieth century, such as *Teoria*, tend to change their focus from state-inflicted physical violence to the permanence of symbolic violence. Lastly, the narratives completely set in the aftermath of independence, such as *Aurélia de Vento* and *Marginais*, tend to give more space to the representation of symbolic violence tempered with physical violence that emerges from members of civil society and not from the state.

Seen from this perspective, these narratives' societal portraits suggest intrinsic connections between violence and political structures in early twenty-first century Portuguese-speaking Africa. The revolutionary violence needed to push colonialism out of their countries was the main resource deployed by the newly independent single-party states in order to secure the revolution. With time and the maturation of democratic structures, state violence dims, and literature seems to turn its critical eye to symbolic forms of violence that maintain social structures of internal dominance. For this reason, issues such as discourse actualisation, performance, ideological apparatus and power, addressed in Chapter 2, are consistent in these novels' representations of the state. Keith Topper's view of Bourdieu's concept of symbolic violence speaks of its relevance as a mechanism 'for investigating vexing problems of democratic theory and practice, and particularly for combating perversions of those political values inextricably linked to democratic forms of life: freedom, equality, and social justice' (2001: 31). Similarly, the analysis in this chapter has shown that the literary registration of change from physical to symbolic violence accompanying the abandonment of more totalitarian forms of government and the development of democratic forms of political organisation registers the perversion of revolutionary political values and the ways in which they live on the new political ideologies. The truculence of the state – be it physically violent as seen in *Teoria* or legally enacted as we see in *Aurélia* – the gendered forms of oppression as the maintenance of gender hierarchies, and the tight control and manipulation of historic memory can only maintain a dynamics of domination that is at odds with the democratic premises adopted in the aftermath of the single-party state regime in the 1990s. In the past, these dynamics were in place to sustain colonial capitalism and then to keep the integrity of single-party socialism; today, they are deployed to maintain the predatory practices of democratic neoliberalism.

CHAPTER 4

The Matter of Wealth

[T]he political issue of our times is not whether there will be a transition from historical capitalism to something else. That is as certain as we can be about such things. The political issue of our times is whether this something else, the outcome of the transition, will be morally fundamentally different from what we have now, will be progress.

– Immanuel Wallerstein, *Historical Capitalism with Capitalist Civilization* (1996: 107)

Seen from a world-systems perspective, the history of modern Portuguese-speaking Africa is embedded in the expansion of European capitalism into a world-system. According to Wallerstein, to the extent in which their role was mainly to provide enslaved labour to plantation colonies elsewhere, African territories were an external force in the arena of the capitalist world economy. However, with the Industrial Revolution (1750) and the stabilisation of British hegemony in Europe after the defeat of France in the Napoleonic Wars (1815), there was a need to expand the consumer markets, which allowed the incorporation of modern African territories to the peripheries of the world-system as colonies (2000: 61–62). Despite requiring some adaptation to the specificity of the Portuguese territorial possessions in Africa, Wallerstein's general model is still valid as a means to understand the basis of wealth generation and distribution in a large portion of the continent. Different from what took place in the core economies of Western Europe, what drove Portugal towards its African colonies was rather the loss of Brazil (1822) than a drive for industrial advance or hegemonic position in the world-system. Yet, even though the process of incorporation of the African territories into Portuguese peripheries came much later (Alexandre 2004: 963) if compared to the British case, the premise of economic inequality underlying the social organisation of the peripheries of the industrialised West has also marked the formation of the newly independent countries of Portuguese-speaking Africa.

To think of the presence of inequality in the various political and economic formations of the five Portuguese-speaking African countries is essential if one is willing to see the themes emerging in their contemporary literature in the *longue durée* of the history of these countries and in the interplay between transnational and local contexts. Understood as a system 'based on a division of labour between its core, its semiperiphery, and its periphery in such a way that there is unequal exchange between the sectors but dependence of all the sectors, both economically and politically, on the continuance of this unequal exchange' (Wallerstein 2000: 56), the capitalist world-economy is a system that fundamentally thrives in material unevenness. This perspective restores the material and concrete dimensions of terms such as colony, single-party state and multiparty democracy that have only recently been rematerialised in the literary critique of the field. After a relatively long hiatus since the emergence of anticolonial literature that gave aesthetic form to the political organisation of the colony and the economic enterprise of colonialism, scholars slowly started developing more in-depth studies of the reverberations of economic and social conditions in literary aesthetics in the aftermath of independence (Rothwell 2004; Owen 2007; Arenas 2011; Martins 2012; Jones 2017; Tavares 2018; Maurits 2022, to name but a few). In this context, terms such as single-party state and multiparty democracy can no longer be dissociated from their counterparts, socialism and neoliberalism, as these specific modes of creation and distribution of wealth shape not only expressions of subjectivity but also the form of these literatures.

The inequality in terms of wealth generation and distribution intrinsic to the modes of production employed by the Portuguese colonial capitalist system was one of the main reasons why the nationalist movements of the Portuguese colonies in Africa opted for socialism. As Cabral puts it, 'whether on the economic level, or on the social and cultural levels, imperialist capital has been a long way from fulfilling in our countries the historical mission carried out by capital in the countries of accumulation' (1979: 127), or as Walter Rodney wittingly left to posterity '[t]he

Portuguese stand out because they boasted the most and did the least' (1982: 206). The level of abandonment of the colonies was alarming, and in a text from1960 published in English under the title 'The facts about Portugal's African colonies', Cabral summarises the situation. In Angola and Mozambique, the most fertile areas of land were taken from Africans and distributed between colonial companies and settlers. In Guinea-Bissau, where the number of settlers was small and the whole of the agricultural work was done by Africans, farmers had to face selling prices that were driven down by authorities and further lowered by colonial buyers. The vast majority of wealth produced in the colonies by colonial companies would be sent to the metropole and not reinvested locally. Protectionist laws forced Africans to buy excessively expensive industrialised products from Portugal while having to pay high taxes. Forced labour was a practice in the colonial farms of São Tomé and in the public sector of Guinea-Bissau, Angola and Mozambique. Workers facing mortality rates as high as 30 per cent were rented out for other in-land activities and exported to work in the mines of South Africa and Rhodesia. In addition, there were few doctors, illiteracy levels were about 99 per cent and Africans that were not assimilated (assimilation rate was 0.3 per cent) had no political rights (Cabral 1979: 17–25).

The situation for Portugal, on the other hand, was not too bad. Despite the argument of a Portuguese colonial exceptionalism, often oscillating between the questionable aggrandisement of its uniqueness and the equally questionable smallness of its colonial exploitative practices, the semiperipheral position of the Portuguese Colonial Empire *vis-à-vis* the British Empire is defended by scholars as established as Boaventura de Sousa Santos (2001). Morier-Genoud and Cahen categorically state that '[e]ssentially, the Portuguese Empire was not different from other empires. … Its difference with other European empires] is a difference of degree, not of nature' (2013: 7). The Portuguese were, according to the authors, 'driven by the same global factors driving [other European] capitalist economic expansion – a search for new markets and primary resources' (2013: 3). As the well-documented study of Pedro Lains titled 'Causas do colonialismo português em África, 1822–1975' [Causes of Portuguese colonialism in Africa, 1822–1975] proposes, the income achieved by Portugal through the exploitation of its African colonies was essential for the growth and development of the colonial metropole. The deal seemed so good for Portugal that, even computing the losses imposed by the African wars of independence fought on three separate fronts on the continent, the author states that '[é] plausível que a contribuição das colónias de África para o financiamento da balança de transacções correntes [da metropole] tenha sido mais importante do que os eventuais efeitos negativos do "sistema colonial"' (1998: 492) ['[it] is plausible that the contribution of Africa's colonies to financing the current account balance [of the metropolis] was more important than the possible negative effects of the "colonial system"] for the structure of Portuguese economy.

Once the gains of Portugal were achieved via extractivism and exploitation of the African populations enforced by white colonial settlers and administrators, little infrastructure was left behind when most Portuguese returned to Europe in the immediate post-independence period. The lack of knowledge transfer, which was characteristic of the Portuguese colonial enterprise, left a legacy of underdevelopment for the recently formed governments to overcome (Birmingham 2002: 150; Forrest 2010: 239–240; Newitt 2002: 203; Malaquias 2007: 34). As discussed in Chapter 3, the experience of the people's war was neither enough to engage all populations with the socialist ideology nor to significantly unite the peoples on the three fronts where it took place. As a consequence, the hurried departure of Portuguese personnel after independence left the ex-colonies in Africa unable to effectively operate modes of wealth generation that were set in place during colonialism, regardless of whether they would fit the economic and societal views of the new sovereign governments. In addition to this, all five newly independent African countries had to face the doubly difficult challenge of planning for the future while being virtually unable to provide for the present. Such a situation entailed a material precariousness that further complicated the possibilities of success for the newly established socialist regimes that would last from the mid-1970s through the early 1990s. The need for survival was to put ideological commitments to the test.

Wealth in the socialist years

Commentators show that the immediate wealth distribution in post-independence Portuguese-speaking Africa did not change greatly when compared to colonial times, leaving room for a pragmatics of subsistence that stretched colonial structures of inequality into post-independence history. As expected, the situation was diverse in each of the five countries. In Angola, Mozambique and Guinea-Bissau, the three fronts where the struggle for independence was fought and colonial presence was visible – although minimally in Guinea-Bissau if compared to what happened in Angola and Mozambique – cultural, ethnic, ideological and regional divides posed obstacles to their development in different ways.

In Angola, the departure of the settlers gave way to the widening of internal divisions that led the country to its twenty-seven-year-long civil war, reflecting a deep ideological divide – the Marxist-Leninist MPLA vs. the Liberal UNITA – that, for scholars such as Assis Malaquias (2007: 65), also represented an ethnic dispute. In the country's capital, Luanda, the ethnic and economic fronts saw a clash for power in the state apparatus between prestigious old *creole* elites, relatively educated black colonial *assimilados* (assimilated), and the growing number of brown *mestiços* (mestizos) who thought themselves racially better than their Black fellow citizens (Birmingham 2002: 148–149). Draining the country of resources and impairing the development of basic infrastructures essential for interlinking the various parts of the country, regional divides became deeper and were intersected by the dichotomy of urban vs. rural. Such intersecting divides clearly influenced the way in which socialism failed to serve the commonwealth.

The lack of socialist consciousness was among the main reasons why Angolan socialism ended up becoming a machine for personal enrichment. Added to all the divides fracturing the social construct of the country, the absence of a socialist education for the masses engendered the general mismanagement of the *res publica* (Bhagavan 1980: 23), and with it the need for further concentration of power in the hands of a central government conceived as always under threat. Within such a climate, the state-party lived under the paranoia of betrayal that resulted in an incredible wave of violence and hardening of the regime, referred to in Chapter 3. Therefore, concentration of power and access to wealth in the hands of those faithful to the party was the course taken by the state during its socialist period.

In the case of Mozambique, the party-state commitment to the Marxist-Leninist doctrine did not interact easily with the traditional forms of organisation present in extensive parts of the country that were left unchanged by the colonial power. As is widely known, colonial settlements and activities were concentrated on coastal cities, and in order to manage the interior, colonial administration would empower local chiefs, leaving their laws and customs in place as long as they would not get in the way of colonial extractivism. The fissures within the country – between regions, ethnicities and ideological orientations – led to a civil war that was primarily a war of destabilisation of the ruling party by destruction of the country's already meagre infrastructure (Newitt 2002: 210–211). Consequently, concentration of wealth in the hands of members of the party-state, despite being less expressive than in Angola, had as motif the war threat and the ideological nature of a political elite that shared little with the majority of the population, which was not as well versed in European episteme nor convinced by Marxist-Leninist secularism (Cahen 1993: 51).

Despite its contextual specificities, the situation in Guinea-Bissau shared two main characteristics with the cases in Angola and Mozambique. Inheritance of the colonial social order was even more of a burden to the recently formed government since the country was so sparsely colonised and the local structures remained in the hands of the de facto indigenous power (Forrest 2002: 237). This situation compromised the effective central planning of resources and investment and benefited the rise of a politics of personalism that marked the division of wealth and political power in the country, stalling the development of the infrastructure necessary for the success of a socialist planned economy. A series of unfortunate infrastructural investments pushed the country into starting its wave of privatisation as early as 1984, and by 1987 it was already borrowing money from the IMF (Forrest 2002: 240–241). The Guinean commitment to socialism can be matched with the other two small economies in this group of five: São Tomé and Príncipe and Cape Verde.

Although the trajectories of these two economies have little in common with the cases of much larger countries like Angola and Mozambique, their participation in the same colonial system ensured the presence of similar structural issues that determined the (un)success of their implementation of socialism. As both territories had a very small presence of White settlers to be catered to – Cape Verde was even less so than São Tomé and Príncipe – both countries had very little infrastructure put in place during colonialism. São Tomé and Príncipe, a country that did not yet know of its oil reserves and whose economy was heavily reliant on its cocoa culture, was underdeveloped and badly managed after independence. The *forro* elite, who seized the place of the White settlers in the country's internal social hierarchy, knew little of the plantation work that was usually delegated to contracted workers who were kept away from administrative posts. Clientelist culture turned the public sector into an inefficient machine plagued by nepotism and misuse, further depleting the scarce resources of the country. In this context, nationalisation worked as a legal way to set the country's assets definitely in the hands of the local elite, and inequality became the social rule (Seibert 2002: 300–301).

In Cape Verde, the neglect of colonial administration allied to the country's climatic challenges threatened the population's well-being to the extent that the newly installed government was obliged to adopt more pragmatic economic measures in line with their domestic needs, despite its professed ideological commitment to socialism. While the mineral-poor- and drought-prone archipelago state of Cape Verde did not encounter major problems in terms of ethnic or ideological divide given its largely *mestiço* population, it faced a problem more fundamental than colonialism: the widespread state of famine. The absence of substantial colonial investment amplified the catastrophic results of the periodic lack of rain of which the country is a victim, pushing its government to rely on international aid to feed its population. For this reason, the government's approach has been seen as 'sustainable human development rather than socialism' (Silva Andrade 2002: 268). On the other hand, as the scarcity of data relating to wealth inequality in the first political and economic period of independent Cape Verde seems to indicate, it was the excessive

concentration of wealth that aggravated the country's poverty during the
years of single-party socialism.

Wealth in the times of neoliberal economy

With the fall of the Soviet Union, the most fragile economies in
Portuguese-speaking Africa were amongst the first to open up politically and economically. São Tomé and Príncipe and Cape Verde were so
dependent on foreign aid and trapped by the conditions it imposed that,
regardless of the ideological commitment to the end of exploitation of
men by men, both started the transition to a nominal market economy
in 1988 and 1987, respectively (Silva Andrade 2002: 260; Seibert
2002: 302), embracing multiparty democracy soon after. Although
the injection of capital from the free market economy helped to improve the lives of the populations of both countries in the short term,
the long-term side effects of wealth inequality are yet to be overcome.
The legacy of kinship and clientelism that continued in the aftermath of
the economic transition has earned the governments of São Tomé and
Príncipe the reputation of a corrupt machine that not only fails to develop the country but also devours the potential gains of its newfound
oil reserves (Conti-Brown 2010). Cape Verde's political and economic
opening, too, seems to have been more profitable for overseas investor
groups than for its populations, as the large gains of the tourism industry
are remitted offshore and cheap imported commodities threaten the fragile informal economy based on diasporic remittances that sustain much
of its population (Fikes 2010). Despite now being able to at least feed
its population in cases of emergency, the neoliberalisation of the Cape
Verdean economy seems to have brought with it a wealth inequality un-
seen during the socialist period (Sangreman Proeça 2009: 39). Similarly
devoid of any economic infrastructure, a situation aggravated by its flagrant political instability, Guinea-Bissau, which embarked on the IMF's
Structural Adjustment Programs of neoliberalisation in 1987 (Forrest
2002: 241), not only lives from international aid but has become an

important point in the international drug trafficking route. The country is now seen as a distribution hub for the cocaine in transit from its manufacturing sites in South America towards its consumer markets in Europe (McGuinn 2015).

These three cases show that while the journey into neoliberalism may have helped these countries mitigate some of the most immediate problems inherited from an utterly extractivist and exploitative form of colonialism, it has either aggravated or created new long-term problems in terms of wealth inequality. The withdrawal of the state from its role in promoting economic and social development at a time when it had not yet managed to guarantee the most basic living standards to its peoples left these countries' populations by and large unshielded against the predatory practices of a capitalism whose international abstraction relies on concrete exploitation at the local level. While some disillusioned critique of these post-colonial single-party regimes would ironically suggest that independence merely afforded the chance to replace one set of foreign exploiters with indigenous ones, the same kind of logic would support the argument that the transition to neoliberalism has given way to a backward movement in which indigenous exploiters are once again replaced by foreign ones, only this time protected by the faceless anonymity of the the international financial system.

The diverse pathways taken by Angola and Mozambique in their transition from socialism to neoliberalism do not mean that they led to less problematic outcomes. One should be careful not to diminish the impact of the destabilisation wars on these countries' state initiatives. Among their disastrous effects were the undermining of existing infrastructure along with the inhibition of the development of new ones, the draining of a vast array of resources, especially manpower, which was affected by the loss of life and life-changing injuries caused by conflict (Cammack 1989). The case of Mozambique demonstrates how conflict-induced debilitation influenced the country's transition into capitalism. As Newitt has put it, '[t]he changes in economic policy had been planned long before the peace process began. It is perhaps more helpful to see the peace process as arising out of the change in political and economic direction rather than the shift in economic direction coming as a result of peace' (2002: 227).

Peace in Mozambique had much to do with the dismantling of the Soviet Union and the gradual decrease of financial support for Frelimo. This international scenario forced the party to confer certain legitimacy to RENAMO once they agreed to discuss peace on the condition of changing the single-party political model into a multiparty one in which RENAMO could legitimately participate. Heavily mediated by the United Nations and the Vatican, the Mozambican peace came wrapped up in Western financial aid under the condition of a quick neoliberalisation of the country's economy, which kept Mozambique from the kind of economic recovery that would allow a faster investment in its industrial infrastructure. The *quid pro quo* for the much needed financial aid to keep the country's ball rolling was a sweeping wave of privatisation and deregulation, further weakening the already fragile local economy that was unable to compete with foreign investors and the wave of imported manufactured products. Despite the country's relative success in borrowing and honouring international commitments, which puts it on the good side of credit institutions such as the IMF and the World Bank, its population still remains largely in poverty.

Caught up in the vicious cycle of foreign aid, external debt and underdevelopment, the country ended up pushing its populations into all forms of economic instability that were, as Pitcher argues, quite good for the consolidation of Frelimo as the ruling party and for the strengthening of the state. '[T]he party has used the privatization process to consolidate its power and to build legitimacy for the state among investors. [… T]he ruling party has redoubled efforts to revive and extend its base and to use the state to provide club goods to supporters and to deliver selective public goods to a larger population' (2012: 185). Whereas the opening of the economy in exchange for foreign aid was a quick fix that delayed the development of the national economy in the long run, it served the state apparatus well. It helped keep the ruling party in power while providing an environment diplomatically intricate enough to allow the government to restrict political liberties and make use of force when deemed necessary, in the name of the country's political and economic stability.

Although it is imperative not to forget the huge impact of the civil wars both countries underwent, an account of the current state of their affairs should not avoid turning a critical eye to government mismanagement of resources either. Unlike Mozambique, which, despite its many obstacles, still managed to build up a good international reputation for its state, Angola is (in)famous for its inequality in wealth distribution as well as its governmental and administrative corruption. Notwithstanding the enormous hindrances caused by a post-independence war that started almost back-to-back with the thirteen-year-long liberation war, even in the aftermath of the 2002 peace, it can be argued that the state continued to focus on the maintenance of its own apparatus in detriment of public investments.

While Angola's production of oil rocketed over the years, the levels of human development remained below acceptable levels. Nonetheless, a 2003 list with the country's wealthiest men, topped by its president, had a total of seven acting government officials, and, in 2013, *Forbes* named the then president's daughter, Isabel dos Santos, as the richest woman in Africa (title kept in 2014 and 2015). Despite all this wealth, the lack of investments in the country's industries – since the main source of income for the state is the exploitation of its minerals – makes the country's food supply still reliant on imports. This fact, allied with the concentration of wealthy people transiting between government buildings and company headquarters, made the capital, Luanda, one of the most expensive cities in the world (Mercer 2015). Originally planned to accommodate 500,000 people, contemporary Luanda has a population of more than 6 million, of which two-thirds live on less than two dollars a day (Manuel and McClelland 2014: 16).

As these numbers add up, we see that the history of wealth in Portuguese-speaking Africa is rather a history of wealth inequality attuned with the capitalist world-system that shaped its actual contours. This brief detour through these countries' key aspects of wealth (mis)management over the last forty years shows that despite attempts by those committed to independence and equality through another form of wealth creation and management such as socialism, the capitalist form of accumulation – this time in the shape of neoliberalism – slowly proceeds to deliver its promises of progress at the expense of the exploitation of these countries' peoples. Given the impact and the material weight of matters of wealth, it is with little surprise that we observe its growing relevance in the fiction of Portuguese-speaking Africa in this century.

The next section looks at how wealth distribution is portrayed in the novels considered in this study. This comparative analysis has revealed that the literary picture of wealth in this phase of these countries' literatures is closely connected to the mode of wealth concentration verified at the social level. This allowed the division of the analysis into the three main sections according to the predominant form of representation of wealth concentration in each narrative. As a result, the remainder of the chapter is composed of three analytical sections and one final, comparative section.

The wealth of the state

Had the eighteenth-century Scottish economist and philosopher Adam Smith read the Mozambican *Campo de Trânsito* and Guinea *Tiara* before writing his *Wealth of Nations*, he would certainly have titled his work *Wealth of States*. Less for how the concept of state wealth would have affected Smith's view of macroeconomics and more for how well these literary conceptualisations of state seem to follow his views, the change of title would certainly match the individualistic ethos driving the state in these novels. John Larson reminds us that in 'the end, the private individual – Smith's primary actor – facilitates the greater good simply by following his self-centered impulses' (2015: 6), as Smith puts it:

> [The individual] intends only his own gain, and he is in this, as in many other cases, led by an invisible hand to promote an end which was no part of his intention. By pursuing his own interest he frequently promotes that of the society more effectually than when he really intends to promote it. I have never known much good done by those who affected to trade for the public good. It is an affectation, indeed, not very common among merchants, and very few words need be employed in dissuading them from it. (Smith 1965:423)

It would be entertaining to watch Smith's reaction to seeing states doing exactly the opposite of what he would expect them to do, which was acting as intervenors in the market for the sake of their people. As Smith's five-volume oeuvre can be seen as the Pentateuch of liberalism, much of its content reflects the capitalist structure of feeling within which the European states as we know them today came into being. It is probably due to this kind of contact, mediated through colonialism, that some states demonstrate, in their postcoloniality, a hunger for wealth closely resembling that of the self-centred individual.

Although the concentration of wealth by the state is a key element in all five narratives considered in this study, the representation of the state as the sole possessor of means in society is found only in *Tiara* and in *Campo de Trânsito*. Even though the state concentration of wealth in *Tiara* can be seen as a side issue within a *Bildungsroman* much more concerned with the protagonist's journey of maturation, *Tiara*'s story is put in parallel to that of the country around which the story develops. Correspondingly to her journey, we have the maturation trajectory of the fictional Muriti's independence movement, evolving from its early idealism into a corrupt party-state in the country's post-independence period. Consequently, it can be said that together with the coming-of-age of its heroine, Embaló's narrative offers us glimpses of what can be seen as the sketch of a *Bildungsroman* of the state. Understood in Franco Moretti's terms as 'one of the most harmonious solutions ever offered to a dilemma conterminous with modern bourgeois civilization', the *Bildungsroman* is perhaps one of the best forms through which 'the conflict between ideal *self-determination* and the imperious demands of *socialization*' (Moretti 2000: 15) can be seen at work as one of the root causes of the voracity with which some states accumulate and concentrate wealth.

To follow the formation of an independent state through a *Bildungsroman* emphasises the state's historicity because of the genre's inherent connection with the concept of youth. The idea that the condensation of the form in eighteenth-century Western Europe is linked to the region's modern revolutionary winds of change, to be materialised by the achievements of its 'dual revolution' (Hobsbawm 1962: ix), has interesting similarities with the historical conditions surrounding the emergence of the state of Muriti. In the twentieth-century, Africa experienced modern political and economic revolutions, eradicating colonialism and experimenting with socialism, similar to Europe in the eighteenth- and nineteenth centuries. In this convoluted scenario, organisations such as the novel's revolutionary movement, formed and led by the country's young intelligentsia, were also being formed under the modern revolutionary premises 'that perceive[d] the experience piled up in tradition as a useless dead-weight, and therefore can no longer feel represented by maturity, and still less by old age' (Moretti 2000: 5).

To the extent that the novel offers elements for a story of the emergence and development of the state of Muriti, it deals extensively with its double tradition of colonial and ancestral origin. The novel shows that, in its roots, the liberation movement that was to give birth to the party responsible for shaping the state inherited a lot from both traditions. From colonialism, the revolutionaries inherited a country lacking the most basic infrastructure, massive indexes of illiteracy and segregationist racism. From ancestral tradition were inherited social norms that, enhanced to survive under the pressures of the colonial regime, reproduced racism alongside practices of gender inequality and violence that became part of treasured aspects of the country's national identity. As discussed in the chapter analysing gender violence, despite their attempt to move away from tradition, both Tiara and Kenum fall victim to traditional practices that doom their marriage to fail. Equally, it can be said that it is the inability, first of the liberation movement and later of the party, to abandon key practices of its double tradition that condemns it to become a self-serving machine.

This is clearer in the characterisation and constitution of the two main antagonists of Tiara, the heroic protagonist embodying values such as justice, moderation, courage and detachment. On the political front, things in the fictional country go from bad to worse. Despite the adoption of multiparty democracy five years following independence, the government was a little democratic. After independence, Kito, the revolutionary who first excluded Tiara on racial grounds upon her arrival in the country, is already deep into the machinery of a state that is heavily controlled by the party stemming from the country's liberation movement. The novel suggests that the state became a means to transform the interests of the high levels of the political caste in policy rather than an institution to pursue the interests of the people. It is interesting to note how the lack of division between party and state is present, almost entirely in episodes related to Kito. As time goes by, every instance where Kito and Tiara's destinies cross shows how the state has distanced itself from its ideological roots, become corrupt and, consequently, rejected the protagonist. After the last confrontation between these two characters, based on Tiara's negative advice on a big state contract with a corrupt company, the euphemistic references to corruption finally give way to a conclusive, disillusioned remark: '[Tiara n]ão via futuro no Instituto, nem em nenhuma empresa estatal. Quanto a isso, admitia que tinha perdido a Guerra. Afinal de contas, nunca ninguém venceu o inimigo na sua própria casa...' ['[Tiara] did not see a future at the Institute, nor at any state company. In that regard, she admitted that she had lost the war. After all, no one has ever defeated the enemy in their own home...'] (Embaló 1999: 234). The first of Tiara's two big defeats in the novel comes with her acceptance of disillusionment and her non-belonging to the country she helped to liberate.

Nonetheless, Tiara's defeat in the public arena is not sufficient to represent the maturation stage of the corrupt state. Together with the colonial legacy of racial segregation, nepotism and concentration of power, the state also inherits an ancestral intransigence consolidated in opposition to colonial acculturation. Therefore, on the ancestral front, Kenum's mother, Mãe Zinga, embodies the continuation of ancestral structures in the country's society. The character's resolve in not letting her son walk away from the family's ancestral traditions, leading Zinga to entrap her son into getting a local, ancestrally acceptable, young woman pregnant to maintain the family's ethnic and social lineage, destroys Kenum and Tiara's marriage. The incident brings to the surface the problematic nature of a break with ancestral tradition among members of the State apparatus: 'Por que teria ele caído na armadilha da mãe? Ele, que decidira tomar em mãos a sua própria vida, fugindo às tradições ancestrais. ... Seria realmente por respeito à mãe, às tradições familiares, que de toda maneira constutuíam os pilares da sua identidade?' ['Why would he have fallen into his mother's trap? He, who had decided to take life into his own hands, escaping ancestral traditions. ... Was it really out of respect for his mother, for family traditions, which in any case constituted the pillars of his identity?'] (Embaló 1999: 244), Kenum thinks with himself. With the end of his relationship, Kenum feels unable to continue exercising his much-needed role of opposition within the ruling party. By breaking his union with

Tiara, Kenum breaks with all she means in the narrative, and, accepting
the irreconciliability between the modernity of the socialist project and
non-modern principles guiding his cultural traditions, he finally detaches
himself from any commitment to a different future for the country. '[Kenum
s]entou-se à secretária e redigiu mecanicamente seu pedido de demissão
do Instituto. Sem Tiara não teria forças para continuar a lutar. ... Iria para
o Senda, viver com a família como queria a sua mãe. Estaria finalmente em
paz com as tradições ancestrais' ['[Kenum] sat at his desk and mechanically
wrote his resignation from the Institute. Without Tiara he wouldn't have
the strength to continue fighting. ... He would go to Senda, live with his
family as his mother wanted. He would finally be at peace with ancestral
traditions'] (Embaló 1999: 245).

    If Kenum represented the best public servant the liberation movement
had formed – the only one deserving the love of the novel's heroine – his
withdrawal from public life is a meaningful sign of how things will develop
in the country. In fact, as the novel ends with the physical and intellectual
separation of all nuclear characters, the logic of the self-centred individual
has prevailed in that society, mirroring the distortions of its state, where one
is incapable of conciliating self-determination with socialisation. Although
the novel tends to describe the state in political terms, it is through its
management of public wealth that a verdict on its nature is delivered.
Even when the party is able to manage its concentration of power through
skilful manipulation of political mechanisms in place, the verdict on its
self-centredness can only come when its fault is verified in the materiality
of the economic sphere through wealth appropriation, an activity shown
in much more length and detail by Coelho's *Campo de Trânsito*.

    While in *Tiara* state, concentration of wealth is the economic, ma-
terial and palpable outcome of the state's political constitution for the
long run of the country's history, in *Campo de Trânsito*, the timeless focus
on the complex of camps offers a much more comprehensive view on the
biopolitical aspects of the production and concentration of wealth by a
totalitarian state. *Campo*'s allegorical narrative conjugates a powerful discursive practice that collectivises individuals and individualises the state,
with an anatomy of the predatory productive process through which the
state disposes of the individual. The novel's representation of the state

through its discursive practice has been analysed in Chapter 2, dedicated to representations of the state, and this section concentrates on the novel's representation of productive processes of wealth based on inequality and exploitation of its people.

The state in *Campo* is openly suggested as a totalitarian and inescapable construct. It is portrayed as an unquestionable, inevitable and unavoidable entity that reproduces itself through the reprocessing of individuals, hence the strong ideological component of the camp and the skilful organisation of prisoners' bodies, minds and time into productive forces. Historically, Coelho's conceptualisation of state production and amassing of wealth could be inspired by both the colonial and post-revolutionary Mozambican states. This possibility is granted by the unspecific ways in which this state is described and also by the historical fact that massive population displacement aimed at ideological and economic development was a strategy carried out by both colonial and post-independence states in the history of Mozambique.

The colonial project of *aldeamentos* [villages] was initiated in the late 1960s as the struggle for independence continued and strategies to fight the revolutionaries in the interior were required. The plan consisted of the creation of new villages in strategic locations with the promise to better feed and educate the population under colonial rule but with the intention of concentrating resources and people in strategic areas to contain the advancement of the revolutionary forces (Coelho 1993: 216–237). The post-independence villagisation project, known as *aldeias comunais* [communal villages], worked differently depending on where they were located. While many new farming communities were built, a number of them inherited the mode of organisation of the colonial *aldeamentos*. Nonetheless, they seem to have been inspired more by the good example of the Ujamaa villages in Tanzania – a project of voluntary peasants for communal agriculture – and by Frelimo's own case of communal organisation carried on during the war in its liberated areas (Coelho 1993: 330–331). Yet, despite the wide range of the programme, reaching almost 20 per cent of the population by 1982 (1993: 345), the initiative failed both during its destruction by RENAMO militants and by the system's own shortcomings related to the incompatibility of Frelimo's Marxist large-scale view of means and objectives with the peasants' subsistence-driven way of life (1993: 436). Additionally, similar to the prison structures developed in the Soviet Union, whose economic dimension proved to be important between the 1930s and 1950s (Ivanova 2000), post-independence Mozambique also had re-education camps. These camps, designed uniquely for the punishment and regeneration of individuals whose activities and morals would not comply with the strict moral code of the party (Thomaz 2008: 187), although in part inspired by the communal villages, had the sole purpose of ideologically transforming their inmates.

Mozambique's history, thus, has many points of contact with what the readers finds in *Campo de Trânsito*. Yet, as much as the novel focuses on the prison camps, the role of the displaced village in the narrative – whence the Chief and the Tea Seller come – enlarges the scope of the story, making it more representative of common traits of this kind of resettlement than a faithful reconstruction of any one in particular. Moreover, to the extent that the Mozambican post-independence resettlement attempts are seen to be related to the colonial ones, the specific contours of Coelho's fictional prison structure show its postcoloniality by taking from both systems' forms of population redistribution. This hypothesis is reinforced by the author's deliberate avoidance to localise the camps in time and space, concentrating only on the notion of state, common to both forms of political organisation thanks to the Portuguese colonial decree of 1951 that changed the status of its then colonies to Overseas Provinces of the Portuguese state. Therefore, when it comes to the production of wealth, the novel paints a critical picture, problematising precisely the relationship between state and individual that relates both to colonial and post-independence production practices on the basis of people's displacement, ideological and cultural re-education and exploitation.

Productivity through alienated work is the material drive behind Coelho's fictional camp complex. The transit camp is the place of arrival, loss of subjectivity and learning – the place in which the worker's alienation of the self must be achieved. Although central, work in that camp is experienced in a light, ludic manner, as if to triage which prisoners are predisposed for the activities of the Old Camp and which would be better suited for the New Camp. The ultimate function of the camp would thus be the creation of a herd of highly specialised types of alienated workers.

The classes of the Teacher on collectivity, the lack of tools with which to find progress and tame nature: 'São cerca de uma dezena [de pessoas], dois ou três com pequenas enxadas, os restantes com paus aguçados que utilizam como se fossem instrumentos de trabalho' ['There are about a dozen [people], two or three with small hoes, the rest with sharpened sticks that they use as if they were work instruments'] (Coelho 2007: 49) – and the most complete lack of objects with which they have to live upon their arrival in the camp all seem to calculatedly promote the idea of progress through production. The lack of food or comfort in which inmates are left, added to the isolation of the place, makes any individual attempt to improve a prisoner's situation into a statement that inspires envy and respect. '[Mungau n]ota que os prisioneiros mais antigos comem com umas toscas colheres de madeira; alguns têm-nas mesmo de alumínio, assim como facas, garfos e outros objectos. ... São esses os mais bem instalados, comportando-se aqui como se estivessem em sua própria casa' [Mungau notes that the oldest prisoners eat with crude wooden spoons; some even have them made of aluminum, as well as knives, forks and other objects. ... These are the best installed, behaving here as if they were in their own home] (Coelho 2007: 45).

Equally, prisoners who do not spontaneously take steps to improve their conditions are noticed, although not yet punished: 'Há evidentemente prisioneiros desprovidos do mínimo de sentido construtivo. Não prestam atenção ao que se vai inventando, comem com as mãos ... . [Mungau n]ota que os prisioneiros mais miserável são também os mais preguiçosos. Finda a refeição deixam-se ficar entregues a arrastadas digestões' [There are evidently prisoners devoid of the slightest constructive sense. They don't pay attention to what is being invented, they eat with their hands... . Mungau notes that the most miserable prisoners are also the laziest. At the end of the meal, they allow themselves to be left in prolonged digestions] (Coelho 2007: 48). Mungau tries to mingle with the agricultural workers, but his intellectual soft skills and ambition are more suited for the information activities that the Director wisely entrusts him with. Through the observation of Mungau's eagerness in fulfilling his task to visit and produce a report on the other two camps, we see how effective the Transit Camp is in finding each inmate a job that would align with their abilities. Such essential activity, carried out at the camp in which the Director – who *is* the state – resides, is one of the factors that determines the success of the camp as a production site. Added to that is the delicate balance that the Director has to achieve between state ideology of alienated production and the tradition that is so dear to the prisoners of the Old Camp and to the Village Chief, who acts as the administrator of the Old and New camps.

The tension between these two forms of societal organisation echoes a similar problem faced by the state in *Tiara*; however, the approach of each novel privileges a different view of the situation. Located at the political and ideological level, *Tiara*'s focus on society's superstructure portrays wealth distribution. *Campo*, in its turn, shows me how this tension operates at society's base, thus concentrating on the portrayal of wealth creation. Therefore, while this tension in *Tiara* is exposed in a moderate and intellectualised way, relying on the systemic avoidance of conflict resulting in a quiet acceptance of defeat by the protagonist, in *Campo* the clash between civilisation and tradition explodes with the intensity of the violence through which it happens. After the Director secretly arranges the disappearance of the skull of the Original Chief, the archaeological artefact that conferred the only symbolic meaning left to the daily lives of prisoners of the Old Camp, the whole system goes off-balance and revolution breaks out.

After losing the symbolic object that materially connected their work with the site of the camp and with the rule of the Village Chief, the Old Camp's prisoners could no longer keep focused on either their productive or archaeological tasks. While the Director's aim was to destabilise the tradition-oriented rule of the Village Chief to try to increase the camp's productivity, such a dramatic disruption in the inmate's carefully crafted routine was the pivotal event that awakened their collective consciousness. Following this incident, the inmates from the Old Camp marched to the New Camp – from which they were kept strategically separated – 'Não queremos unir o músculo à perspicácia, a força à inteligência. Tonar-se-ia perigoso' ['We don't want to combine muscle with insight, strength with intelligence. It would become dangerous'] (Coelho 2007: 117) – to summon the remaining prisoners and march together towards the Transit Camp. As it turned out, the camp complex could not prescind entirely from the forces of tradition to keep arms and brains alienated from one another, as the state wanted.

In his allegory of a totalitarian state eager to use its populations to produce a wealth that is not to be shared, Coelho seems to indicate that a state's biggest mistake is to underestimate its populations' subjectivity and agency. Estranging its peoples' customs and traditions was not only the Director's mistake but also that of the colonial administration and of the post-independence government in Mozambique. In common with colonialism's disregard and disapproval of local customs as an excuse for the system of labour and wealth exploitation it brought, was the Mozambican party-state's intolerance to ancestral customs disconnected from Marxism-Leninism, as well as its opposition to the peasants' traditional mode of production, based on familiar subsistence rather than industrial large-scale necessary to serve a whole country (Coelho 1993: 434–437).

When it comes to how these two novels approach the theme of wealth, their supplementary view is historically connected to the early days of both states within which they have been conceived. *Tiara* shows the slow process of condensation of a postcolonial single-party state, from its roots in the liberation struggle through to its establishment in the post-independence period, which is marked by the concentration of political power and control over public wealth. *Campo de Trânsito*, on the other hand, paints a picture of a totalitarian state and the exploitative processes through which this state produces its wealth to the detriment of the well-being of its populations, grouped as prisoners in the exceptional space of the camp. Notwithstanding the differences inherent to each local specificity, these portraits relate to political and economic formations in postcolonial Portuguese-speaking Africa, as these countries share an important history. In each case, their revolutionary nationalism is followed by single-party states with central-ised economies characterised by the concentration of wealth around the states and in the hands of the local elites, be they revolutionary or not.

Wealth in transition

Establishing a curious continuum with *Tiara* and *Campo de Trânsito*, the Santomean *Aurélia de Vento* and the Angolan *Teoria Geral do Esquecimento* relate to each other in a way that parallels the kind of relationship found between the first two novels, while also advancing into postcolonial times. *Aurélia* and *Teoria*, too, establish supplementary relations given that one is more concerned with a portrait of wealth in society's superstructure and the other seems to dig deeper in society's economic base. Similarly to the previous section, one novel covers a long time span and the other covers a brief, unspecified interval in time. However, contrary to the previously analysed pair of novels, the two narratives studied in this section take the cultures within which they emerge as the main setting for their plots, explicitly referring to them. In terms of their relation to history, this set of novels seems to pick up where the previous two left off. *Aurélia* offers portraits of a society where the state is reluctantly letting go of its position as the sole proprietor of wealth in society, having to negotiate with an emerging and empowered bourgeoisie that is not afraid to point at its failures and shortcomings. *Teoria*, in turn, takes a more historical approach and, addressing just very briefly the revolutionary nationalist movement of Angola, concentrates on the practices of the single-party socialist regime, when wealth is concentrated in the hands of the state, and on the country's transition towards the neoliberal practices of market economy. This comparative frame is the basis for an analysis that will 'follow the money' in order to complete the larger picture of wealth drawn by these five narratives of Portuguese-speaking Africa.

Although crucial to the development of its plot, wealth and class in *Aurélia de Vento* are never openly discussed, being diluted as unproblematic components in a social fabric that, despite its many layers, articulates itself with a large degree of harmony with the only exception of the state, personified by one politician: Minister Ventura. Yet, even implicitly, the trail of wealth in the novel does follow what has been proposed by other narratives in this corpus. Wealth is distributed first between settler colonisers, after whose departure wealth is nationalised and redistributed amongst members of the political elite who, after the adoption of a market economy, face challenges in appropriating resources. This is the main premise of the dispute between Santos and the state. Even when this process is not at all strange among the novels of our corpus, in *Aurélia* it is placed against an explicit background of the class system.

Aurélia de Vento is a novel centred on the perspective of a relatively multiethnic emerging bourgeoisie, portraying its relations with the state and with the country's class of workers. As a result, for an agricultural country like São Tomé and Príncipe that has considerable levels of poverty, all nuclear characters are in very good economic shape. Aurélia is regarded as a 'doctor', reflecting her access to tertiary education, and is in a good enough position to allow herself to work in a charity association. Santos, arguably as central a character as Aurélia, owns productive land. Minister Ventura is a wealthy politician, and Castro is an independent and successful lawyer. However, despite these characters' centrality, the lower local class is essential for the development of the story, for it seems to be only in relation to these and against the state that a bourgeoisie maintains its core position in the plot of the novel.

The general support of the people belonging to the working class legitimised the bourgeois cause for justice in *Aurélia*'s two subplots. In the first, Santos' victory sees popular support for the landowner's plea against the state, and in the second, popular support turned against traditional customs as it was essential to bring justice to the attempted murder of Aurélia, ordered by her stepmother. The association between the working class and the bourgeoisie was already indicated in Chapter 2, and the representation of the state in the novel was analysed. While the state is constituted from a general opposition in the face of those deprived of political power and that the alliance of the population with the main characters of the novel points towards a constructive future, viewed from the perspective of wealth distribution, the type of collective consciousness from which the wealthier benefitted from their opposition to state power in the narrative also contains elements capable of engendering its own end. Considering this, whereas the state can be seen as an institution separated from the idea of a nation or people in the novel, the societal divides portrayed go beyond further and just superficially disguise the divide separating the bourgeoisie (political and/or economic) and working class, whose difference is marked throughout the narrative. The following passage refers to a scene in which Santos stops quickly at a bar in a poor area to buy cigarettes, respectfully greeting the men present and then leaving:

– Há pessoa, preto ou branco, que respeito parece estar colado nele. É como esse senhor Pedro Santos! Branco que respeita toda a gente, grande ou pequeno, e com bom coração como ele, parece que não há mais!

– Chê, você não vê que ele é branco que ficou aqui não foi p'a terra dele depois de dependência. Pessoa que mesmo 'ntempo de Cívica nunca ninguém incomodou ele ... . (Bragança, 2011: 103)

[There are people, black or white, to whom respect seems to stick to. It's like this Mr. Pedro Santos! A white man who respects everyone, important or not, and with such a good heart, seems like they don't exist anymore!

Chê, can't you see that he's white and he stayed here and didn't go to his country after the independence. A person who, even when at the times of Cívica, no one ever bothered... .]

Later on, after hearing of Aurélia's murder attempt, one of the working-class men present in the previous scene at the bar is restless enough to lose his sleep. His wife then tries to reason:

– Mas Kununo, essa doutora é da tua família? Qué que ela é p'a você, p'a você perder sono dessa maneira? Essa coisa de você ir procurar homem que atacou ela é bem pensada mesmo? Cuidado, nós temos filho p'a criar...!

Kununo nada lhe respondia. Ele sabia que a mulher tinha razão, até porque, ao fim e ao cabo, nada o prendia a Aurélia, gente de outro meio social. Ele sabia-o, mas reconhecia que aquela mulher era especial. Havia nela qualquer coisa que raramente se encontrava nas outras da sua classe, a fraternidade que dela irradiava, essa facilidade de relacionamento com as gentes em toda a Trindade e arredores. Para ele não contava apenas o dinheiro e outros bens materiais: a amizade, o respeito, a consideração valiam muito mais do que isso. E aquela mulher comprava-o como ninguém. (Bragança 2011: 127)

[But Kununo, is this doctor part of your family? What is she to you, for you to lose sleep like that? Is this thing about you going to look for the man who attacked her really well thought out? Be careful, we have children to raise...!

Kununo didn't respond to her. He knew that his wife was right, especially because, in the end, nothing tied him to Aurélia, someone from another social background. He knew it, but he recognized that this woman was special. There was something about her that was rarely found in others in her class, the fraternity that radiated from her, this ease of relationship with people throughout Trindade and its surroundings. For him, it wasn't just money and other material goods that counted: friendship, respect, consideration were worth much more than that. And that woman bought him out like no one else.]

These passages demonstrate that the bond connecting the working class and the bourgeoisie in *Aurélia de Vento* is a notion of mutual recognition and respect strong enough to overcome class differences that are very well marked in the text. The most visible index of these differences is materialised in the register of these characters' speech. While the bourgeois portions of direct speech are written in an educated norm of Portuguese also referred to as standard (or *norma culta*) – the same as the one used by the narrator – the speech of characters belonging to the working class shows numerous written renditions of spoken and colloquial registers of Portuguese and is represented in their use of interjections, contractions and syntactic inversions to show the influence of the local language landscape on their speech, which works as a visible mark of class in the novel. Furthermore, as the narrative uses descriptions of places, habits and customs to confer local colour to the story, we get glimpses of the concrete dimension of the difference between classes. Santos drives to buy cigarettes, but the working-class men observing him do not own a car and get their cigarettes from a simple cigarette case made out of an old newspaper. While Aurélia and Clotilde sleep on comfortable beds, Nununo and his wife share a narrow bed and their kids sleep on the floor. Yet, as we see in the second quote, these differences, of which the working class shows itself to be very aware, are not enough to set them completely apart if they understand there is a moral code of mutual respect, which is portrayed as more important than class.

It is precisely this solidarity of the working class with the bourgeois in the novel that will bring the man who attempted to murder Aurélia to justice. As it happens, Kununo and his friends, following a trail of rumours, end up tracking down and delivering the wrongdoer to justice, much to the shame of the police and the state. In the face of these facts, as far as the plot goes, it seems that the novel draws a somewhat harmonious picture in which the bourgeoisie and working class are together in a struggle against a corrupt, suspicious and inefficient state. Even though more sceptical readers could attribute this somewhat utopic scenario to an eventual authorial intervention aiming at the canonisation of this struggle-free class society, a closer look at the narrative reveals that the structural unevenness is never overcome in the novel. The way it is laid out, this interclass solidarity relies heavily on commitment from the working classes, whose efforts are neither reciprocated nor substantially recognised or rewarded.

Upon Aurélia's return home from her many days in hospital, she is overwhelmed by visitors. Nonetheless, whereas her father, a lawyer, the bishop, two ministers and other members of the local high society are invited into her house, members of the working class who were eager to see Aurélia alive and well are allowed just to agglomerate on the street outside, in the rain. In fact, Aurélia only goes to the balcony to wave to her popular supporters following a request from the Director of the Police Department – one of the visitors invited in – who asked her to do so to avoid extended popular gatherings and their subversive potential. Additionally, none of the working-class captors of her assassin are called in for personal thanks or given any sign of public recognition, nor are they mentioned by their names again through the end of the narrative.

Seen from this perspective, the novel's picture of an apparently harmonious coexistence between classes in contemporary São Tomé and Príncipe is built up on rather fragile foundations that have historical precedents. Just as the people once supported a class of intellectual revolutionaries who promised them freedom in exchange for their trust, only to later see them become a distant and corrupt class of governors, it seems now that by putting their hopes in the emerging bourgeoisie, the working class is committing the same mistake. Regardless of the righteousness and well-meaning intentions of some of its members, and despite its disputes with the state, the bourgeoisie is still depicted as much closer to the state and much further away from the members of the working class – both physically and culturally. Despite their differences, enacted mostly when it comes to wealth distribution, in *Aurélia de Vento*, the state and bourgeoisie are much closer than the bourgeoisie and the working class, on whose support the bourgeois privileges rely.

If taken as a story that shows the contemporary dynamics of class, *Aurélia de Vento* constitutes a still-life picture of a society in a whirlwind of change. In terms of wealth distribution and inequality, despite the emergence of a culture of solidarity, divisions remain and seem to become deeper. Yet, wealth and influence appear to be in transition, changing from the hands of the state to the hands of a bourgeoisie, which finds the support of a working class willing to accept an elite that, although irreconcilably different, can still give them a degree of respect and recognition. However, this far echo of Cabral's plea for an alliance between bourgeoisie and peasantry, discussed in Chapter 2, loses its strength when the novel's representation of wealth inequality comes to the fore. The tensions presented in the narrative open possibilities for a gloomy future, as the abyss between the classes does not seem to be bridged by episodes of solidarity, and the bourgeoisie seem unwilling to accept Cabral's advice and suicide as a class to give way to the rise of the local working class. In its portrait of the rise of a Santomean bourgeoisie, *Aurélia de Vento* captures the pivotal moment where an alliance between the working class and the bourgeoisie is still possible but its future remains uncertain.

Similarly to what happens in *Aurélia de Vento*, wealth and transition, as well as wealth in transition, are important themes in Agualusa's *Teoria Geral do Esquecimento*. References to wealth in various forms, along with the continuous change of hands to which it is subjected, are meaningful features of this narrative of transition. Yet, this novel diverges from its Santomean counterpart in its approach. It treats the theme of wealth explicitly, turning it into one of the central threads connecting the trajectories of all the characters together, and it focuses on the processes involved in the acquisition of material wealth rather than on its condensation in social classes. For this reason, to grasp the type of changes that take place in Angolan society during the twenty-eight years of the narrative, 'follow the money' here demands the reader follow a trail of diamonds.

The importance of wealth in *Teoria Geral do Esquecimento* is clear from the outset of the story, which is comprised of brief passages taking place right before the independence of Angola, between the Carnation Revolution in April of 1974 and the country's independence in November of 1975. The narrative is filled with vivid illustrations that depict the wealth of the settlers who were rushing to leave Luanda:

Os primeiros tiros assinalaram o início das grandes festas de despedida. Jovens morriam nas ruas, agitando bandeiras, e enquanto isso os colonos dançavam ... .

O que não conseguirmos beber deixamos com vocês, disse [Rita], mostrando a Orlando a despensa onde se amontoavam caixas com os melhores vinhos portugueses: Bebamnas. O importante é que não fique nenhuma para os comunistas festejarem.

Três meses mais tarde o prédio estava quase vazio. Em contrapartida, Ludo não sabia onde colocar tantas garrafas de vinho, grades de cerveja, comida enlatada , presuntos, postas de bacalhau ... . Orlando recebera de um amigo, colecionador de carros desportivos, um *Chevorlet Corvette* e um *Alfa Romeo GTA*. Outro entregara-lhe as chaves do apartamento. (Agualusa 2012: 17, emphasis of the original)

[The first gunshots signaled the start of the big farewell parties. Young people were dying in the streets, waving flags, and meanwhile the settlers danced ... .

'Whatever we can't drink we'll leave for you,' she said to Orlando, pointing at the pantry stacked high with cases of the finest Portuguese wines. 'Drink them. The important thing is that there mustn't be anything left over for the communists to celebrate with.

Three months later, the apartment block was almost empty. Ludo, meanwhile, didn't know where to put so many bottles of wine, crates of beer, tins of food, hams, pieces of salt cod ... . Orlando had received from one friend – a collector of sports cars – a Chevrolet Corvette and an Alfa Romeo GTA. Another had given him the keys to his apartment.] (Agualusa 2015: 8)

Yet, as the narrative shows, regardless of Rita's – Ludo's neighbour – will, wealth changed hands in postcolonial Angola, just as their apartments in the luxurious *Prédio dos Invejados* were later to be occupied by humble families and their husbandry. Perhaps the most striking example of this process is represented by the trajectory of Ludo's brother-in-law, Orlando, or, to put it better, the trajectory of his diamonds. The sometimes nationalist, some-times settler-sympathising wealthy mestizo, whose name clearly draws from the multiplicity of Viginia Woolf's character of the same name, was a man caught up in the ambivalences of his society: 'Compreendia a necessidade de maior justiça social, mas os comunistas, ameaçando nacionalizar tudo, assustavam-no. Expropriar a propriedade privada. Expulsar os brancos. Partir os dentes à pequena burguesia. Ele, Orlando, orgulhava-se do sorriso perfeito, não queria usar dentadura.' (Agualusa 2012: 16–17) [He under-stood the necessity for greater social justice, but the communists, who were threatening to nationalise everything, alarmed him. Expropriating private property. Expelling the whites. Knocking out all the petite bourgeoisie's teeth. He, Orlando, took pride in having a perfect smile, and he had no desire for dentures.] (Agualusa 2015: 7). An engineer employed by the co-lonial company responsible for the extraction of diamonds, Orlando was reluctant to leave Angola alongside other members of the colonial elite until he managed to steal a bunch of high-quality diamonds. These stones, first sought after by the fearful captain of the Portuguese Army, Jeremias Carrasco, who accidentally kills Orlando while trying to get to the stones, end up in the hands of Ludo. After running out of food in the isolation of her apartment, she uses the stones as shining bait in the hunt for pigeons. One of the pigeons eats a couple of stones but escapes Ludo's pan only to be caught by an equally starving, though much poorer, Pequeno Soba, who eats the pigeon and keeps the stones. A revolutionary at heart whose true devotion to the revolutionary cause and the people made him a threat to both old and new political regimes, Pequeno Soba's story includes homelessness, arrest and torture. The stones, which he kept for many years despite the tribulations he suffered, were later used to open a courier company that thrives in neoliberal Angola. At the end of the narrative, we are told that Ludo still has some of the stones left behind, as they were too big for the palate of any pigeon. These are then given to Jerónimo, which is the new identity of Jeremias after spending almost three decades with the Mucubal peoples of the south of the country, as he begs for help to buy his adoptive people the land necessary for their subsistence, which is now being divided between members of the country's elite, formed mainly by politicians and military who once were revolutionaries fighting in the name of their peoples.

The long, contorted story of Orlando's diamonds and their impact on people's lives is the most consistent example of Agualusa's portrayal of wealth creation and distribution in this novel. Its focus on the transmission of wealth between individuals rather than institutions evidences the novels' attention to the lower strata of society. Matching the novel's focus on a more granular view of systems and institutions traditionally conceived as faceless and autonomous, state wealth is not portrayed as such. As discussed in Chapter 1, the state in *Teoria* is perceived as a performative institution, existing to the extent that active individuals enact it. So here, state appropriation of wealth is the appropriation by individual state representatives, such as what happens with the land of the Mucubal people, now the property of a general. Hence, the emphasis is on the neoliberal system as a root cause of the uneven distribution of wealth in that society:

A guerra terminara. Nos hotéis de Luanda acotovelavam-se empresários vindos de
Portugal, Brasil, África do Sul, Israel, China, todos à procura de dinheiro rápido
num país em frenética reconstrução.

...

Tudo o que é sólido se desmancha no ar, murmurou Monte, pensando em Marx, e
pensando, como Marx não em aviões, mas no sistema capitalista, que ali, em Angola,
prosperando como bolor em ruínas, vinha já apodrecendo tudo, corrompendo tudo,
e, dessa forma, engendrando o próprio fim. (2008: 151)

[The war had ended. In the hotels of Luanda, businessmen from Portugal, Brazil,
South Africa and Israel all rubbed shoulders, in search of quick money in a country
going through a process of frantic reconstruction. ...

'All that is solid melts into air,' muttered Monte, thinking about Marx, and thinking,
like Marx, not about planes but about the capitalist system, which there in Angola,
thriving like mould amid ruins, had already begun to rot everything, to corrupt
everything and, thus, to bring about its own end.] (2015: 153)

As a result, the Luanda of *Teoria* is one of the new money acquired
through the redistribution of wealth expropriated from the people by colonialism to the post-independence political and military elites. Reflecting
the country's history of infrastructural underdevelopment, a lack of industrial parks or a legitimate economy raised from production and reinvest-
ment, the economic development of the characters who are not engaged
in governmental activities seems to be determined by chance, luck, favour
and opportunism. The presence of a wealth dissociated from productive
economic activities gives way to an economic culture of insecure labour
and exploitation. Together with foreign businessmen comes the prostitution of girls (*catorzinhas*), the recruitment of boys to crime – such as
what happened to the character of Sabalu – and the general impoverishment of the local populations, as salaries are low and profits are not reinvested locally. With the passing of the years, no character in *Teoria Geral
do Esquecimento* who improved their economic situation significantly
succeeded entirely due to the remuneration of their work. Pequeno Soba
was favoured by luck when eating the right pigeon; Pappy Bolingô and
Nasser Evangelista – not to mention Ludo and Sabalu – counted on the
kindness of Pequeno Soba. Monte, who refuses illicit enrichment by up-
holding ideological principles still in line with Marxism, managed to use

his prestige to save his father-in-law from prison. The diamonds stolen by Orlando as he planned to flee his country, costing both his and his wife's lives, are the main source of wealth for the characters of the lower classes to succeed in this story.

The wealth distribution in *Teoria Geral do Esquecimento* shows a diverse process with points of contact with the economic transition portrayed in *Aurélia de Vento*. In the Santomean novel, an established state agricultural economy is becoming private and complemented by other sectors, more traditionally associated with liberal bourgeoisies. In the novel, Minister Ventura, representing the state, not only loses the law suit for Santos, who is a private farmer, but also fails to force the lawyer Castro to take a case he does not want. The slow concentration of wealth in the hands of individuals in this story indicates that the country is about to have a silent bourgeois revolution, which, like many others before it, is founded on claims of moral righteousness and strength of character but which, in reality, excludes the lower classes on whose very support it relies.

On the other hand, in *Teoria*, the representation of a system of production and class is not visible. The population of Luanda is divided between the haves and have-nots, between those who inherited the spoils of colonial exploitation along with its modes of exploitation and those relying on their favour. This makes Agualusa's Angola much more open to transnational neoliberal exploitation than Bragança's self-contained São Tomé and Príncipe. The rise of a local economy is only depicted in *Teoria* towards the end of the novel, when Pequeno Soba invests in various areas such as services, real estate and the craft industry. Despite promising, these investments are revealed to be a small effort in a largely depleted economy that would require many people like himself to develop a social class capable of changing the country.

These two narratives of economic transition provide more detailed accounts of the ways in which national state wealth becomes private wealth in the aftermath of single-party state regimes and socialism in Portuguese-speaking Africa. Although they differ in terms of the angle, they take on the topic and, as each narrative brings up important elements of the reality of each respective context of production, their views of national economy in the historical background of societal change from colonialism to independence, socialism and capitalism provide little insight on the possibilities opened by individuals' agency in the brave new world of neoliberal economies of these contemporary postcolonial societies. The approach to the impact of wealth on individuals' lives and subjectivities is taken more clearly in Rocha's *Marginais*.

Private wealth

Wealth in *Marginais* is no longer portrayed as in the hands of the state or in transition to the pockets of the political elite. In this novel, wealth is pictured as a private asset belonging to a fragmented lower-middle class. Set between the mid-1980s and late-1990s, it speaks of a society divided between exploiters and exploited (Rocha 2010: 13), in a country at the mercy of transnational neoliberalism. If we take Jason W. Moore's proposition that 'the production of surplus value is not only the proletarization of labor and accumulation of capital but the production of global spaces of appropriation' (2015: 222), we find a match for the role that this novel gives to the Island of Sal in this economic system. For Sérgio 'a ilha do Sal está infestada de sanguessugas, coronéis que só pensam no vil metal e cultuam o desprezo pelos marginalizados' ['the island of Sal is infested with leeches, colonels who only think about money and cultivate contempt for the marginalized'], whose inhabitants live 'sob a ditadura dos operadores turísticos e dos governos corruptos' ['under the dictatorship of tourism operators and corrupt governments'] (Rocha 2010: 29;30). This statement, uttered early on in the novel when the Pitboys are deciding on a representative idol – Che Guevara's revolutionary enthusiasm was chosen over Jesus' 'disposable miracles and hopes' (2010: 29;30) –, reveals one of the greatest problems of the country: a careless, enriched bourgeoisie that sells the country and its underprivileged inhabitants to the transnational tourism industry.

As discussed in Chapters 1 and 2, although the role of the state in *Marginais* is minimal, it is still an essential agent for the marginalisation of its populations' lower strata. The novel depicts a society devoid of a welfare state, where the state is only visible through its ideological and repressive apparatuses. As such, people are first made to believe that they can only occupy a subaltern place in society, crushing any dreams and mining their potential, so that later on they become disciplined by an implacable coercive apparatus. By this process, the poorest fraction of the country's population is devoid of their full citizenship and systematically marginalised to the point they are dissocialised and dehumanised to be appropriated as a resource by the system: 'Somos maltratados pela lei, duplamente maltratados pela miserável condição de vida que levamos. (Rocha 2010: 30) ['We are mistreated by the law, doubly mistreated by the miserable living conditions we lead.']

Here, again, Jason W. Moore helps to understand the impact of transnational capital on the industrial manner through which people are formatted to serve as fuel for its engine in *Marginais*. Drawing on Marx's proposition that capitalism demands the appropriation of nature, Moore argues that the system is, in fact, *'a way of organizing nature'* (2015: 2, emphasis of the original) and that the separation between nature and society is not arbitrary but historically conceived precisely to allow the appropriation of nature, understood as non-human nature. This, Moore continues, was at the core of the colonial enterprise when African peoples were necessarily dehumanised in order to be appropriated and capitalised as assets in the form of enslaved labourers, just as nature was (2015: 13–18). Returning to our object of analysis, set more than a century after the end of slavery in the Portuguese-speaking world, which was driven, as we know, by the impact of industrialisation on transnational capitalism worldwide, it is the process of marginalisation that dehumanises people enough to have them serve as cheap labour in the age of global capitalism.[1]

This complicity between the state, heavy ideological coercive apparatus, and private initiative – represented mainly by tourism in the narrative – is decisive in the lives of all the characters surrounding Sérgio. The poverty at

---

1   Moore sees cheap labour as one of the four main pillars of capitalism: 'Capital … must ceaselessly search for, and find ways to produce, Cheap Nature: a rising stream of low-cost food, labor-power, energy, and raw material to the factory gates (or office doors, or…). These are the Four Cheaps. The law of value in capitalism is a law of Cheap Nature.' (2015: 53)

home, the disdain at school and the lack of opportunities were key to his early involvement in theft, vandalism, drug consumption and trafficking. His friend, Pianista, sharing the same structural conditions but amassing the trauma of being raped by police officers, soon enters a life of crime that includes drug trafficking for an Italian boss and prostitution, where he is used to recruit girls to sexually please European tourists. Mirna, the only strong female presence in Ségio's friendship group, was also victimised by poverty, domestic violence and sexual abuse, dying young and disillusioned in prostitution. One after the other, Sérgio's closest friends fall victim to a system of exploitation that disposes of their lives. Few are the characters that remain alive by the end of the novel. As Sérgio tells us, despite the growing tourism industry, 'os filhos da terra dificilmente conseguiam um bom trabalho' (Rocha 2010: 88) ['the locals could hardly get a good job']. In this scenario, young people were easy prey for illegal drug and sex industries, or for small business owners such as those running restaurants and clubs, serving as 'lavandaria – para lavagem de dinheiro sujo, claro' (2010: 91) ['laundry – for laundering dirty money, of course'].

The setting up of Sal as a place of appropriation and of its people as dehumanised commodities had yet more dramatic costs for other characters in the novel. The most widely known consequence of the state politics of neglect of the poor evoked in the narrative is immigration. Affecting Sérgio's mother, who left the country to become cheap labour in Italy, the push to immigrate caused the abandonment that was one of the most important factors in the protagonist's involvement with crime, as he was left by the only person with whom he had a true emotional tie at the critical age of sixteen, rather a meaningful time, as Althusser (1971: 155–156) has shown. The novel problematises this phenomenon as it exposes its two-fold impact. Locally, immigration contributes to the further impoverishment of the local economy by draining it of a substantial workforce and flooding the internal economy with the unsustainable practice of money remittances; internationally, immigration provides wealthy countries with a fresh wave of cheap workers necessary to keep their privileges on track. However, the most shocking of these consequences in the narrative is the industry of human trafficking and organ harvesting. The book tells us stories such as that of 'indigentes como Adalgisa, Paula, Astrogildo, Elton e tantos outros que foram raptados por vendedores de órgãos humanos que facturam milhares de contos nos bancos de órgãos para acidentados no estrangeiro' (2010: 30) ['indigents like Adalgisa, Paula, Astrogildo, Elton and many others who were kidnapped by human organ sellers who make thousands in organ banks for victims of accidents abroad'], or that of Mirna's mother who 'vendera a filhinha de dois anos a um casal de turistas alemães' ['sold her two-year-old daughter to a couple of German tourists'] (2010: 100) to afford bandages for her other daughter, who had accidentally been badly wounded during an episode of domestic violence. Still, we read that this kind of fate is not considered the worst that can happen in the wretched universe of *Marginais*. As Sérgio puts it:

> Ela iria ter uma boa educação, viveria longe dessa miséria dissimulada. Meu lamento é para aqueles que ficaram para trás. Havia rumores que os estrangeiros raptavam ou compravam crianças para extraírem órgãos e faziam fortunas aos vendê-los na Europa. Não me importava vender um dos meus rins em troca de uma pequena fortuna. Dizem que há um médico que vem de vez em quando e oferece um passaporte europeu a quem doar um rim. (2010: 101)

> [She would have a good education, she would live far from this poverty. I am actually sorry for those left behind. There were rumors that foreigners were kidnapping or buying children for organ harversting, making fortunes selling them in Europe. I didn't mind selling one of my kidneys in exchange for a small fortune. They say there is a doctor who comes from time to time and offers a European passport to anyone who donates a kidney.]

The contemplation of organ donation as a way out can be seen as one of the most dramatic consequences of the insertion of the Island of Sal into Cape Verdean neoliberalism and its role in the uneven system of distribution of wealth under the capitalist world-system. Aided by the state and a small local elite fully enmeshed in government, as the candidature of Dr Apolinário to the local administration demonstrates, Sal is made into a space for appropriation *par excellence*. Since the island, as well as the country as a whole, lacks wealth in the form of mineral deposits, fertile land or industry, we see the transformation of its people into the actual raw material to feed the international system of exploitation of nature and men alike. The novel shows how the systematic process of marginalisation of its poor population dehumanises them to the point in which, for survival, they agree to sell each other, as well as themselves, as units or in parts. Poverty is a vital condition in this industry of people, as the unavoidability of inequality is essential in making these people believe there is no alternative but to succumb to the available routes of subsistence.

Alongside the four other novels analysed, *Marginais* offers a grim view of neoliberal postcoloniality. Its utterly deregulated economy, combined with the lack of natural resources to supply extractivist transnational industrial activities, constitutes a successful recipe for the commodification of the very bodies of its populations to serve as raw materials in extractivist transnational enterprises legal or illegal such as sex tourism and organ harvesting. The novels' naturalist aesthetics and determinist approach to Sérgio's wretched coming-of-age narrative, curiously enough, establish a close aesthetic relationship with the function of the *Bildungsroman* in *Tiara*. While in the Guinean novel we have the rather disillusioned trajectory of a romantic heroine into another ordinary, failure-prone second-class citizen diminished by the rise of the institution of the state, in *Marginais* the submission of a state, that has become minimal to international capitalism seems to point to the unavoidable end of the revolutionary time that marks the outset of Tiara's journey. In this respect, Franco Moretti's conceptualisation of the end of the *Bildungsroman* follows the same general lines. According to him, '[t]he world of the late *Bildungsroman* has solidified into impersonal institutions' (2000: 233), so the heroes of this type of *Bildungsroman* become younger and younger 'because, historically, the relevant symbolic process is no longer growth but regression' (2000: 31). This regression, very much connected to the traumatic effects of the tragedy of World War I on European subjectivity, 'would thus be the narrative form that liberal Europe saw as an anthropological reversal from the individual as an autonomous entity to the individual as mere member of a mass' (2000: 232).

Taken as a form of *Bildungsroman*, *Marginais* certainly shows an important number of the characteristics highlighted by Moretti as inherent to works of the late phases of the genre. However, whereas Moretti's reflection on the European *Bildungsroman* is wrapped up by the clash of the ideal of modern man and the cruelties of World War I, the tragedy in Portuguese-speaking Africa is that of the fall of a revolutionary anticolonial ideal in the face of the unavoidable return of a highly exploitative form of international capitalism. Therefore, Sérgio's narrative is one centred on youth because these characters seem stuck in their subjective development as, while they move forward in time, their country seems to move backwards in history, towards a more cruel and painful form of exploitation since this regression happened despite the lessons learned during colonialism.

Consequently, regardless of the novel's undeniable differences when compared to its other four counterparts in this study, given the very peculiar historical development of its context of production, it advances important discussions when it comes to contemporary portrayals of wealth in the literatures of Portuguese-speaking Africa. As the fever of consumerism and globalisation spreads under the regime of neoliberalism in each of the five countries represented in this corpus, a literary representation of its systemic malaise, intra- and internationally speaking, supplements a critical tradition of the current state of affairs, already existing in the literatures of the countries included in this study, by going back to its principles. If the countries of Portuguese-speaking Africa successfully get rid of colonialism, they still have to live with its basic and underlying problems, as the capitalist world-system still thrives on their population's miserable condition.

The matter of postcolonial wealth

In 'What postcolonial studies doesn't say', Lazarus retailors one of his longstanding critical stances on postcolonial studies that is present, in many ways, throughout his body of work. In this article, Lazarus reclaims that 'postcolonial theory [and criticism] is inclined to conflate categories of "colonialism" and ' "imperialism", but that it tends to construe "colonialism" as an exercise solely in *political* domination, of the global projection of *power*' (2011: 11; emphasis in the original), and that 'postcolonial *criticism*, as an institutionalized mode of academic practice, has tended to turn a blind eye to what this body of literature has notably been concerned to put on display', which comprises 'the specifically capitalist dimensions of colonial experience' (2011: 14; emphasis in the original). Certainly pertinent for the field of contemporary postcolonial African literatures in Portuguese, Lazarus' critique is echoed by the novels analysed here. As this chapter shows, these contemporary works from Portuguese-speaking Africa confer a key role on wealth creation and division, which, besides their differences, indicate a growing awareness that the roots of the structural malaise afflicting their histories are systemic and run deeper than political forms of colonialism.

Written and published on average three decades after the independence of their respective countries, each of these novels attests to the undeniability of the material weight of wealth production, circulation and distribution in their contemporary postcolonial condition. With the political and economic departure of the coloniser, new forms of articulation of these two complementary realms of society had to be re-engineered from within. As a result, each of these five countries has come up with its own unique postcolonial trajectory of reconstruction and distribution of wealth that, nonetheless, shares a historical commonality. In one way or another, they are all written palimpsestic over a history of colonialism, which is but a chapter of the *longue durée* of the capitalist world-system.

This comparative approach has demonstrated that no novel has managed to draw a picture of society disregarding the relevance that wealth distribution, or better yet, wealth inequality, has for the state of affairs of their late postcolonial condition. Even if wealth cannot be said to constitute the central theme of at least four of the five novels analysed, it constitutes an inescapable structural factor in each of the narratives. Whereas wealth distribution, poverty and its consequences in the lives of postcolonial subjects are indeed central in *Marginais*, the same cannot be said of *Tiara*, whose main theme is the coming-of-age of revolutionary dreams by a revolutionary elite. Although barely mentioned until very late in the narrative, when evoked, bad wealth management and distribution are taken as the ultimate proofs of the demise of Tiara's revolutionary ideal, constituting the pivotal moment when the protagonist decides to abandon the cause that drove her journey of maturity. *Campo de Trânsito*, in its turn, is a novel in which biopolitics and state apparatus are the central themes; nonetheless, the argument simply could not be made without mention of the ultimate reason for such a highly organised form of physical exploitation: the generation of wealth for the state. The same is true in *Aurélia de Vento* and *Teoria Geral do Esquecimento*. No picture of the Santomean society could be painted without continuous allusions to the material cement of wealth sticking its social organisations together, and no predictions of its future reconfiguration should be made without attention to it. For this reason, wealth and social organisation are openly used in the Angolan narrative as the thread that links people from the past, present and future together. Agualusa's depiction of wealth transference in a country of constant change playfully reminds us that although Love goes by, 'diamonds are forever'.[2]

Each of these five novels points to diverse, yet interlinked, economic postcolonial unfoldings that conjugate intra- and international economic dynamics. The colonial past is undeniably present in the contemporary forms of wealth generation and distribution that they depict. The *longue durée* of a system of exploitation is clearly seen in each of the analysed fictional constructs. Colonialism is plainly addressed in *Tiara*, *Teoria* and *Aurélia*; in *Campo*, the perpetuation of the system at the end of the narrative leaves us with an idea of *durée*; similar to what happens in *Campo*, in *Marginais*, the idea of *durée* is given by an end that entails a new, cyclical beginning. Nonetheless, differently from the Mozambican story, the Cape Verdean narrative names, from its outset, the system of exploitation in place: international capitalism and neoliberalism.

As we approach the end of this study in the realm of comparative literature in Portuguese-speaking Africa, we return to the proposition of Lazarus with which this section was opened. The works included in this study do support his claim for a change in shifts in postcolonial theory and criticism. These novels demonstrate that, at least when it comes to contemporary Portuguese-speaking Africa, a change in the postcolonial critical paradigm is imperative. It is clear that a critique of systemic modes of wealth accumulation and division is part and parcel of how these novels

---

2   Amor (Love), is the name of the pigeon used as a mode of correspondence between Monte and his girlfriend in the beginning of Agualusa's novel. This is the pigeon that eats some of the diamonds – stolen by Orlando – used as bait later on by Ludo and flies away before she can catch him. He is caught later on by Pequeno Soba (Little Chief), who finds the stones and acquires a small fortune that he uses to change his life and the course of the lives of many in the story.

project reality into fiction. It is also evident that these changes are perceived in a *durée*, which seems to be an inherent condition of postcoloniality in its material and cultural unfolding. Nonetheless, the change that these literatures demands from theory and criticism does not seem to stop there. They also require changes when it comes to the ways in which these material tensions are seen in their political and cultural aspects. For, with the departure of the settlers and rearranging of internal systems, newly situated challenges were added to the old lingering ones, composing intricate and sophisticated scenarios that cannot be understood only with the help of a set of theoretical and critical tools designed to understand oppositions almost strictly in the realm of colonisers and the colonised. Which is to say that, together with a much-needed material revolution to equip postcolonial theory and criticism to account for the *longue durée* of exploitation in the global theatre of the capitalist world-system, there is also a need for an ideological shift to take into account the impact of the local dynamics of politics and power in the understanding of contemporary complex and diverse forms of postcoloniality.

Conclusion: Towards a *Late Postcoloniality*

> I would go as far as saying that it is the critic's job to provide resistances to theory, to open it up toward historical reality, toward society, toward human needs and interests, to point up those concrete instances drawn from everyday reality that lie outside or just beyond the interpretative area necessarily designated in advance and thereafter circumscribed by every theory.
>
> – Edward W. Said, *The World, the Text, and the Critic* (1983: 242)

This book opened with the question of whether national identity is still the main phenomenon registered by literary works conceived across Portuguese-speaking Africa at the turn of the twenty-first century. To answer this question, in Chapter 1 we started with a reflection on the role of the critic and of theoretical apparatus in the development of master narratives of critical reading and established that both the fields of criticism of the African literatures in Portuguese and the field of postcolonial studies need to extend their concerns to the postcolony's internal axis of tensions, whose relevance is essential for the comprehension of contemporary challenges in these spaces of entangled time. Taking on the challenge of reading *inter*national phenomena via the advantage point of *intra*-national peripheral postcolonial literary registrations, we analysed a selected corpus of novels from the literatures of Portuguese-speaking Africa published around the first decade of this century to chart some of the ways in which this transnational space can offer important coordinates if to reassess the contours of the concept of the postcolony today.

The literary projections of state, violence and wealth that emerged from the comparative analysis in this study answer our initial question by indicating that nation-building is no longer the main axis for these literary registrations. While they still show how structural issues at a societal level are linked to colonial practices, their approach takes an inward-looking stance, no longer interested in capturing a national identity but one that, relying on stable senses of national identity, is now ready to focus on the agency of their respective societies in the maintenance of exploitative practices. The

fact that these twenty-first-century texts, each attuned to the situated realities of very different countries such as Angola, Cape Verde, Guinea-Bissau,
Mozambique and São Tomé e Príncipe, still share structural and thematic
features decades after the end of their bond under Portuguese colonial
rule, evidences a postcolonial *longue durée* still uncharted in postcolonial
studies. Through a myriad of aesthetic resources involving *Bildungsroman*,
allegory, fragmentation and naturalism, these novels weave commentaries
on the structural features of their respective and diverse societies that con-
verge and interrelate.

Chapter 2 has shown that literature now conceives of the idea of nation
apart from the idea of state. While the nation is perceived in the uses and
customs of people regardless of the fashioning of the narrative, the state
is fictionalised as repressive, distant, corrupt and elitist. If in the past, the
nation was represented in literature as the home of its local inhabitants,
clearly separate from colonial settlers along tangible racialised lines, the
novels analysed have problematised the nation as an ideologically loaded
discursive device deployed by an intra-colonial state, whose agents are
conveyed in separation from the idea of the nation's 'people'. As a result,
this movement of dissociation of the idea of nation from the idea of state
evidences the abandonment of canonic literary projects of nation-building,
indicating a movement towards a constructive critique of the process of
state-building. Despite the colossal role of the various literary projects of
nation-building in the cultural history of these countries, the gradual withdrawal from them is not to the detriment of the national project. On the
contrary, it evidences the consolidation of ideas of nation that are plural,
multilayered and at peace with their colonial history. On the other hand,
the display of awareness of the existence of a state in need of criticism
shows an increase in political awareness, marking a critical turn towards
the *intra*-national aspects of social experience that compose one of the
main features of the latest phase of their postcoloniality.

The second theme running through all five narratives of our corpus
that was isolated in this study is the ongoing violence as a structural force in
the current organisation of the social formations portrayed in the novels. In
Chapter 3, we have seen how, despite the undeniable changes that took place
in the fabric of these novels' fictional societies since the end of colonialism,

violence did not recede in terms of prominence or reach. The corpus shows that, as the years passed in the aftermath of independence, the representations of state violence portrayed as typically physical and explicit gave way gradually to less overt and more symbolic forms of repression and social control performed by members of civil society. This movement, as we have highlighted, seems to be intimately connected with the demise of the authoritarian single-party state and with the rise of a dominant class stemming from it. Seen through this prism, symbolic violence increases as the socialist experiment is abandoned, the political system is opened and neoliberal economic practices are adopted, which leads to the theme of wealth.

Chapter 4 argues that wealth is the missing element in the equation involving state and violence in these novels' portrayal of contemporary postcolonialities. The three stages of wealth accumulation identified among the narratives not only match these countries' historical development but also correspond to how violence evolved from physical to symbolic in a context of massive opposition to an intra-colonial state no longer seen in consubstantiation with the nation. The chapter calls attention to the depictions of the process of class formation that are present in the analysis and how they point to diverse pathways for the postcolonial phases to come.

Together, the ways in which state, violence and wealth are registered in the literatures of Portuguese-speaking Africa evidence that a turn from an *inter*-national perspective to an *intra*-national perspective has already taken place. This does not mean, however, that these novels are blind to the forces of international capitalism, but it demonstrates their emphasis on the denunciation of internal factors and actors who facilitate the exploitation of these countries and their peoples on the international stage of the capitalist world-system. These novels' portrayal of societal problems perceived primarily as a result of internal forms of state intra-colonialism escapes the scope of a concept of postcoloniality primarily grounded on the interaction between former colonisers and former colonised, which is still a defining characteristic of postcolonial studies. Therefore, in order to address the mismatch between a postcolonial sovereign contemporaneity and a conceptual language conceived to handle foreign domination, I propose the concept of *late postcoloniality*.

The concept of *late postcoloniality*, or *late postcolonial condition*, recuperates the much needed episodic perspective on the dynamic space of entangled temporalities that is the postcolony. Its proposition does not cancel or affect the idea of postcolonial as a *longue durée*, but it prevents the postcolonial from becoming a concept evolving infinitely 'through a homogeneous, empty time' (Benjamin 2007: 261). Departing from our case study in the realm of the African literatures in Portuguese, the 'late' in late postcolonial condition is not in function of these countries' position in late capitalism, even when it relates to it. Late postcoloniality describes a postcolonial phase in which tensions within postcolonial societies are no longer perceived solely as a result of the opposition between colonisers and colonised. Located necessarily after the political stabilisation of the postcolony, which is characterised by the demise of organised military threats to a postcolony's sovereignty, the idea of late postcolonial condition seeks to imbue the concept of postcoloniality with a timeliness that is lost as soon as the foreign invader, around which the concept has been developed, departs for good.

The connection of late postcoloniality with the consolidation of a postcolony's secure political status is necessary for two reasons. Firstly, since the postcolony's economic subjugation is an underlying factor of its position within the capitalist world-system – from colonialism to neoliberalism – its economic subaltern situation constitutes a determinant condition of its postcoloniality. Secondly, given the essential relevance that political autonomy has in the postcolony's internal material conditions, such as organisation of power and distribution of wealth, its impact is first felt by national subjects as they carry out the structural reorganisations of their societies *vis-à-vis* a colonial order premised on the presence of the colonial settler. Hence, the concept is productive as it does not deny the lingering of economic practices related to colonialism in kind, but it focuses on the changes that take place as local elites seize power and reconfigure structures of privilege and oppression under which the capitalist world-system is enabled to operate at its best. Its relevance lies in its supplementary nature, given that its main proposal is to reinstitute the importance of a postcolony's political sovereignty in this process.

The concept of late postcoloniality is innovative in its urge for an emphasis on postcolonial agency. It makes way to a generative take on the postcolonial condition by inviting critical approaches capable of registering postcolonial innovation, thus recuperating the place of the postcolony and of its peripheral aesthetics as a privileged site from which to chart major worldwide changes of systemic proportions. Late postcolonial writing constitutes an advantaged point from which to see the interlocking threads of interests by core and semiperipheral agents in the seams of contemporary global capitalism. The postcolony's always already global locality provides rich and nuanced insights on the cultural and ideological processes underpinning peripheral societal organisations, such as those involved in racialisation, class organisation, the distribution of power and resources, as well as accountability and reconciliation. As such, late postcoloniality is a concept whose efficacy lies in its ability to adequately trace the lingering of coloniality, taking the aftermath of political independence as a foundational point.

The idea of a postcolonial literary aesthetic moulded within and around a post-independence, internal or intra-colonial context as *late* postcoloniality is inspired by Young's use of the term 'late postcolonialism'.[1] Discussing the 'relevance of postcolonial theories for the understanding of world-systemic transformations and the shifts in geopolitics in terms of conflict, transitional justice and cosmopolitanism' (2013: 1), Young's coinage of the term speaks of how postcolonialism's intrinsic lateness 'comprises its peculiar characteristic and power' (2013: 1) to examine these questions. Drawing attention to how situations of conflict and transnational justice, such as the case in Israel and Palestine, Tibet and Kashmir, 'could be described as being late, out of time and out of joint with the times, still living anachronistically in conditions that seem more of a piece with the politics

---

1   'Late Postcolonialism' is the title of a keynote address delivered by Young at the conference 'Postcolonial Transitions in Europe: Conflict, Transitional Justice and Cosmopolitanism', organised by the Postcolonial Europe Network (PEN) and held at the University of Utrecht on 18 April 2013. While the ideas developed in this paper have not yet been published, upon contact, Young kindly shared a document containing the first three pages of the address, which have been quoted in this section.

of the 19th or earlier 20th century' (2013: 3), Young's focus on the lateness
of postcolonialism is important to recuperate the field's ability to operate
'with historical anachronisms which persist today, and through which it
defines itself'(2013: 3).

While differing from Young in terms of object – he speaks of the analytical potential of lateness to postcolonial studies (or postcolonialism)
as a field of enquiry and this book proposes lateness as an index of the
postcolonial condition in the aftermath of independence – Young's invitation to revisit Edward Said's understanding of the term in his posthumously published book *On Late Style* (2006) was an essential contribution
to this study. *On Late Style* collects Said's essays on late style inspired by
Theodor Adorno's observation of the phenomenon in the compositions
of Beethoven (2002). Late style, for Adorno, is a controversial, dissonant
aesthetic achieved by certain artists at the end of their productive lives. For
Said, however, the idea of lateness trespasses the simple circumscription of a
parcel in a lifetime and takes on the contours of a more general style, which
can be more prominent throughout the works of certain artists who live in
specific historical contexts, as was the case of Adorno. Therefore, lateness for
Said – as well as for Adorno – is '"*lost totality*", and therefore *catastrophic…*
is the idea of *surviving beyond what is acceptable and normal*; in addition,
lateness includes the idea that one *cannot really go beyond* lateness at all,
cannot transcend or lift oneself out of lateness, but can *only deepen* the lateness' (2006: 13; emphasis added). In the light of our concept, therefore, the
late postcolonial condition is one that denotes the *lost totality* of a finished
idea of colonialism, to which the exploiter is, necessarily, an invader whose
outside status is connected to the idea of 'foreign'. It is *catastrophic* because
it denounces the pervasiveness of its underlying system of material exploitation. It expresses the *survival* of coloniality *beyond* the end of its system of
political dominance. It also includes the idea that upon the dissociation of
exploitation from any specifically visible markers, such as race, one *cannot
really go beyond it* as it is perceived in its ubiquity. Finally, the idea of late
postcoloniality *interrupts the hope for a redemptive sublation, transcend-
ence or escape*. The colonial exploitation trace, in late postcoloniality, is no
longer contested; colonialism cannot be undone, and, as such, it comes to
integrate the genetic code of the postcolony as a space of entangled time.

Nonetheless, if in Adorno this lateness was perceived as a mark of decay, here late postcoloniality is proposed as a departure point for a beginning capable of embracing the generative potential of postcolonial episteme.

Originating from observations drawn from early twenty-first century literary texts from Portuguese-speaking Africa, the late postcolonial condition draws the attention of the critic to the relevance of matters of timeliness and lateness, which allow no one writing in the present the comfort of settled certainties in the rapidly changing environment of cultures and societies. It also reaches out to the field of postcolonial studies by demonstrating that, if it is to have a future as an area of academic inquiry, it has to inform itself with situated analyses drawn from the myriad of postcolonies in the world, as this future certainly lies in peripheral loci of theorisation.

Bibliography

Adorno, Theodor Wiesengrund, 'Late Style in Beethoven', in Richard Leppert, ed., Susan H. Gillespie, trans. *Essays on Music* (Berkley, Los Angeles, and London: University of California Press, 2002), 564–568.

African Development Bank and African Development Fund, 'Cape Verde: A success story.' Regional–West 2 Department (ORWB) Report (2012), <https://www.afdb.org/sites/default/files/documents/projects-and-operations/cape_verde_-_a_success_story.pdf>, accessed 01 August 2023.

Agamben, Giorgio, *Homo Sacer: Sovereign Power and Bare Life* (Stanford: Stanford University Press, 1998).

Agualusa, José Eduardo, *Teoria Geral do Esquecimento* (Alfragide: Dom Quixote, 2012).

—. *A General Theory of Oblivion*, Daniel Hahn, trans. (London: Harvill Secker, 2015).

Ahmad, Aijaz, 'Jameson's Rhetoric of Otherness and the "National Allegory"', *Social Text* 17 (1987), 3–25.

—, 'The Politics of Literary Postcoloniality', in Mongia, Padmini, ed., *Contemporary Postcolonial Theory: A Reader* (London: Arnold, 1996), 276–293.

Alexandre, Valentim, 'O império português (1825–1890): ideologia e economia', *Análise Social* 38/169 (2004), 959–979.

Althusser, Louis, *Lenin and Philosophy and Other Essays*, Ben Brewster, trans. (New York and London: Monthly Review Press, 1971).

Anderson, Benedict, *Imagined Communities: Reflections on the Origin and Spread of Nationalism* (London and New York: Verso, 1991).

Anderson, Perry, 'Portugal and the End of Ultra-Colonialism 2', *New Left Review* 1/16 (1962), 88–123.

Arenas, Fernando, *Lusophone Africa: Beyond Independence* (Minneapolis: The University of Minnesota Press, 2011).

Arendt, Hannah, *The Origins of Totalitarianism* (San Diego, New York and London: Harcourt, 1979).

Ashcroft, Bill, Gareth Griffiths, and Helen Tiffin, *Post-Colonial Studies: The Key Concepts* (New York: Routledge, 2000).

—, *The Empire Writes Back* (London and New York: Routledge, 2002).

Assman, Aleida, 'Canon and Archive', in Astrid Erll, and Ansgar Nünning, eds, *Cultural Memory Studies: An International and Interdisciplinary Handbook* (Berlin: Walter de Gruyter, 2008), 97–107.

Barthes, Roland, *S/Z: An Essay*, Richard Miller, trans. (New York: Hill and Wang, 1974).

Batalha, Luís, *The Cape Verdean Diaspora in Portugal: Colonial Subjects in a Postcolonial World* (Maryland: Lexington Books, 2004).

Benjamin, Walter, 'Critique of Violence', in Walter Benjamin, ed., *Reflections*. Edmund Jephcott, trans. (New York: Schoken Books, 1986), 277–300.

—, 'The Storyteller: Reflections on the Work of Nikolai Neskov', in Walter Benjamin, ed., *Illuminations*, Harry Zohn, trans. (New York: Schoken Books, 2007a), 83–110.

—, 'Theses on the Philosophy of History' in Walter Benjamin, ed., *Illuminations*, Harry Zohn, trans. (New York: Schoken Books, 2007b), 253–264.

Bhabha, Homi, *Nation and Narration* (New York: Routledge, 1990).

___, *The Location of Culture* (London and New York: Routledge, 1994).

Bhagavan, Malur Ramanna, *Angola: prospects for socialist industrialisation*. Research report. (Uppsala: Nordiska Afrikainstitutet, 1980).

Birmingham, David, 'Angola', in Chabal, Patrick, ed., *A History of Postcolonial Lusophone Africa* (Bloomington and Indianapolis: Indiana University Press, 2002), 137–184.

Blackey, Robert, 'Fanon and Cabral: A Contrast in Theories of Revolution for Africa', *The Journal of Modern African Studies* 12/02 (1974), 191–209.

Bloom, Shelah S, 'Violence Against Women and Girls: A Compendium of Monitoring and Evaluation Indicators', Measure Evaluation (2008), <https://www.measureevaluation.org/publications/pdf/ms-08-30.pdf.html>, accessed 1 August 2023.

Boer, Pim den, 'Loci memoriae - Lieux de mémoire', in Astrid Erll, and Ansgar Nünning, eds, *Cultural Memory Studies* (Berlin: Walter de Gruyter, 2008), 19–26.

Bourdieu, Pierre, and Loïc J. D. Wacquant, *An Invitation to Reflexive Sociology* (Chicago: University of Chicago Press, 1992).

Bragança, Albertino, *Aurélia de Vento* (São Tomé: Tipografia Lousanense, 2011a).

—, *Um Clarão sobre a Baía* (São Tomé: Tipografia Lousanense, 2011b).

—, 'Dia de Amador', Téla Non (2013), <https://www.telanon.info/cultura/2013/01/10/12206/dia-de-amador/>, accessed 1 August 2023.

Braudel, Fernand, 'History and Social Sciences: The Longue Durée', in Richard E. Lee, ed., *The Longue Durée and World Systems Analysis* (Albany: State University of New York Press, 2012), 214–276.

Brennan, Timothy, *Borrowed Light: Vico, Hegel and the Colonies* (Stanford: Stanford University Press, 2014a).

—, 'Subaltern Stakes', *New Left Review* 89 (2014b), 67–87.

Brugioni, Elena, *Literaturas Africanas Comparadas: Paradigmas Críticos e Representações com Contraponto* (Campinas: Editora Unicamp, 2019).

—, Marie-Manuelle Silva, Joana Passos, and Andreia Sarabando, eds, *Itinerâncias: Percursos e Representações da Pós-colonialidade* (Ribeirão: Edições Húmus, 2012).

Cabaço, José Luís de Oliveira, 'Moçambique: Identidades, Colonialismo e Libertação', PhD Thesis, Universidade de São Paulo, 2007.

Cabral, Amílcar Lopes, *Unity and Struggle: Speeches and Writings*, Michael Wolfers, trans. (New York: Monthly Review Press, 1979).

—, 'A Arma da Teoria', in Amílcar Lopes Cabral, and António E. Duarte da Silva, eds, *Documentário (Textos Políticos e Culturais)* (Lisboa: Edições Nova Cotovia, 2008a), 167–202.

—, 'O Papel da Cultura na Luta pela Independência' in Amílcar Cabral Lopes, and António E. Duarte da Silva, eds, *Documentário (Textos Políticos e Culturais)* (Lisboa: Edições Nova Cotovia, 2008b), 203–236.

—, 'Resistência armada', in Amílcar Lopes Cabral, and António E. Duarte da Silva, eds, *Documentário (Textos Políticos e Culturais)* (Lisboa: Edições Nova Cotovia, 2008c), 115–144.

Cahen, Michel, 'Check on Socialism in Mozambique — What Check? What Socialism?', *Review of African Political Economy* 57 (1993), 46–59.

Calafate Ribeiro, Margarida, and Maria Paula Meneses, eds, *Moçambique das Palavras Escritas* (Porto: Edições Afrontamento, 2008).

—, and Odete Costa Semedo, eds, *Literaturas da Guiné-Bissau: Cantando os Escritos da História* (Porto: Edições Afrontamento, 2011a).

—, and Sílvio Renato Jorge, eds, *Literaturas Insulares: Cabo Verde e São Tomé e Príncipe* (Porto: Edições Afrontamento, 2011b).

Cammack, Diana, 'The "Human Face" of Destabilization: The War in Mozambique', *Review of African Political Economy* 14/40 (1987), 65–75.

Campos, Haroldo de, *O sequestro do barroco na formação da literatura brasileira: o caso Gregório de Matos* (Salvador: Fundação Casa de Jorge Amado, 1989).

Can, Nazir Ahmed, 'Para além da História: *Campo de Trânsito* de João Paulo Borges Coelho', *Via Atlântica* 16 (2009), 105–117.

Candido, Antonio, *Formação da Literatura Brasileira (momentos decisivos)* (Belo Horizonte and Rio de Janeiro: Editora Itatiaia Limitada, 2000).

—, 'A personagem do Romance', in Antonio Candido, Anatol Rosenfeld, Décio de Almeida Prado, and Paulo Emílio Sales Gomes, eds, *A Personagem de Ficção* (São Paulo: Editora Perspectiva, 2005), 51–80.

Casanova, Pascale, *The World Republic of Letters*, M. B. DeBevoise, trans. (Cambridge and London: Harvard University Press, 2004).

Césaire, Aimé, *Une Tempête* (Paris: Éditions du Soleil, 1969).

CG, 'Evel Rocha regressa poemas de "Cinzas Douradas"', A Nação (2015), <https://www.anacao.cv/noticia/2015/04/19/evel-rocha-regressa-poemas-de-cinzas-douradas>, accessed 1 August 2023.

Chabal, Patrick. 'People's War, State Formation and Revolution in Africa: A Comparative Analysis of Mozambique, Guinea-Bissau and Angola', *The Journal of Commonwealth & Comparative Politics* 21/3 (1983), 104–125.

—, ed., *The Postcolonial Literature of Lusophone Africa* (London: Hurst & Company, 1996).

—, ed., *A History of Postcolonial Lusophone Africa* (Indiana: Indiana University Press, 2002a).

—, 'Lusophone Africa in Historical and Comparative Perspective', in Patrick Chabal, ed., *A History of Postcolonial Lusophone Africa* (Bloomington and Indianapolis: Indiana University Press, 2002b), 3–134.

Chaves, Rita, 'O passado presente na literatura africana', *Via Atlântica* 7 (2004), 147–161.

—, 'A Pesquisa em Torno das Literaturas Africanas de Língua Portuguesa: Pontos para um Balanço', *Revista Crioula* (2010), <https://www.revistas.usp.br/crioula/article/view/55236>, accessed 1 August 2023.

Cheeseman, Nic, 'Nationalism, One-Party States, and Military Rule', in Nic Cheeseman, and David M. Anderson, eds, *Routledge Handbook of African Politics* (London: Routledge, 2013), 11–23.

Coelho, João Paulo Borges, 'Protected villages and communal villages in the Mozambican province of Tete (1968–1982): A history of State resettlement policies, development and war', PhD Thesis, University of Bradford, 1993.

—, 'Da violência colonial ordenada à ordem pós-colonial violenta: Sobre um legado das guerras coloniais nas ex-colônias portuguesas', *Lusotopie* 10 (2003), 175–193.

—, *Campo de Trânsito* (Lisboa: Editorial Caminho, 2007).

—, 'Entrevista a João Paulo Borges Coelho', Buala (2010), < https://www.buala.org/pt/cara-a-cara/entrevista-a-joao-paulo-borges-coelho>, accessed 1 August 2023.

—, 'Lugares da escrita, lugares da crítica' in Elena Brugioni et al., eds, *Itinerâncias: Percursos e Representações da Pós-colonialidade*, (Ribeirão: Edições Húmus, 2012), 193–201.

—, 'Writing in a Changing World: The Difficult Relationship with Reality', *Luso-Brazilian Review* 50/2 (2013), 21–30.

Comaroff, Jean, and John L. Comaroff, 'Law and Disorder in the Postcolony: An Introduction', in Jean Comaroff, and John L. Comaroff, eds, *Law and Disorder in the Postcolony* (Chicago: The University of Chicago Press, 2006), 1–56.

Connell, R. W., *Gender and Power: Society, the Person and Sexual Politics* (Stanford: Stanford University Press, 1987).

—, and James W. Messerschmidt, 'Hegemonic Masculinity: Rethinking the Concept', *Gender Society* 19 (2005), 829–859.

Conti-Brown, Peter, 'Increasing the Capacity for Corruption: Law and Development in the Burgeoning Petro-State of São Tomé e Príncipe', *The Berkeley Journal of African-American Law & Policy* 12/1 (2010), 33–65.

Damrosch, David, 'World Literature in Postcanonical, Hypercanonical Age', in Haun Saussy, ed., *Comparative Literature in an Age of Globalization* (Baltimore: John Hopkins University Press, 2006), 43–53.

Davidson, Basil, 'African Peasants and Revolution', *Journal of Peasant Studies* 1/3 (1974), 269–290.

de Man, Paul, *Blindness & Insight: Essays in the Rethoric of Contemporary Criticism* (New York: Oxford University Press, 1971).

Derrida, Jacques, *Positions* (Chicago: The University of Chicago Press, 1981).

—, *Limited Inc*, Samuel Weber, trans. (Evanston: Northwestern University Press, 1988).

—, *Of Grammatology*, Gayatri Spivak, trans. (Baltimore and London: The Johns Hopkins University Press, 1997).

—, *Writing and Difference*, Alan Bass, trans. (London: Routledge, 2001).

—, and Eric Prenowitz, 'Archive Fever: A Freudian Impression', *Diacritics* 25/2 (1995), 9–63.

Dirlik, Arif, 'Third World Criticism in the Age of Global Capitalism', *Critical Inquire* 20/2 (1994), 328–356.

—, 'Rethinking Colonialism: Globalization, Postcolonialism, and the Nation', *Interventions: International Journal of Postcolonial Studies* 4/3 (2002), 428–448.

Doyle, Don H., and Marco Antonio Pamplona, *Nationalism in the New World* (Athens: University of Georgia Press, 2006).

Downard, Lisa, 'Female Developments in the Nineteenth Century: Neera's *Teresa*, *Lydia* and *L'indomani*, George Eliot's *Middlemarch*, Charlotte Brontë's *Jayne Eyre*', in Giovanna Summerfield, and Lisa Downward, eds, *New Perspectives on the European Bildungsroman* (London: Continuum, 2010), 109–142.

Embaló, Filomena, *Tiara* (Lisboa: Instituto Camões Coleção Lusófona, 1999).

—, 'O que representa para mim o projecto Guiné-Bissau Contributo', Didinho. Org (2009), <https://www.didinho.org/Arquivo/PROJECTOGUINEBIS SAUCONTRIBUTOSEISANOSAOSERVICODAGUINEBISSAUEDO SGUINEENSES.htm>, accessed 1 December 2015.

Engels, Friedrick, *The Origin of the Family, Private Property and the State*, Lawrence and Wishart, trans. (London: Penguin Books, 2010).

Erll, Astrid, and Ansgar Nünning, eds, *Cultural Memory Studies: An International and Interdisciplinary Handbook* (Berlin and New York: Walter de Gruyter, 2008).

Fanon, Frantz, 'Algeria Unveiled', in Frantz Fanon, ed., *A Dying Colonialism*, Haakon Chevalier, trans. (New York: Groove Press, 1965), 35-67.

—, *Toward the African Revolution*, Haakon Chevalier, trans. (New York: Grove Press, 1967).

—, *The Wretched of the Earth*, Constance Farrington, trans. (London: Penguin Books, 2001).

—, *Black Skin White Masks*, Charles Lam Markmann, trans. (Sidmouth: Pluto Press, 2008).

Ferreira, Ana Paula, 'Home Bound: The Construct of Femininity in the Estado Novo', *Portuguese Studies* 12 (1996), 133–144.

Ferrell, Jeff, 'Urban Graffitti: Crime, Control and Resistance', *Youth & Society* 27/1 (1997), 73–92.

Fikes, Kesha, 'Late Capitalism in Cape Verde', *Transition* 103 (2010), 56–67.

Fonseca, Ana Margarida, 'A Invenção do Futuro: (Re) Escritas do Passado nos Contos de José Eduardo Agualusa', in Elena Brugioni et al., eds, *Itinerâncias: Percursos e Representações da Pós-colonialidade* (Ribeirão: Edições Húmus, 2012), 357–37.

Fonseca, Maria Nazareth Soares, 'Percursos da memória em textos das literaturas africanas de língua portuguesa', *Gragoatá* 10/19 (2005), 45–63.

—, 'Mulher-Poeta e Poetisas em Antologias de Literaturas Africanas de Língua Portuguesa: O Feminino como Exceção' in Inocência Mata, and Laura Cavalcante Padilha, eds, *A Mulher em África: Vozes de uma Margem Sempre Presente*, (Lisbon: Edições Colibri, 2007), 489–518.

Forrest, Joshua B, 'Guinea-Bissau', in Patrick Chabal, ed., *A History of Postcolonial Lusophone Africa* (Bloomington and Indianapolis: Indiana University Press, 2002), 236–263.

—, 'Anatomy of State Fragility: The Case of Guinea-Bissau', in Necla Tschirgi, Michel S. Lund, and Francesco Mancini, eds, *Security and Development: Searching for Critical Connections* (Boulder: Lynne Rienne, 2010), 171–210.

Foucault, Michel, *Discipline and Punish: The Birth of the Prison*, Alan Sheridan, trans. (New York: Vintage Books, 1995).

Freyre, Gilberto, *The Masters and the Slaves: A Study in the Development of Brazilian Civilization*, Samuel Putnam, trans. (Berkley, Los Angeles and London: University of California Press, 1986).

—, *Casa-grande e Senzala: formação da família brasileira sob o regime da economia patriarcal* (São Paulo: Global Editora, 2003).

Gellner, Ernest, *Nations and Nationalism* (Ithaca: Cornell University Press, 2006).

Giddens, Anthony, *The Nation-State and Violence: Volume Two of A Contemporary Critique of Historical Materialism* (Cambridge: Polity Press, 1985).

Gilroy, Paul, *Postcolonial Melancholia* (New York: Columbia University Press, 2005).

Graham, James, Michael Niblett, and Sharae Deckard, 'Postcolonial Studies and World Literature', *Journal of Postcolonial Writing* 48 (2012), 465–471.

Hall, Stuart, 'Quando foi o pós-colonial? Pensando no limite', in Stuart Hall, ed., *Da diáspora: Identidades e mediações culturais*, Liv Sovik, trans. Adelaine La Guardia Resende (Belo Horizonte: Editora UFMG, 2003) 101–130.

Hamilton, Russell G., *Voices from an Empire: A History of Afro-Portuguese Literature* (Minneapolis: University of Minnesota Press, 1975).

—, 'African Literature in Portuguese', in F. Abiona Irene, and Simon Gikandi, eds, *The Cambridge History of African and Caribbean Literature* (Cambridge: Cambridge University Press, 2004), 604–625.

Hegel, G. W. F., *Philosophy of Right*, T. M. Knox, trans. (New York: Oxford University Press, 1978).

—, *Philosophy of Nature*, M. J. Petry, trans. Vol. 1 (London: George Allen & Unwin Ltd., 1970).

—, *Phenomenology of Spirit*, A. V. Miller, trans. (Oxford: Oxford University Press, 1977).

Heimer, Franz-Wilhelm, 'Estrutura social e descolonização em Angola', *Análise Social* 40 (1973), 621–655.

Hobsbawm, Eric, *The Age of Revolution: 1789–1848* (London: Abacus, 1962).

hooks, bell, *The Will to Change: Men, Masculity and Love* (New York, Toronto, London and Sydney: Atria Books, 2004).

Huggan, Graham, *The Post-Colonial Exotic: Marketing the Margins* (London and New York: Routledge, 2001).

Hutcheon, Linda, *A Poetics of Postmodernism: History, Theory, Fiction* (New York: Routledge, 1988).

—, *The Politics of Postmodernism* (London and New York: Routledge, 2002).

Ivanova, Galina M., *Labor Camp Socialism: The Gulag in the Soviet Totalitarian System*, Carol Flath, trans. (London and New York: Routledge, 2000).

IBGE, 'Características étnico-raciais da população: um estudo das categorias de classificação de cor ou raça: 2008' Coordenação de População de Indicadores Sociais (IBGE: Rio de Janeiro, 2011) <https://biblioteca.ibge.gov.br/index.php/biblioteca-catalogo?view=detalhes&id=249891>, accessed 01 May 2024.

Jameson, Fredric, 'Third-World Literature in the Era of Multinational Capitalism', *Social Text* 15 (1986), 65–88.

Jones, Eleanor K., *Battleground Bodies: Gender and Sexuality in Mozambican Literature* (Oxford: Peter Lang, 2017).

Lacan, Jacques, 'The Mirror Stage as Formative of the Function of the I', in Jacques Lacan, ed., *Écrits: A Selection,* Aland Sheridan, trans. (London and New York: Routledge, 1989), 1–6.

Lains, Pedro, 'Causas do colonialismo português em África,1822–1975', *Análise Social* 33/(146–147) (1998), 463–496.

Langenohl, Andreas, 'Memory in Post-Authoritarian Societies', in Astrid Erll, and Ansgar Nünning, eds, *Cultural Memory Studies: An International and Interdisciplinary Handbook* (Berlin and New York: Walter de Gruyter, 2008), 163–172.

Laranjeira, Pires, *De letra em riste: identidade, autonomia e outras questões na literatura de Angola, Cabo Verde, Moçambique, São Tomé e Príncipe* (Porto: Afrontamento, 1992).

—, 'Ficção com ajuste de contas', *Jornal de Letras, Artes e Ideias* 940 (2006).

—, 'Bragança: crítica do mal-estar político e social', *Jornal de Letras, Artes e Ideias* 1072 (2011).

Larson, John Lauritz, 'An Inquiry into the Nature and Causes of the Wealth of Nations', *Journal of the Early Republic* 35 (2015), 1–23.

Lawrence, Bruce B., and Aisha Karim, *On Violence: A Reader* (Duke University Press, 2007).

Lazarus, Neil, 'What Postcolonial Theory Doesn't Say', *Race and Class* 53/1 (2011a), 3–27.

—, *The Postcolonial Unconscious* (Cambridge: Cambridge University Press, 2011b).

Leite, Ana Mafalda, *Literaturas Africanas e Formações Pós-coloniais* (Lisboa: Cotovia, 2003).

—, 'Breve história, tópicos e questões sobre o ensino das Literaturas Africanas de Língua Portuguesa', *Revista Cerrados* 19 (2010), 77–90.

—, Hilary Owen, and Rita Chaves Livia Apa, eds, *Nação e Narrativa Pós-Colonial I: Angola e Moçambique* (Lisboa: Edições Colibri, 2012a).

—, eds., *Nação e Narratiava Pós-Colonial II: Angola e Moçambique* (Lisbon: Edições Colibri, 2012b).

—, *Narrating the Postcolonial Nation: Mapping Angola and Mozambique*, Luis R. Mitras, trans. (Oxford: Peter Lang, 2014a).

—, *Speaking the Postcolonial Nation: Interviews with Writers from Angola and Mozambique*, Luis R. Mitras, trans. (Oxford: Peter Lang, 2014b).

Leite, Débora David, 'Inocência Mata: A Essência dos Caminhos que se Entrecruzam', *Revista Crioula* 5 (2009), <https://www.revistas.usp.br/crioula/article/view/54948>, accessed 7 March 2022.

Lima, Redy Wilson Duarte, 'Thugs: Vítimas e/ou Agentes da Violência?' Portal do Conhecimento de Cabo Verde (2010), <http://www.portaldoconhecimento. gov.cv/stats?level=item&type=access&page=views-series&tab=3&pyear= 2021&anofim=2021&anoinicio=2021&start=01-06-2021&mesinicio= 01&end=30-06-2021&pmonth=06&mesfim=06&object=item&object-id= 10961/457>, accessed 5 December 2015.

Linz, Juan J., 'State Building and Nation Building', *European Review* 1/4 (1993), 355–369.

Loughlin, Martin, 'Why Sovereignty?', in Richard Rawlings, Peter Leyland, and Alison Young, eds, *Sovereignty and the Law: Domestic, European and International* (Oxford: Oxford University Press: 2013), 35-49.

Lugarinho, Mário César, 'O homem e os vários homens: masculinidades nas Literaturas Africanas de Língua Portuguesa', Post-doctoral Thesis, Universidade de São Paulo, 2012a.

—, 'Em Cabo Verde, os Marginais, de Evel Rocha: justiça social e gênero', *Via Atlântica* 22 (2012b), 219–233.

Lugones, María, 'Heterosexualism and the Colonial/Modern Gender System', *Hypatia* 22/1 (2007), 186–209.

Lukács, Georg, 'O Romance como Epopéia Burguesa', *Revista Ad Hominem 1* Tomo III, Música e Literatura (1999), 87–117.

Ly, Aliou, 'Promise and Betrayal: Women Fighters and National Liberation in Guinea-Bissau', *Feminist Africa* 19 (2014), 24–42.

Lyotard, Jean-François, *The Postmodern Condition: A Report on Knowledge.* Geoff Bennington and Brian Massumi, trans. (Minneapolis: University of Minnesota Press, 1991).

Machel, Samora, *Mozambique: Sowing the Seeds of Revolution* (Angola & Guinea: Committee for Freedom in Mozambique, 1975).

Magee, Glenn Alexander, *The Hegel Dictionary* (London and New York: Continuum, 2010).

Malaquias, Assis, *Rebels and Robbers: Violence in Post-Colonial Angola* (Stockholm: Nordiska Afrikainstitutet, 2007).

Marcuse, Herbert, *Reason and Revolution: Hegel and the Rise of Social Theory* (London: Routledge, 1955).

Martins, Ana Margarida Dias, *Magic Stones and Flying Snakes: Gender and the 'Postcolonial Exotic' in the Work of Paulina Chiziane and Lídia Jorge* (Oxford, Bern, Berlin, Bruxelles, Frankfurt am Main, New York and Wien: Peter Lang, 2012).

Marx, Karl, *A Critique of Hegel's 'Philosophy of Right'*, Annete Jolin and Joseph O'Malley, trans. (Cambridge: Cambridge University Press, 1977).

—, *Capital,* Volume 1 (London: Penguin, 1990).

—, and Frederick Engels, *The German Ideology: Part One*, Lawrence and Wishart, trans. (New York: International Publishers, 1970).

Mata, Inocência, *Diálogo com as Ilhas: Sobre a Cultura e Literatura de São Tomé e Príncipe* (Lisboa: Edições Colibri, 1998).

—, *A Suave Pátria: Reflexões Político-Culturais sobre a Sociedade São-Tomense* (Lisboa: Edições Colibri, 2004).

—, *A literatura africana e a crítica pós-colonial: reconversões* (Luanda: Editorial Nizila, 2007).

—, *Polifonias Insulares: Cultura e Literatura de São Tomé e Príncipe* (Lisboa: Edições Colibri, 2010).

—, 'A Utopia Cosmopolita na Recepção das Literaturas Africanas', *Mulemba* 1/4 (2011), 3–15.

—, 'Literaturas em portguês: encruzilhadas em África', *1616: Anuario de Literatura Comparada* 3 (2013), 107–122.

—, 'Literaturas em português: encruzilhadas atlânticas', *Via Atlântica* 25 (2014): 59–82.

Mata, Inocência, and Laura Cavalcante Padilha, *A mulher em África: vozes de uma margem sempre presente* (Lisboa: Cotovia, 2007).

Mayer, Tamar, *Gender Ironies of Nationalism: Sexing the Nation* (London and New York: Routledge, 2000).

Mbembe, Achille, *On the Postcolony* (Los Angeles: University of California Press, 2001).

—, 'What is Postcolonial Thinking?', Eurozine (2008), https://www.eurozine.com/what-is-postcolonial-thinking/#:~:text=Postcolonial%20thought%20demonstrates%20that%20colonialism,merchandise%20of%20the%20modern%20kind, accessed 1 August 2023.

—, *Sortir de la Grande Nuit* (Paris: Éditions La Découverte, 2010).

McClintock, Anne, 'The Angel of Progress: Pitfalls of the Term "Post-Colonialism"', *Social Text* 31/32 (1992), 84–98.

—, *Imperial Leather: Race, Gender and Sexuality in the Colonial Contest* (London and New York: Routledge, 1995).

McGuinn, Bradford, 'Understated Yet Turbulent: Narcotics Trafficking and the Criminalization of Guinea-Bissau', in Marten W Brienen, and Jonathan D. Rosen, eds, *New Approaches to Drug Policies: A Time for Change* (New York: Palgrave Macmillan, 2015), 73–88.

McGuirk, Bernard, 'Intra-Colonialism or l'Animotion Mosaïque of the Black Atlantic: Re(p)tiling Angola', in J. E. Agualusa's "O Vendedor de Passados"/ The Book of Chameleons', in Cristina Demaria, and Macdonald Daly, eds, *The Genres of Post-Conflict Testimonies* (Nottingham: CCC Press, 2009a), 278–311.

—, 'Laughing Again He's Awake: de Campos à l'oreille de l'autre celte', in Bernard McGuirk and Else R. P. Vieira, eds, *Haroldo de Campos in Conversation: In Memoriam 1929–2003* (London: Zoilus Press, 2009b), 126–152.

McWilliams, Ellen, *Margaret Atwood and the Female Bildungsroman* (London and New York: Routledge, 2009).

Medeiros, Paulo de, '7 Passos (para pensar uma Europa pós-imperial)', in Ana Mafalda Leite, et al., eds, *Nação e Narrativa Pós-Colonial I: Angola e Moçambique* (Lisboa: Edições Colibri, 2013), 323–338.

Memmi, Albert, *Decolonization and the Decolonized*, Robert Bononno, trans. (University of Minnesota Press: Minneapolis, 2006).

Mendonça, Fátima, 'Ovídio e Kafka nas margens do Lúrio', Ma-Schamba (2007), <https://ma-schamba.blogs.sapo.pt/fatima-mendonca-sobre-campo-de-trans ito-554369>, accessed 1 August 2023.

Meneses, Maria Paula G, 'O "Indígena" Africano e o colono "Europeu": A Construção da diferença por processos legais', *e-Cadernos CES 7* (2010), <https://doi.org/ 10.4000/eces.403>, accessed 1 August 2023.

Mercer, 'Cost of Living City Rankings', Mercer (2015), https://info.mercer.com/ Cost-of-Living-Ranking-2015.html, accessed 20 November 2015.

Mignolo, Walter D., *Local Histories/Global Designs: Coloniality, Subaltern Knowledges, and Border Thinking* (Princeton: Princeton University Press, 2012).

Moore, Jason W., *Capitalism in the Web of Life: Ecology and the Accumulation of Capital* (London and New York: Verso, 2015).

Moreira, Teresinha Taborda, 'Memória e História em *Campo de Trânsito* de João Paulo Borges Coelho', *Afro-Ásia* 42 (2010), 109–124.

Moretti, Franco, 'Conjectures on World Literature', *New Left Review* 1 (2000a), 54–68.

—, *The Way of The World: The Bildungsroman in European Culture* (London and New York: Verso, 2000b).

Morier-Genoud, Eric, and Michel Cahen, eds, *Imperial Migrations: Colonial Communities and Diaspora in the Portuguese World* (London: Palgrave Macmillan, 2013).

Mosse, George L, *Nationalism and Sexuality: Respectability and Abnormal Sexuality in Modern Europe* (New York: Howard Fertig, 1985).

Nascimento, Augusto, 'O crescendo da violência em São Tomé e Príncipe' *Nova Cidadania* Jan-Mar (2007), 54–55.

—, '"Poverty…, of course we have it…" Notes for the Analysis of an Institutional Conscience about Poverty and Micro-violence in Cape Verdean Contexts', in Cristina Udelsmann Rodrigues, and Ana Bénard da Costa, eds, *Pobreza e paz nos PALOP* (Lisboa: Sextante Editora, 2010), 160–179.

Nascimento, Naira de Almeida, 'Despojos da guerra, rastros de identidade: Alguns dilemas da literatura africana de expressão portuguesa pela voz de Tiara', *Muitas Vozes* 1/1 (2012), 29–47.

Neto, Agostinho, … *Ainda o meu sonho… Discursos sobre a cultura nacional*, Edições 70 (1980).

Newitt, Malyn, 'Mozambique', in Patrick, Chabal, ed., *A History of Postcolonial Lusophone Africa* (Bloomington and Indianapolis: Indiana University Press, 2002), 168–235.

Nora, Pierre, *Realms of Memory: Rethinking the French Past under the Direction of Pierre* Nora, Arthus Goldhammer, trans. (New York: Columbia University Press, 1996).

—, and Marc Roudebush, 'Between Memory and History: Les Lieux de Mémoire', *Representations* 26 (1989), 7–24.

Owen, Hilary, *Mother Africa, Father Marx: Women's Writing of Mozambique 1948–2002* (Lewisburg: Bucknell University Press, 2007).

—, and Anna M. Klobucka, eds, *Gender, Empire, and Postcolony: Luso-Afro-Brazilian Intersections* (London: Palgrave Macmillan, 2014).

—, and Philip Rothwell, eds, *Sexual/Textual Empires: Gender and Marginality in Lusophone African Literature* (Bristol: University of Bristol, 2004).

Padilha, Laura Cavalcante, *Novos Pactos, Outras Ficções: Ensaios sobre Literaturas Afro-Luso Brasileiras* (Lisbon: Novo Imbondeiro, 2002).

——, 'O Ensino e a Crítica das Literaturas Africanas no Brasil: um caso de Neocolonialidade e Enfrentamento', *Revista Magistro* 1 (2010a), 2–15.

—, 'Os estudos literários africanos no Brasil: percursos e desafios', *Revista Cerrados* 19 (2010b), 207–216.

Paredes, Margarida, 'Deolinda Rodrigues, da Família Metodista à Família MPLA, o Papel da Cultura na Política', *Cadernos de Estudos Africanos* 20 (2011), 11–26.

Parry, Benita, 'What is Left in Postcolonial Studies', *New Literary History* 43/2 (2012), 341–358.

Pepe, Paulo, and Ana Raquel Fernandes, *Beyond Binaries: Sex, Sexualities and Gender in the Lusophone World* (Oxford: Peter Lang, 2019).

Pina, Leão Jesus de, 'Cordialidade e Democratização: da Morabeza às tendências actuais da cultura política cabo-verdiana', Repositório of ISCTE (2010), <https://repositorio.iscte-iul.pt/bitstream/10071/2301/1/CIEA7_13_PINA_Cordialidade%20e%20Democratiza%C3%A7%C3%A3o.pdf>, accessed 1 August 2023.

Pitcher, M. Anne, *Party Politics and Economics: Reform in Africa's Democracies* (New York: Cambridge University Press, 2012).

Poggi, Gianfranco, *The State: Its Nature, Development and Prospects* (Cambridge: Polity Press, 1990).

Poiraud, Cyrielle, 'Equality, Recognition and Social Justice: A Hegelian Perspective Announcing Amartya Sen', Œconomia (2019), <https://doi.org/10.4000/oeconomia.5178>, accessed 1 August 2023.

Proença, Carlos Sangreman, *A Exclusão Social em Cabo Verde: Uma Abordagem Preliminar* (Lisbon: Centro de Estudos sobre África e do Desenvolvimento, 2009).

Quilan, Susan Canty, and Fernando Arenas, eds, *Lusosex: Gender and Sexuality in the Portuguese-Speaking World* (Minneapolis and London: University of Minnesota Press, 2002).

Rocha, Evel, *Marginais* (Praia: Gráfica da Praia, 2010).

Rodney, Walter, *How Europe Underdeveloped Africa* (Washington D.C.: Howard University Press, 1982).

Rose, Susan D., *Challenging Global Gender Violence: The Global Clothesline Project* (New York: Palgrave Macmillan, 2014).

Rothbergh, Michael, *Multidirectional Memory: Remembering the Holocaust in an Age of Decolonization* (Stanford: Stanford University Press, 2009).

—, 'Between Memory and Memory: From Lieux de mémoire to Noeuds de mémoire', *Yale French Studies* 118/119 (2010), 3–12.

Rothwell, Phillip, *A Postmodern Nationalist: Truth, Orality, and Gender in the Work of Mia Couto* (Lewisburg: Bucknell UP, 2004).

Said, Edward W., *The World, the Text and the Critic* (Cambridge: Harvard University Press, 1983).

—, *Beginnings: Intention and Method* (New York: Columbia University Press, 1985).

—, *Power, Politics and Culture* (London: Bloomsbury, 2001).

—, *Orientalism* (London: Penguim Books, 2003).

—, *On Late Style: Music and Literature Against the Grain* (London: Bloomsbury Publishing, 2006).

Sklar, Richard L., 'Democracy in Africa', in Patrick Chabal, ed., *Political Domination in Africa: Reflections on the Limit of Power* (Cambridge: Cambridge University Press, 1986), 17–29.

Santos, Boaventura de Sousa, *Toward a New Comon Sense: Law, Science and Politics in the Paradigmatic Transition* (New York: Routledge, 1995).

—, 'Entre Próspero e Caliban: Colonialismo, pós-colonialismo e inter-identidades', in Maria Irene Ramalho, and António Sousa Ribeiro, eds, *Entre Ser e Estar: Raízes, Percursos e Discursos da Identidade* (Porto: Edições Afrontamento, 2001), 23–86.

Santos, Boaventura de Sousa, and Maria Paula Meneses, eds, *Epistemologias do Sul* (Porto: Edições Afrontamento, 2010).

Santos, Emanuelle, and Patricia Schor, eds, 'Brazilian Postcolonialities', *P: Portuguese Cultural Studies* 4 (2012), <https://scholarworks.umass.edu/p/vol4/iss1/>, accessed 1 August 2023.

Saul, John, *The State and Revolution in Eastern Africa* (London: Monthly Review, 1979).

Schwarz, Roberto, 'As idéias fora do lugar', in *Cultura e Política* (São Paulo: Paz e Terra, 2005a), 59–83.

—, 'Nacional por subtração' in *Cultura e Política* (São Paulo: Paz e Terra, 2005b), 109–136.

Seibert, Gerhard, 'A política num micro-Estado: São Tomé e Príncipe, ou os conflitos pessoais e políticos na génese dos partidos políticos', *Lusotopie* 2 (1995), 239–250.

—, 'São Tomé e Príncipe', in Patrick Chabal, ed., *A History of Postcolonial Lusophone Africa* (Bloomington and Indianapolis: Indiana University Press, 2002), 291–315.

—, 'São Tomé and Príncipe: Political Instability Continues', *Lusophone Countries Bulletin* III (2013), 1–5.

Shohat, Ella, 'Notes on the "Post-Colonial"', *Social Text* 31/32 (1992), 99–113.

—, and Robert Stam, 'The Culture Wars in Translation', in Manuela Ribeiro Sanches, Fernando Clara, João Ferreira Duarte, and Leonor Pires Martins, eds, *Europe in Black and White* (Bristol and Chicago: Intellect Books, 2011), 17–36.

—, '"Brazil is not Travelling Enough": On Postcolonial theory and Analogous Counter-currents', *P: Portuguese Cultural Studies* (2012a), 15–40.

—, *Race in Translation: Culture Wars Around the Postcolonial Atlantic* (New York: New York University Press, 2012b).

—, 'Whence and Whither Postcolonial Theory?', *New Literary History* 43 (2012c), 371–390.

Silva Andrade, Elisa, 'Cape Verde', in Patrick Chabal, ed., *A History of Lusophone Africa* (Bloomington and Indianapolis: Indiana University Press, 2002), 264–290.

Smith, Adam, *An Inquiry into the Nature and Causes of the Wealth of Nations*, Edwin Cannan, ed. (New York: Modern Library, 1965).

Smith, Anthony D, 'Memory and Modernity: Reflections on Ernest Gellner's Theory of Nationalism', *Nations and Nationalism* 2/3 (1996), 371–388.

Soque, Manuel, and Collin McClelland, 'In Luanda, the rich feast, the poor scramble', *Bloomberg Business Week* (29 December 2014).

Sousa Ribeiro, António, 'Vítima do próprio sucesso? Lugares comuns do pós – colonial', in Elena Brugioni et al., eds, *Itinerâncias: Percursos e Representações da Pós-colonialidade* (Edições Húmus, 2012), 39–48.

Strath, Bo, *Europe and the Other and Europe as the Other* (Brussels: Peter Lang, 2000).

Tavares, Maria, *No Country for Nonconforming Women: Feminine Conceptions of Lusophone Africa* (Oxford: Legenda, 2020).

Thaler, Kai M., 'Ideology and Violence in Civil Wars: Theory and Evidence from Mozambique and Angola', *Civil Wars* 14/4 (2012), 546–567.

Thomaz, Omar Ribeiro, 'Campos, aparato repressivo e construção social do inimigo: notas sombre a cooperação da RDA em Moçambique', in K. C. Silva, ed., *Timor Leste por trás do palco: cooperação internacional e a dialética da formação do estado* (Belo Horizonte: Editora da UFMG, 2007), 383–416.

—, '"Escravos sem dono": a experiência social dos campos de trabalho em Moçambique no período socialista', *Revista de Antropologia* 51 (2008), 177–214.

Topper, Keith, 'Not so trifling nuances: Pietter Nourdieu, symbolic violence and the pervasions of democracy', *Constellations* 8/1 (2001), 30–56.

Veiga, Abel, '"Aurélia de Vento" mais um romance de Albertino Bragança', *Tela Nón* (2011), <https://www.telanon.info/cultura/2011/06/28/7583/%E2%80%9Caurelia-de-vento%E2%80%9D-mais-um-romance-de-albertino-braganca/>, accessed 7 March 2022.

Xavier, Lola Geraldes, 'São Tomé e Príncipe: um olhar endoexógeno a partir da literatura', *Actas do Colóquio Internacional São Tomé e Príncipe numa perspectiva interdisciplinar, diacrónica e sincrónica* (2012), <http://hdl.handle.net/10071/3924>, accessed 7 March 2022.

Wallerstein, Immanuel, *Historical Capitalism with Capitalist Civilization* (London: Verso, 1996).

—, 'Africa in a Capitalist World', in Immanuel Wallerstein, ed., *The Essential Wallerstein* (New York: The New Press, 2000), 39–68.

Weber, Max, 'Politics as a Vocation', in H. H. Gert, and C. Wright Mills, eds, *Max Weber: Essays in Sociology*, H. H. Gert, and C. Wright Mills, trans. (London and New York: Routledge, 2009), 77–128.

Woloch, Alex, *The One vs. the Many: Minor Characters and the Space of the Protagonist in the Novel* (Princeton and Oxford: Princeton University Press, 2003).

Young, Robert J. C., *Postcolonialism: An Historical Introduction* (Oxford: Blackwell Publishing, 2001).

—, 'Postcolonial Remains', *New Literary History* 43/1 (2012), 19–42.

—, 'Late Postcolonialism' (2013), Unpublished draft shared via private correspondence on 4 June 2021.

Yuval-Davis, Nira, *Gender and Nation* (London: Sage Publications, 1997).

—, *The Politics of Belonging: Intersectional Contestations* (Los Angeles, London, and New Delhi: Sage, 2011).

Index

RECONFIGURING IDENTITIES IN THE PORTUGUESE-SPEAKING WORLD

Edited by

Paulo de Medeiros and Cláudia Pazos-Alonso

The series publishes studies across the entire spectrum of Lusophone literature, culture and intellectual history, from the Middle Ages to the present day, with particular emphasis on figurations and reconfigurations of identity, broadly understood. It is especially interested in work which interrogates national identity and cultural memory, or which offers fresh insights into Portuguese-speaking cultural and literary traditions, in diverse historical contexts and geographical locations. It is open to a wide variety of approaches and methodologies as well as to interdisciplinary fields: from literary criticism and comparative literature to cultural and gender studies, to film and media studies. It also seeks to encourage critical dialogue among scholarship originating from different continents.

Proposals are welcome for either single-author monographs or edited collections (in English and/or Portuguese). Those interested in contributing to the series should send a detailed project outline to oxford@peterlang.com.

VOL. 1   Ana Margarida Martins: Magic Stones and Flying Snakes: Gender and the 'Postcolonial Exotic' in the Work of Paulina Chiziane and Lídia Jorge.
ISBN 978-3-0343-0828-1. 2012

VOL. 2   Ana Mafalda Leite, Hilary Owen, Rita Chaves, Livia Apa (eds): Narrating the Postcolonial Nation: Mapping Angola and Mozambique.
ISBN 978-3-0343-0891-5. 2014